Sarah Daniels
Plays: 2

**The Gut Girls, Beside Herself, Head-Rot Holiday,
The Madness of Esme and Shaz**

The Gut Girls: 'Humane and hugely funny, throwing a generous and affectionate arm around women who walked abroad with outrageous hats and no underwear, who counted their free hours in pints of ale, and who were quite up to shaming a second-rate comedian off the stage.'

Claire Armistead, *Financial Times*

Beside Herself: 'Sarah Daniels' important and red-hot new play is the dramatic analogue of a contemporary social tragedy which exists on a scale we are only just beginning to comprehend.'

Michael Coveney, *Observer*

'There is a fine, hard humour, as well as compassion, in the way *Head-Rot Holiday* examines the contradictions entangling these women's lives . . . entertains as much as it enlightens.'

Paul Taylor, *Independent*

The Madness of Esme and Shaz: 'As always, Daniels' writing crackles with good jokes, the gallows humour of ordinary women who have only just recognised the depths of their desperation . . . A passionate and compassionate piece of theatre.'

Lyn Gardner, *Plays International*

Sarah Daniels' plays include *Ripen Our Darkness* (Royal Court Theatre Upstairs, London, 1981); *Ma's Flesh is Grass* (Crucible Studio Theatre, Sheffield, 1981); *The Devil's Gateway* (Royal Court Theatre Upstairs, London, 1983); *Masterpieces* (Manchester Royal Exchange, 1983; Royal Court Theatre, London, 1983/4); *Neaptide*, winner of the 1982 George Devine Award (Cottesloe, National Theatre, London, 1986); *Byrthrite* (Royal Court Theatre Upstairs, London, 1986); *The Gut Girls* (Albany Empire, Deptford, 1988); *Beside Herself* (Royal Court, London, 1990); *Head-Rot Holiday* (Clean Break Theatre Company, 1992); *The Madness of Esme and Shaz* (Royal Court Theatre Upstairs, London, 1994); and *Blow Your House Down*, based on the novel by Pat Barker (Live Theatre, Newcastle-upon-Tyne, 1995).

by the same author

Sarah Daniels Plays: 2
Beside Herself, Gut Girls, Head-Rot Holiday,
The Madness of Esme and Shaz

Masterpieces
Beside Herself

For a complete catalogue of Methuen Drama titles
write to:

Methuen Drama
Michelin House
81 Fulham Road
London SW3 6RB

SARAH DANIELS

Plays: 2

The Gut Girls
Beside Herself
Head-Rot Holiday
The Madness of Esme and Shaz

Introduced by the author

Methuen Drama

METHUEN CONTEMPORARY DRAMATISTS

This collection first published in Great Britain in 1994
by Methuen Drama
Methuen Publishing Limited
215 Vauxhall Bridge Road
London SW1V 1EJ

3 5 7 9 10 8 6 4

ISBN 0–413–69040–7

A CIP catalogue record for this book is available from the British Library.

Typeset by Deltatype Limited, Ellesmere Port, Cheshire
Printed and bound in Great Britain by
Cox & Wyman Ltd, Reading, Berkshire

Contents

	page
Sarah Daniels: A Chronology	vii
Introduction	ix
THE GUT GIRLS	1
BESIDE HERSELF	95
HEAD-ROT HOLIDAY	189
THE MADNESS OF ESME AND SHAZ	263

A Chronology

Ripen Our Darkness, Royal Court Theatre Upstairs,
London 1981

Ma's Flesh is Grass, Crucible Studio Theatre, Sheffield 1981

Masterpieces, Manchester Royal Exchange 1983

The Devil's Gateway, Royal Court Theatre Upstairs,
London 1983

Neaptide, Cottesloe, Royal National Theatre, London 1986

Byrthrite, Royal Court Theatre Upstairs, London 1986

The Gut Girls, Albany Empire, London 1988

Beside Herself, Royal Court Theatre, London 1990

Head-Rot Holiday, Clean Break Theatre Company,
touring 1992

The Madness of Esme and Shaz, Royal Court Theatre
Upstairs, London 1994

Blow Your House Down (based on the novel by
Pat Barker), Live Theatre, Newcastle-upon-Tyne 1995

Introduction

It was such a chore writing the introduction to *Plays: One* that as soon as I'd finished it, I thought I'd start on one for *Plays: Two*. This might seem arrogantly optimistic but it was done in the spirit of stock-piling for a crisis. And so, convinced that I couldn't possibly start this introduction without them, I've spent a ludicrous amount of time searching, frantically, for the notes I wrote then, only to find that they give a detailed account of how I came to write the plays which I thought would appear in this volume. Unfortunately, I hadn't written the plays then. Even more unfortunate: I still haven't.

Still, 'Life', as John Lennon immortalised, 'is what happens while you're busy making other plans.'

At least I now know how I came to believe what I had always suspected: that if I talk or write about a play when it's in its embryonic stage, it is then exorcised from the system and becomes impossible to write at all.

But, displacement activities aside, the fact that this time the introduction is being written from the memory of existing plays, rather than from floating ideas, seems to have made it more rather than less difficult to write.

Having said that, it's easy to describe how *The Gut Girls* came to be written because it was virtually handed to me on a plate with side orders of title and deadline by Teddy Kiendl, then the Artistic Director at the Albany Empire Theatre, Deptford. In May 1988, he asked me if I'd like to write a piece set in Deptford at the turn of the century about the young women who worked in the Cattle Market and were turned into domestic servants by the Duchess of Albany. He had scheduled rehearsals for the beginning of October of the same year. Never before had I been given the idea for the story and a production date before writing a word and I found the experience of both was alternately tyrannical and luxurious.

The ordeal of writing *Beside Herself* couldn't have been more different. A couple of years previously, I'd received a commission from the Women's Playhouse Trust to write anything I liked. I didn't deliver *Beside Herself* until June 1988 and Jules

Wright, director of WPT, organised a rehearsed reading in the Royal Court, Theatre Upstairs in August of the same year. Several drafts later, the play opened in March 1990 on the main stage.

Unknown to me at the time, *Beside Herself* was to become the first of three plays in this volume with the theme of 'Women and Madness'. Long before I started it, I became interested in how women's mental health is defined and I wanted to write something specifically about a woman detained in Broadmoor or a 'special hospital' – the new euphemism for an institution for the 'criminally insane'.

I'd discussed this with Paulette Randall, a trainee director at the Royal Court at the time when I was resident writer, with a view to us working together on it. It went to the same place as all the other unwritten plays. (If I look hard enough, I'll probably find an introduction to it somewhere.)

Almost eight years later Alex Ford, director of Clean Break Theatre Company[1], mentioned to Paulette that the company was looking to commission a writer for their next play which was to be about the issues facing women in special hospitals. Paulette, remembering my interest, suggested me. (Thankfully, someone very wisely stipulated a delivery date.)

With the help of WISH (Women in Special Hospitals)[2], Clean Break set up a research period, during which I was able to talk to ex-patients, psychiatrists, clinical psychologists, social workers and solicitors, which enabled me to find a focus for writing about the treatment women receive in those places.

The result was *Head-Rot Holiday*, which was directed by Paulette – so we did eventually get to do a play together about 'special hospitals' after all.

The Madness of Esme and Shaz changes the focus. Somehow, out of the bleakness and horror, a love story emerged; not a

[1] Clean Break Theatre Company, 37–39 King's Terrace, London NW1 0JR (Tel: 071 383 3786)

[2] WISH (Women in Special Hospitals) is a registered charity working on behalf of women released from Special Hospitals, Regional Secure Units and prison psychiatric units WISH, 25 Horsell Road, London N5. (Tel: 071 700 6684)

romantic or sexual one but one of friendship. I suppose it's a sort of fable about two people who've never experienced love and don't even recognise it when they do, but their lives are irredeemably changed by it.

I overheard the director, Jessica Dromgoole, describe it as a collection of ugly things brought together and transformed into something beautiful. I felt I couldn't have been paid a higher compliment.

Following which, I got the idea for a new play, and now that I've discovered the secret is not to write the introduction first, there's every chance that it will be written before *Plays: Three* is published. Now that *is* arrogantly tempting fate.

Sarah Daniels
October 1994

THE GUT GIRLS

The Gut Girls was first performed at the Albany Empire, London on 2 November 1988, with the following cast:

Maggie/Nora/Edna	Eve Bland
Polly	Joanna Mays
Ellen/Priscilla	Cathy Shipton
Kate	Janet Steel
Annie/Emily/Eady	Gillian Wright
Lady Helena	Claire Vousden
Harry/Arthur/Len/Mad Jacko	Graham Cull
Jim/Edwin	Peter Seton

Directed by Teddy Kiendl
Designed by Kate Owen

The action takes place in Deptford at the turn of the century.

Act One

Scene One

The Gutting Shed.

Ellen, Maggie, Polly *and* **Kate** *are working.* **Harry,** *the foreman, comes in.*

Harry I've got a new 'un for yer, gils. To replace Maud. (*Calls behind him.*) Come on, petal, they won't eat yer. (*He shoves* **Annie** *into the shed.*) That's the least of yer problems. (*He goes.*)

Annie *stares at the sight before her in horror. She sways.* **Maggie** *steps neatly behind her, catching her before she falls.*

Maggie Stand yerself up girl, and whatever you do don't take no deep breaths, that won't do yer no good in here.

Annie I think I'm going to be sick. (*She puts her hand over her mouth.*)

Kate *hovers with the mop, in anticipation.*

Maggie (*to* **Annie**) Don't think about it. Think about getting paid, think about buying a new hat, being the Queen of England, anything.

Kate We got enough insides to deal wiv here without clearing up yourn.

Ellen (*to* **Kate**) Alright little 'un, we've not forgotten how you was on your first day.

Kate Stop calling me that. Me name's Kate.

Annie (*holds her nose, gasps*) It's awful.

Polly Nothing wrong with your eyesight, then. That's right. Offal by name, awful by nature. (*Holds up a piece of liver.*) Feeling a bit liverish meself.

Annie *continues to look horrified.*

Maggie Ain't you never seen meat before?

Annie Not a lot.

Kate You never seen a butcher's then? C'mon now, we can't stand around all day waiting to ketch yer if yer decides to fall down again.

Ellen Give her a chance.

Maggie What's yer name?

Annie Annie.

Maggie I'm Maggie. She's Ellen. Her with the offal jokes is Polly and the little madam here is Kate. You start by helping Kate. Then when we get a chance we'll show you what else you got to do, but you've got to keep your eyes and brain on what you're doing, otherwise you'll end up like Maud.

Kate (*to* **Annie**) Fer now, we just got to keep the floor clean on account of it gets all bloody and it's very bad fer yer health once it gets jellified around yer ankles.

Jim, *terrified of humiliation, enters staggering under the weight of a heavy carcass.*

Maggie Having trouble lifting yer meat, Jimbo? Here let me give yer a hand.

Kate Leave him alone.

Maggie *takes the carcass, by contrast handling it with ease, and hangs it up.* **Jim** *starts to load pieces of meat into a barrow as fast as he can. The others carry on as though he wasn't there.*

Ellen (*to* **Maggie**) What you doing helping him? You know what they're like – give 'em an inch and they tek a yard.

Polly More like they think they got a yard when they only got an inch.

Jim, *head down, works even faster.*

Maggie This girl, Maud, used to work here. Best one with the knives she was. Leaves when she gets married. Day after her wedding night, nearly cuts her fingers right off.

Annie How?

Polly She was playing cards and she threw her hand in. How d'you think?

Annie But . . .

Maggie With the bread knife.

Annie Oh. I thought you said she was the best one . . .

Maggie She was. I'm telling you, right.

Ellen Shock of getting married.

Maggie See, all her life she'd been led to believe that something this big (*Indicates two inches.*) was really this big. (*Indicates twelve inches.*) When she finds out on her wedding night – well, severely impaired her judgement.

Jim *goes.*

Kate I don't know why you always have to start up like that in front of Jim.

Polly I feel sorry for him an' all. It's not right at that, that a frail young lad like that should be having to do this sort of work.

Ellen Don't forget he's getting paid half again what we are.

Maggie Oh Christ, don't start up on that bleedin' union business.

Annie What happened to her?

Polly God told her in a dream: Ellen, you are a leader of women – get them interested in the unions.

Annie No, that woman, Maud.

Kate They're talking about unions as in trade not as in marriage.

Polly She went into production – of offspring.

Annie (*to* **Ellen**) You got children, then?

Ellen No, I work here.

Maggie No, Maud has. She's like the rest of 'em – a one woman baby show.

Ellen What you talking about. She ain't even had her first one yet.

Maggie Give her time.

Ellen She don't want no more. I met her down Church Street on Sunday, she said when this one was born she ain't having no more.

Polly What's she planning on – becoming a widow?

Ellen No, her sister works in the sausage skin factory. That gave her the idea. She tells me if them sausage skins can hold sausages and not split then what's the betting . . .

Maggie Not in front of the nipper.

Kate Who are you calling a nipper? I'm fifteen next birthday and I wouldn't care but you ain't never even got yourself a chap.

Maggie And you've got one so frail that he has trouble carting his own intestines around never mind a hundred weight of cattle tubes.

Annie I still don't understand, what trade are you in, Ellen?

Ellen Eh?

Polly You mentioned trade unions, remember?

Maggie Polly, did you have to bring that up again?

Ellen (*to* **Annie**) Oh, right. No, I'm not in one but I'm trying to get one started.

Maggie Leave it out, Ellen, you're worse than a dog with a bone you are. None of us want to go to your boring meetings and read boring books and drink tea with boring people called Jasper, Sebastian and Beatrice.

Ellen (*to* **Annie**) But I've had a little bit of trouble getting anyone interested.

Annie I only just got here, I don't want to go on strike.

Ellen Oh, and do you want to go on working a thirteen hour day in terrible conditions?

Maggie (*to the others*) Here she goes. Ignore her. Pretend you can't hear.

Ellen Being treated like you're not worth a light. No pay when you're ill. No compensation when you chop your hand off. Laid off with no warning.

Harry *comes in.*

Harry I'm sure Mr Cuttle-Smythe would be very interested to hear your views.

Ellen Oh, blimey, I never heard you come in.

Harry 'Course you never.

Maggie She was only joking, Harry.

Harry Mister Dedham to you. None of you are indispensable – right, not one, so just remember that. (*To* **Annie**.) Don't let them corrupt you dear, they're scum this lot, each and every one of them. How come a little flower like yerself couldn't do better than this?

Annie I don't know Mister Dedham.

He tweaks **Annie's** ear.

Polly (*winks at* **Kate**) Oh, Harry, some fat's got stuck in the bloody gully, quick.

Harry Let's have a look then.

Polly (*picks up the fat*) Oh. I've got it. (*Offering it to* **Harry**.) You going outside?

Harry (*takes it*) Oh, give it here.

Polly Ta.

Harry *goes.*

Kate (*to* **Annie**) You gotta watch him. Always hold the mop like this. Wiv the handle sticking out at the end. If he comes up behind you, pretend you don't know and then just jab the broom right back inter his turkey gristle.

Annie Do you get turkeys here then?

Maggie Yeah, 'cept they're still walking around on two legs, giving orders.

Kate (*to* **Annie**) 'Ere, how old are you?

Annie Sixteen.

Kate Oh. Aye. Where you bin?

Annie Nowhere.

Pause.

Maggie Where d'you live now?

Annie St John's.

Ellen Oh? St John's, eh? You still live with your mum and dad? (**Annie** *shakes her head.*) What you got, a room then? (**Annie** *doesn't respond.*)

Maggie Leave it Ellen.

Ellen Well, where . . . Oh, you in that house, ain't yer, fer friendless girls.

Annie *nods but hangs her head in shame. Pause.*

Maggie So you had a baby then?

Annie Born dead.

Ellen What you looking at the floor for? We ain't judging you.

Annie Everybody else does.

Polly Expect they do while you got that address.

Maggie You'd be better off getting yerself a decent place to live.

Ellen There's a room going, in the house where I am, if you want, you can come and see it this evening.

Annie They say I got to stay where I am.

Maggie What fer?

Annie Prevention. Stop me being loose living. That's why I couldn't go back into service an' had to work here.

Silence. **Annie** *has offended them.*

Polly Ellen was in service, weren't yer Ellen? Gave it up specially so as she could work here.

Annie What happened to you then?

Ellen It suited neither my health nor my temperament. In fact I only lasted a day.

Annie Lord Jesus, you must have done something terrible.

Ellen They done something terrible to me. I was thirteen right, and the boy was a year younger than me. His mother was in the room, mind, she didn't turn a hair. He threw his shoes at me and said, 'clean these at once.' I said 'Excuse me, poppet, but may I suggest you shove 'em up your arse hole.'

Annie You was lucky you had somewhere else to go.

Maggie (*to* **Annie**) I tell you girl, you may think this place is hell but we get paid in one week nearly what you get for a whole year in service, so by comparison it makes this place seem more like paradise.

Polly Except the only difference is, you didn't have to wear no clothes in the Garden of Eden. If you don't wear two coats in this cold hole you'll be in a wooden overcoat before you can say foot and mouth.

Jim *tries to enter without them seeing him. They pretend they haven't although they start a conversation for his 'benefit.'* **Annie** *looks worried, frightened that they may say something about her past in front of* **Jim**.

Ellen Now this place in St John's, didn't I read in the Kentish Mercury, I think it was, that they was pulling it down and going to put in its place a building so enormous it could fit the whole cattle market into it.

Maggie (*looks at her*) Did yer?

Ellen *winks at* **Maggie**.

Polly Oh yeah. Now you come to say it, I remember that an' all.

Ellen It's going to be changed into a refuge for loose and fallen men.

Kate Pull the other one.

Polly That's right. Any man who's so much as showed himself to anyone other than the midwife who delivered him is going to have to live there.

Jim *glances at* **Kate**. **Kate** *is looking at* **Polly**, *but* **Maggie** *sees* **Jim**.

Maggie (*to* **Kate**) And even ones who look at women will have to go there, for prevention is better than cure. (**Ellen** *joins in.*)

Kate Huh, that'll be the day.

They laugh. **Jim** *scurries out.*

Annie Please, please don't say nothing about me in front of the men.

Ellen Don't worry. We know what it's like if they find out, they think you're fair game.

Kate What you on about? Most blokes out there think we're rubbish. I mean as far as they're concerned, there's only one thing worse than being a gut girl and that's being a whore.

Ellen Time for tea. Kate tek Annie with yer so as you can show 'er.

Kate (*looks round to make sure they're not overheard*) You don't want to mind their talk. They're all right.

Annie Polly seems nice. The other two frighten me. Seem real hard.

Kate Listen, right, 'cos I thought that. I still do, especially about that Ellen. Then last Christmas me Mother died. I was right upset. She made us promise she wouldn't have no pauper's burial. I tried to reason with her. I says, you never would've spent that much money on yerself when you was alive, why worry when you ain't even going to be there to see it.

Annie I know but the old 'uns are funny that way aren't they?

Kate We done everything, but we never had enough money. It was Ellen, what stood outside the gate here on payday 'til she'd collected enough. And she jus' give it to me. Not a word, nothing. C'mon they'll all be moanin' an' groaning fer their tea. Don't worry you'll be all right.

They go. Crossfade to **Maggie, Polly** *and* **Ellen.**

Maggie Where have they got to?

Ellen Wherever it is, if they don't get back here soon they'll have me to answer to, never mind Harry.

Maggie Oh, hark at you.

Polly (*sings*) The working class can kiss my arse. I've got the foreman's job at last.

Ellen Oh, yes. How can a woman become a foreman?

Maggie Can't you talk about anything other than rights and wrongs and this way, that way, state of how-things-should-be nonsense.

Kate *and* **Annie** *return carrying the cans of tea.*

Polly (*looking at the tea*) Bloody hell. It isn't weak, it's helpless.

Maggie (*taking a mouthful*) And it's cold.

Kate (*excited*) Forget the tea. Forget the tea. Guess who we just saw – only Lady Helena and Lord Tartaden.

Polly What was they doing – walking on the water?

Kate No, they're here. In the market.

Maggie Butcher's shut – and she's run out of devilled kidneys.

Kate No, no, she's come to look at us all working.

Polly What does she think we are, a side show?

Ellen It'll be about that club she set up – a non-starter if ever I heard one.

Annie What club?

Maggie We don't rightly know. Some do-goody thing run by some interfering ladies with Jesus between the ears. We're supposed to go down there but we don't really fancy it.

Polly By all accounts, she's never shown her face in there and I bet my life she won't bother to poke her nose in here either.

Lady Helena *and* **Lord Edwin Tartaden** *appear at the other end of the shed.* **Harry** *seems intent on preventing them from entering.*

Harry Oh no, me lady. I implore you. You don't want to come in here. It's not fer someone of your sensibilities.

Lady Helena My good man. I am the best judge of my sensibilities. The very purpose of my visit is to meet these young ladies.

Harry Ladies? Oh your highness, how you compliment them. Why their language would knock you sideways – it's enough to stagger a horse.

Lady Helena I think you are forgetting that I experienced my poor husband bleed to death. His language was choice, forgivable in the circumstances, but choice.

Edwin (*to* **Harry**) I shall see that no harm befalls the Duchess. So be a good chap and allow us through.

Harry (*nervously*) Well, of course.

Lady Helena *and* **Edwin** *advance.* **Harry** *goes.* **Polly, Maggie** *and* **Ellen** *work with vigour and perhaps a little unnecessary vulgarity.* **Annie** *gazes, stunned by admiration.* **Kate** *too, is a little in awe. She mops the floor frantically trying to make it a more acceptable place for* **Lady Helena's** *feet.* **Edwin** *takes one look.*

Edwin Oh my. (*Softly.*) Oh my. (*Faintly.*) Oh my.

He collapses on the floor. **Maggie** *is near enough to him to have caught him but she continues with her work.*

Lady Helena Oh dear, dearie me. (*Calls.*) Foreman. Would it be possible to give Lord Tartaden a cup of tea?

Harry *rushes in, puts his hands under* **Edwin**'s *armpits and drags him off.*

Lady Helena I really must apologise for Lord Tartaden. Oh please carry on with your work.

Annie (*blurts out*) That nearly happened to me this morning. It's my first day like so I know what it feels like.

Lady Helena I suppose in time one becomes accustomed to it. I don't suppose you ever find it pleasant though. What's your name?

Annie Annie. And – er – this is Ellen, Polly, Kate and Maggie.

Lady Helena Pleased to meet you. How many young women are there working in this market?

Silence.

Ellen Well, there's about fifty in each shed and there's ten sheds in all, so it's above five hundred.

Lady Helena And what sort of work, I mean, what does your job entail?

Polly Put your finger right on it, madam, entrails.

Maggie Chop up animal flesh, sorting and cleaning the tubes from the hearts, livers, kidneys, lungs and that.

Ellen Getting the meat ready for how you find it in the butcher's basically.

Lady Helena Hence the collective noun for you all: The Gut Girls. (*They look at her.*) Oh I'm quite *au fait* with the word 'gut' – and I often have to use the word belly – in the context of asking my cook occasionally if we may have (*Whispers.*) belly of pork.

Polly Oh right. (*Wraps up a piece of pork.*) There you go. (*Gives it to* **Lady Helena**.) Don't say nothing.

Lady Helena Thank you very much, but no, (*Giving the meat back.*) I don't think so. The purpose of my visit was to talk to you.

Maggie Oh?

Lady Helena Are all the women working here as young as you?

Kate Mostly, 'cos of course they leave when they gets married and that, but there a few old 'uns like nearly thirty.

Lady Helena And do you become rather demoralised working here?

Polly We got as much morals as the next person, lady.

Ellen Yes we do. The conditions we work in, as you can see, leave a lot of room for improvement.

Maggie Shut it, Ellen. Lady Helena don't want to know about that.

Lady Helena But I do. I have heard about this place. And I wanted to see it for myself. I agree with you, it is gruesome work.

Annie Someone's got to do it, I suppose.

Lady Helena I don't know if you know but I have set up a club for you, for any young women working here – in Creek Road, not two minutes walk away.

Maggie We did hear about it.

Lady Helena I am baffled as to why it's been so poorly attended.

Polly To be honest with you, we don't have the time.

Ellen Life's too short.

Maggie Life's for the livers.

Lady Helena But it's in the evening. It doesn't start until seven.

Polly But we don't knock off 'til eight.

Lady Helena So then what do you do?

Maggie Most of us have to go home, help get the tea, put our younger brothers and sisters to bed.

Ellen Sleep. We have to be back here at seven in the morning.

Lady Helena Don't you have any time for yourselves at all?

Polly We might have a drink after work, go to the music hall occasionally.

Lady Helena But the club, the whole purpose of it, is for you. To give you some time for yourselves, something specially for you. Not work, whether it's here or at home but a place to go that's warm and safe and great fun.

They all look rather unsure.

Lady Helena There's a piano, we have coffee and cake. And plenty of other things.

Maggie What d'you want ter go wasting yer time with us fer? We got jobs and homes. There's them far worse off than us. You've no need to bother yerself we're all right as we is, honest.

Lady Helena Your unselfish attitude is commendable but I have done other things in this area, for other people and I thought it was time that you, the young ladies of Deptford got a piece of the cake. Your well-being is now, well, my concern.

Polly No need to concern yerself further, now you've seen us. (*Holds up her arm to display her biceps.*) See, we're strong as oxes.

Lady Helena Please say you'll think about it.

Maggie We'll do that all right.

Ellen (*mutters*) That's about all we'll do.

Kate Oh, we will, madam.

Lady Helena Well, next port of call, the sheep-gutting sheds.

Polly No, they ain't got no morals, what they got is offal.

Lady Helena Pardon?

Polly Offal.

Lady Helena Sorry?

Polly Entails only entrails. Just a joke like.

Lady Helena I'll say goodbye for now but I do hope you give the club a try. You won't regret it. It was nice to talk with you. (*She shakes hands with them all.*) Polly, Kate, Annie, Maggie, Ellen.

They all look aghast as her white glove becomes bloodstained but she appears not to notice. She goes.

Annie (*looks at her hand in wonderment*) I don't think I'll ever wash it again.

Ellen If you carries on looking at it like that, boggled-eyed, and you starts chopping, you won't have to wash it, you'll hack it off.

Kate She was lovely though weren't she? See that dress on her – what it must've cost.

Ellen Hark at yer. I thought you didn't like toffs.

Kate She ain't no toff. She's related to royalty. Yer saw how she was with us, spoke to us like we was taking tea with her or something.

Annie She might be dressed expensive but didn't she look comical.

Polly Yeah, she never even had no earrings – poor cow.

Ellen If you ask me, she wants us out of here, so men can have our jobs.

Kate Don't talk stupid – they wouldn't do this job. It's only a club she's set up.

Harry *comes in.*

Harry Fancy her stooping to visit you lot. I bet you showed us up good and proper.

Ellen She were asking after you Harry, weren't she gils?

Harry You. How many times do I have ter tell you. You call me Mister Dedham. (*Then.*) What d'you mean, asking after me?

Maggie She says ter us, she says, with a little like shiver in her voice, who's that handsome bulky foreman?

Harry Go on wiv yer.

Ellen She reckons to us that she'd really like to let her hair down with a body like yourn.

Harry That's quite enough. (*But preening himself.*)

Maggie So you'd better watch out Mister Dedham 'cos it's been two years since her husband bled to death. Maybe she wants to see it 'appen again.

Harry Now you've all stopped to have a good boggle at a lady, something you lot will never be if yer lives to be a hundred, don't think you'll be stopping again for yer dinner break. Also we don't want yer sloping off outside 'cos they're unloading. We don't want the cows getting frightened before they reach the slaughtering pens. (*He goes.*)

Ellen But Harry, we need some fresh air.

Harry (*comes back*) Well, if yer go out there the air wouldn't be fresh no more. You lot would turn it rancid.

Maggie (*bringing her knife down*) Time we done something about him.

Ellen Well, what have I been on about these weeks, eh? Organising ourselves.

Polly Right girls, it's pork sandwiches tomorrow.

Maggie Say no more.

Annie Do they, like, give us a discount then?

Polly Very generous discount. Don't you worry.

Ellen I don't know how you can possibly eat the stuff when yer see what happens to it all day.

Polly Except Ellen, who'll be sticking to her lettuce sandwiches through thick and thin.

Maggie She only eats rabbit food, 'er. If she's not careful she'll end up with rickets.

Ellen You don't know what you're talking about, you don't.

Polly (*to* **Annie**) It's these modern people she's acquainted with.

Maggie She'll be riding one of them bicycles next, you wait.

Ellen Leave it out.

Annie What modern people?

Polly Troublemakers.

Maggie This little band of educated pilgrims what go round stirring up folks. First she fell in with the fish filleting lot, then with the fur pullers. She tries to do fer workers what John Wesley done fer Methodists.

Annie What's that got to do with eating lettuce?

Polly Oh my dear, they wouldn't be seen dead eating flesh.

Annie (*gags*) I don't feel . . .

Ellen Go outside.

Annie But he . . . oh, hell! I'll have ter . . . (*She goes.*)

Ellen I suppose I'd better go and see . . .

Maggie Leave it. You heard what Harry said.

Kate She won't want us standing over her anyway.

Polly I thought she'd got used to it. I never meant to . . . well.

Maggie It weren't you mentioning meat what done it. It was you mentioning bleeding lettuce.

Ellen Some of us will never get used to it. Don't you think it's cruel, what happens to those defenceless animals?

Polly At least they got the chance to run away. You should spare a thought for them poor lettuces, Ellen, just sitting there waiting for you to rip 'em up, without hope of escape.

Kate We're bleeding lucky we get to eat meat. Before I worked here, if we saw any at home, it would go to me Dad and me brothers.

Maggie And, Ellen, if no bugger ate meat, we wouldn't have no jobs would we?

Scene Two

Lady Helena's *drawing room. She has changed her clothes. The clothes she wore to the Foreign Cattle Market are in a pile on the floor.*

Lady Helena Enter.

Emily Lord Tartaden is here to see you, madam.

The clothes stink to high heaven and **Emily** *tries not to sniff obviously, but at the same time tries to work out what the smell is.*

Lady Helena Thank you, Emily. Show him in, please.

Emily Very good, madam. (*She goes.*)

Lady Helena (*calls*) Oh Emily . . .

Emily (*comes back*) Yes, madam?

Lady Helena Would you please take these clothes to Johnson and instruct him to burn them.

Emily (*looking at the pile*) As you say madam. (*She bends to pick them up but then looks up.*) Begging your pardon, but all of them, madam?

Lady Helena Yes, yes. (*Then.*) Oh I see what you mean.

Yes, there are one or two delicate items of undergarment there. (*These should be the most enormous, heavy-boned corsets imaginable.*) Not an altogether savoury task for a man. No not at all. Would you perhaps take it upon yourself to dispose of them for me?

Emily Yes, madam. (*She picks up the pile of clothes, staggers to the door, the smell nearly knocking her over.*)

Lady Helena Oh Emily.

Emily (*turns*) Yes, madam?

Lady Helena They, the others, call you Emy – don't they?

Emily (*unnerved*) Why, yes, madam.

Lady Helena Could you spare a couple of moments of your time. Take a seat. Emy. I like that. It sounds friendly.

Surprised, **Emily** *does so. Still carrying the clothes throughout the conversation it appears that* **Lady Helena** *can't smell anything, while* **Emily** *tries not to show that she is reeling from the stench.*

Lady Helena I've had a rather interesting morning, Emy. I've been on a jaunt around Deptford.

Emily (*aghast*) Deptford?

Lady Helena Umm. Do you come from there?

Emily Why no, M'lady, I come from (*Proudly.*) Hatcham Park.

Lady Helena Well, I have set up a club for the young ladies working in the Foreign Cattle Market and this morning I paid them a visit.

Emily (*blurts out*) The Gut Girls? Begging your pardon, madam, I don't know what you want to go bothering with them for.

Lady Helena That is it, isn't it? The world knows what they do for a living and has labelled them accordingly. By themselves they are hardly likely to find the incentive to fight against becoming rough and unladylike.

Emily Well, come to think of it, no other employer would want to touch them with a barge pole.

Lady Helena What I cannot understand is why they are so reluctant to attend the club. They gave me one reason, and I'm seeing Mr Cuttle-Smythe this afternoon about that, but I wondered if you had any suggestions.

Emily I would think that if you were there in person, as it were, it would make a world of difference.

Lady Helena But the ladies who run it are so much better at it than me.

Emily But they're not you.

Lady Helena Umm. No, you're quite right, they're not. Thank you Emily.

Emily What for, madam?

Lady Helena An excellent idea. I'm not going to give up on this. Every time I think of those poor creatures my heart goes out to them.

Emily Poor is one thing they're not. Not really, madam.

Lady Helena Oh my goodness, I'd forgotten all about Lord Tartaden. Please tell him to come straight through.

Emily *goes.* **Edwin Tartaden** *comes in. He kisses* **Helena's** *hand by way of greeting.*

Edwin Helena . . . (*He kneels.*)

Lady Helena Oh Tarty, please stop making a fool of yourself.

Edwin If I were a brave man I would ask for your hand.

Lady Helena Get up this instant, stop being so ridiculous.

Edwin (*stands up*) You are peeved at my untimely departure from the cattle market. My manhood has let you down.

Lady Helena Your manhood is neither here nor there to me. I have asked you here to enlist your support. As a friend. That's all.

Edwin I will do anything to win your affection.

Lady Helena Time to drop this toddle talk Tarty. To

business. Now you didn't meet those poor children this morning.

Edwin No, how impolite of me, I forgot to ask, how did it go?

Lady Helena I met a good number. Their talk was, well, strangely ill-mannered.

Edwin In what way?

Lady Helena Well, they spoke to me as if I was any old body.

Edwin Oh how dreadful, Helena.

Lady Helena It wasn't really. Actually, it was rather refreshing.

Edwin Oh.

Lady Helena It was a revelation. Really, I don't know what I'd expected. I suppose, a rather mind-numbed, dreary collection of girls, but they were full of vigour, actually laughed and chatted with me. I think, well I hope, that they were as intrigued with me as I was with them. But those sheds, the airlessness, the smell.

Edwin Don't remind me.

Lady Helena Covered in stomach linings. Some of them working up to their ankles in blood.

Edwin Please, Helena, spare me.

Lady Helena How would you like to sort through livers, lungs, hearts, kidneys.

Edwin Offal.

Lady Helena Yes, it is. Awful. (*Pause, then giggles.*) Oh, that was it, the joke about being offal, I see now.

Edwin Sorry?

Lady Helena Just something they said. Imagine, Edwin, being pushed into those working conditions at a tender age. No wonder they appear so rough. They have to be. It's disgraceful. I cannot believe what we're breeding.

Edwin Or not breeding. The fact of the matter is that there is a grave concern for the high infant mortality rate among the lower echelons *vis-a-vis* will there be enough healthy young men for the Army in the next generation?

Lady Helena And where does the fault lie?

Edwin With the women, who else? They go out to work like men, drink like men, curse, well – you met them. Some even have started to deny, and here you must excuse my unpardonable frankness, deny their menfolk marital relations for fear of . . .

Lady Helena I should imagine, when one has very little money, feeding one's children and oneself becomes an arduous task.

Edwin Lack of money may indeed affect the mortality rate but it is a poor excuse for having no . . .

Lady Helena I'm not concerned about their relations, but about them *vis-a-vis* their squalid existence.

Emily *enters*.

Emily Mr Cuttle-Smythe to see you, madam.

Lady Helena Please show him in.

Emily *goes*.

Edwin If it makes you happy you shall have my support.

Lady Helena Thank you.

Emily *enters with Mr Cuttle-Smythe*.

Lady Helena Mr Cuttle-Smythe, how lovely to see you. It's so kind of you to call by at such short notice.

Arthur Not at all. The pleasure is all mine, Lady Helena, Lord Tartaden.

Lady Helena I'll come straight to the point Mr Cuttle-Smythe. I've asked you here because my information tells me that you own a large proportion of the Foreign Cattle Market.

Arthur You elevate my status too highly. I wish I did, alas, I am merely a partner of a firm which owns some of the gutting sheds.

Lady Helena Ah, that's what I'm interested in.

Arthur Really? You'd like to make me an offer?

Lady Helena Pardon?

Arthur I thought, sorry. That you were interested in buying –

Lady Helena I am sorry to disappoint you, but what I actually wanted to ask you for was a favour.

Arthur Oh, well, by all means. If I can be of help–

Lady Helena I would like you to give the girls permission to leave work an hour earlier on a Thursday evening as an incentive for them to attend my girls' club.

Arthur But that's a lot of working hours, Mam. With due respect. Do you realise what you are asking for?

Lady Helena I'm sure you could use your influence.

Arthur And, I was going to say, that it's not really up to me. (*Pause.*) Of course, I will ask.

Lady Helena Thank you. And your wife, how is she? I was rather hoping she might accompany you this afternoon.

Arthur She – er – I'm afraid she – er – had another commitment.

Lady Helena I did meet her at Lady Somerville's. We were given a talk about the life and work of Dr Garrison, the Argentine missionary extraordinaire – a thoroughly inspiring evening it was too.

Arthur Oh, yes?

Lady Helena It occurred to me that your wife, Priscilla, if I remember correctly, might like to help me with my work in Deptford?

Arthur Well, you see, how can I put it, my wife is rather withdrawn, not a person who is readily at ease in social situations. I don't mean to undermine her, but I don't think she'd be suited to that sort of thing. To be brutally frank, she suffers from melancholy.

Lady Helena Please just ask her to call on me. After all, it's not really a social situation we're talking about.

Arthur Certainly, I will, Lady Helena. (*Shakes her hand.*) Lord Tartaden.

Arthur *goes*.

Edwin Even our Lord only turned water into wine not –

Lady Helena I was born to privilege and I am aware of it. Please don't hold a candle for me, Tarty. I will never marry again. I am going to dedicate the rest of my life to charitable work.

Edwin You will forgo your own happiness for the sake of the lowest of the low. Oh yes, Helena, even by their own kind they are seen as marginally better than whores.

Lady Helena Edwin Tartaden, may I remind you that you are speaking to me.

Edwin It is my broken heart talking.

Lady Helena Well curb it. And, if you want my opinion it is the men who live off those unfortunate women who are the lowest of the low.

Edwin You are so exquisite when you're serious.

Lady Helena And so would you be. If you really knew of the plight of these poor, wretched, miserable girls.

Scene Three

Those poor miserable girls, wearing wonderful hats and earrings, are laughing and giggling on their way out of work. **Maggie** *and* **Ellen** *support* **Annie** *who appears to be unable to walk unaided.*

Harry Oi!

Ellen Hold up. Keep still. Harry's here.

They stop, terrified. All look serious. **Annie** *looks terrified.*

Polly (*to* **Annie**) Look down at the floor, gil, it shows on yer boat.

Harry What's going on here? Oi, what's the matter with her?

Ellen Are you a doctor now then, Mr Dedham?

Harry Oh no. What's happened? We renounce all liability.

Maggie Well, in this case, rest easy, 'cos it ain't under no circumstances your responsibility.

Harry What is?

Maggie You ought to be ashamed of yerself, grown man not bein' able to guess. (*Whispers.*) Women's troubles.

Harry (*embarrassed*) Oh. (*Disgusted.*) Well, don't just stand there, shift yourselves.

He goes. They continue walking.

Polly Come on Annie, we only got ter get as far as the Brown Bear.

Annie Can't we just go to that one – The Seaman's Arms?

Polly You're joking.

Kate Come on gel, best foot forward.

Man (*off, shouts*) You're quiet tonight gels!

Maggie Sing! Sing something.

Annie *starts singing, quite seriously, 'Jesus bids us shine, with a pure, clear light.' The others stop, horrified.*

Maggie Bloody hell! No, not that, Jesus Christ. (*She starts singing 'Joshua, Joshua . . .' The others join in.*)

Bert (*voice off*) Oh Gawd, Charlie, the gut girls is out.

Charlie (*voice off*) Quick, duck down Queen Street.

Maggie (*calls after them*) You goin' to stand us all a drink then, mate?

The women laugh.

Ellen (*calls*) Where are you off to in such a hurry? Come back here.

They go into the Brown Bear. **Len** *the Publican, is less than welcoming. He is also rather intimidated by them.*

Len Now look girls, how many more . . .

Maggie (*interrupting him. Leans across at him menacingly.*) We ain't girls, right Len? We're ladies, got it?

Len Oh yeah, since when?

Ellen Since today. When the Duchess of Deptford took lunch with us.

Len Oh yeah. (*About their bloodstained coats.*) Spilt her best claret down yer did she?

Maggie Less lip and more service is called for Len.

Len Listen girls, ladies. Whatever. You've got your own places to have a drink in. Since you bin coming in here, chaps don't feel safe. It's killing off me custom.

Kate We're better custom than the blokes. Where's our beers?

Len Ladies drink gin.

Ellen Ah, now that's the thing about being a lady, you have the choice and you know what ours is.

Annie My leg, my leg, I think it's broken.

Maggie Now look what you made us forget. Don't look, have a bit of decency, turn yer back.

Len *turns obediently and gets the drinks.* **Kate** *and* **Polly** *bend down and untie the piece of meat strapped to* **Annie's** *leg.*

Annie It's numb. I can't feel it.

Polly Give it a rub.

Ellen (*to* **Len**) What you gawping at? Mek yerself useful and bolt the door.

Maggie (*to* **Annie**) Is that better?

Annie (*nods*) Ouch. Pins and needles.

Polly It'll go off. (*She lifts the piece of meat.*)

Ellen Newspaper, Len.

Len Oh, mind me tables, girls.

Polly (*drops the meat none too delicately onto a stool which then collapses under the weight*) Oops.

Len Watch it. Watch it. The furniture doesn't grow on trees. Bleedin' hell.

Ellen Stop bellyaching Len. Them things are riddled. Wonder the woodworm ain't soiled the meat.

Polly *lifts the meat to the next table more gently.* **Maggie** *takes her knife and swiftly chops it into pieces.*

Maggie Stinking joint.

Ellen I'm pleased you're coming round to my point of view. (*She wraps the meat.*)

Kate What you grumbling 'bout. This was fresh in today.

Maggie I weren't meaning the meat, I was talking about Len's piss pot of a pub.

Polly Well, we ain't stopping in here much longer, are we.

Len *brings them their pints.*

Maggie You can unlock the door now, Len.

Len No point, nobody's going to come in while you lot are still in here.

Ellen *and* **Maggie** *lift* **Annie** *onto the table.*

Polly Here's to your first day, Annie.

They all raise their glasses. **Annie** *takes a delicate sip. The rest of them down it in one.*

Len (*sees* **Annie**) Bleedin' hell.

Annie Let's go down that club on Thursday.

Ellen You'd be better off coming to the Union Meeting, you would.

Maggie (*to* **Ellen**) You know why you don't like ol' Lady Helena – 'cos you're a bit the same. She's trying to get us in one club and you're trying to get us in another.

Polly An' if Harry had his way, we'd all be in the club.

Awkward silence. **Annie** *cringes.*

Ellen Come on Annie, me and you going to find you a new place to live.

Annie I told yer – they won't let me leave.

Ellen We'll see about that.

Polly I better get off home meself.

Kate C'mon then.

They finish their drinks and stand.

Len 'Ere, where you off to?

Polly Somewhere where the stools ain't shit, and can stand up by themselves.

Maggie You want a couple of bottles to tek away, Polly?

Polly Yeah, ta.

Maggie And four to tek out, Len.

Polly *picks up the broken table and puts it under her arm.*

Len (*with four bottles in his hand*) What you doing, you can't mek off with that.

Polly Getting out of your way, Len. It's only littering up your establishment, lowering the tone.

Len That's a shilling you owe me all told.

Maggie Behave yourself you mutton head. (*She puts a packet of meat on the bar.*) Since when did we shortchange you?

Polly, Ellen, Annie *and* **Kate** *go.*

Len 'Ere Maggie, you ain't looking fer a husband yet are yer?

Maggie I ain't likely ter find one if I stop in here jawing with you, am I? What anyone would be wanting one for beats me.

Len Oh.

Maggie What's it to you anyway?

Len Ter tell the truth, we get some rough fellas in here and that. I don't mind admitting it, they fair put the wind up me, but with you here like beside me, I don't think I'd ever feel frightened again.

Maggie Oh Len, you're such a lump of lard. (*She ruffles his hair, accidentally nearly knocking his head off and goes.*)

Len (*with admiration*) What a woman.

Lady Helena, *who has been sitting in her corner, reading the Bible throughout this, now closes it and her eyes.*

Lady Helena Dear Father, who knowest all things, please hear your servant at this time. Give me the strength and comfort which helped to sustain me through my husband's illness. That I, who know the despair and ugliness which suffering brings, might use my knowledge to thy purpose. Please, I ask that you might grant me the grace to overcome my awkwardness with these girls and give me the humanity to remember that we are all your children, equal in your eyes. Guide me along the path thou has chosen for me. That I might share the gifts which in thy graciousness thou hast bestowed upon me. In the hope that through me they will learn of thy everlasting love. Amen.

Scene Four

*Polly's Mum (***Edna***) sits in a chair, peeling potatoes. Although she doesn't let it show, she is really pleased to see her daughter.* **Polly** *comes in, two bottles of stout in one hand, the broken table in the other and the meat under her arm.*

Polly Oi! Mother!

Edna Taken up totting, 'ave we? (*Meaning the table.*)

Polly Jus' fell apart in me hands down Len's.

Edna How come you got to take it home?

Polly Public bar ain't it? Public's entitled to it. Thought them next door be glad of it fer firewood.

Edna They chopped up the shutters today. Ain't got one stick of furniture in there now. I offers him that chair we got upstairs, says look it's no use to me, I can't get up there but he wouldn't hear of it. Pride, pride, pride. It's a good thing God knows, but it'll carry 'em all off ter the workshouse.

Polly I'll chuck it over their yard right. Then you go out an' do one of your carry ons about this street bein' used for tipping rubbish, and that way he'll think by burning it he'll be doing us a favour.

Edna I said to him, I said, what you going to do when the vicar comes round and he ain't got nothing but bare floorboards to rest his arse on.

Polly I'm sure if Jesus stooped to a stable, the vicar can manage. 'Ere now talking of stooping guess who came round and spoke to us all today – Our Lady of Deptford.

Edna What fer?

Polly I dunno. So as she could have a butchers I s'pose.

Edna She didn't want no quarter of tripe. It smells.

Polly Thank Gawd you reminded me. (*She takes the meat from under her arm and puts it in* **Edna's** *lap.*)

Edna Well, that'll have plenty of flavour that will, feels half cooked already.

Polly I'll go and start it shall I?

Edna In a minute, sit down and tell us about your day.

Polly Where's the boys?

Edna Misbehaved at school today, so I sent 'em to bed without no supper.

Polly Oh, you never.

Edna Don't worry, I weakened about half an hour ago – took 'em up some bread and a scrape. So, have you got any more gossip?

Polly New girl started – Annie – ter take Maud's place. Fallen woman like.

Edna Public bars, fallen women, appearances from the gentry. You sure you been to work and not to the music hall.

Polly What do you mean it 'smells'?

Edna Them types poking their noses in. Oh, yes, with the best intentions granted, but mark my words, they always end up making things worse.

Polly I don't see how they can though. I mean as long as people eat meat, I'll always have a job. The only thing that could make anything worse is the barmy idea that you've only got to eat vegetables.

Edna Well, don't waste no time worrying over that – it'll never catch on. Talking of daft ideas, how is Ellen the mouth?

Fade to **Annie** *and* **Ellen**.

Scene Five

Ellen This is my room.

Annie Blimey, it's so tidy.

Ellen When I moved in I, well, I wanted it to look different than me home. Everything there was so cluttered.

Annie And all them books. Was them shelves here?

Ellen No, I made them. I'll show you how if you want some in your room.

Annie I can hardly believe it. You didn't half stand up to her – Mrs Pickles at the home.

Ellen (*mimicking Mrs Pickles*) Are you sure, Annie dear child? Deptford is such a grotesquely insalubrious area with all manner of temptations to corrode a young woman's moral conduct.

Annie I know she was a silly bat and that, but she can't help the way she talks and she done all right by me.

Ellen What? Shut up in a prison with the Holy Trinity for breakfast, dinner and tea and a load of hoity-toity nonsense in between.

Annie I never 'ad no place else to go did I? It was them, or the streets, or the workhouse. Yeah, so I got the lectures, the looking down the nose, but I tell you one thing, it's a lot easier to stomach when you ain't starving hungry. I was fed proper there, they saw to that.

Ellen What about yer chap then? Buggered off I suppose. (*Pause.*) Would you like me to help paint your room?

Annie No, no it's all right. I like that paper. (*Suddenly.*) He weren't my chap were he? And he's not buggered off nowhere. He's still living the life of Riley fer all I knows.

Ellen Listen, you don' have to say nothing. You just have to say 'Ellen, you got too much of what the dog sniffs its arse with,' and I'll hold me mouth. I won't take offence.

Annie I was in service, oh, not round here, no, in a beautiful house in Blackheath, and I was real proud of meself, oh, I was. The master and mistress was all right, never thrashed you or anything, they was above that. Had a son at Oxford University, really nice spoken, educated gentleman. When he came home in the holiday, he wouldn't let me be. In front of anybody, I mean, he treated me like dirt, but would creep up on me when no one was about. I fought him. I pleaded with him, I threatened him, but he'd laugh. His Mama would never believe it of her darling son. Oh, and I wasn't the only one, and it didn't only happen once and when I fell, that was it – got shot of me. I 'ad nowhere ter go, nowhere. I walked the streets and I was picked up and taken to be examined – six months gone I was – for diseases; to them I was a prostitute and the way they treat you and the way they look at you, and the way they hate you, and the way they blame you and everyone blames me. But I never cried, not one of them saw me cry and when I got to that home, it was awful but it was heaven. And even when I was told it was dead I never cried. Why don't they tell you birth is such an awful, bloody, terrible, painful thing. It was born with the cord round its neck. It had strangled itself the poor, poor, little tiny thing and I looked at it before they took it away and I thought, you lucky, lucky bastard, how much better if I'd have been born like that.

She starts to sob for the first time since the baby was born. **Ellen** *looks at her and puts her arms round her and lets her cry.*

Scene Six

Fade to **Kate** *and* **Jim**.

Jim What was Lady Helena talking to you lot for this morning?

Kate She's set up some poxy club.

Jim Where? Why don't we go there now 'stead of being out here by the river?

Kate It's only for girls.

Jim That's not fair.

Kate You earn more than me.

Jim So?

Kate That's not fair either.

Jim You've been listening to that Ellen. She's not right in the head.

Kate Don't say that. She's been a good friend to me, you know it. I like her.

Jim I wish we could get married now, then you wouldn't have to work there at all.

Kate I'd have to work somewhere. We couldn't live off your money and I'm not taking in washing and ending up me veins all bulging like Maggie's ol' girl.

Jim But when the children come along . . .

Kate 'Ere, they was saying something today – umm – about sausage skins.

Jim Katie. How could you? I'm not putting no sausage skin on my . . . fer no one. I'm really shocked at you, you've got jus' like them and you used to be real nice.

Kate I am real nice ain't I, but if you think I'm going to spend me life working like a horse fer nothing you'd be better off marrying a horse.

Jim I'd have to put a saddle and bridle on yer so as I could ride you down the street like a real gent.

Kate (*suddenly tightening her hold round his neck aggressively*) What you talking about? I'd squash the breath outta yer.

Jim (*struggles*) Leggo.

Kate (*laughs and lets go*) Sorry.

Jim Lucky none of the blokes could see me. They'd make mincemeat outta me.

Kate You don't like working there either do you?

Jim I hate it. To the others, it's just a job. They get used to it don't think about it – they're lucky. I don't seem to be able to get used to it.

Kate Best just to try and think of something else. I do, except when we get the meat and it's still warm. That's horrible.

Jim What do you think about, then?

Kate Daydreams mostly, but then there's always quite a lot of chat.

Jim You know what I dream about? Having a shop.

Kate What, a bleeding butcher's shop?

Jim No, a toy shop, with sweets, gobstoppers, lucky bags.

Kate (*joining in*) And ballad sheets and jumping jacks.

Jim And proper toys made of wood. I could make them.

Kate And I could paint 'em.

Jim But people like us don't get shops. I mean we don't know where to start.

Kate 'Course we do. Look at Mrs Jones in Prince Street, she turned her front parlour into a shop.

Jim Didn't last long.

Kate Only 'cos her old man come back to her.

Jim We don't know enough about it.

Kate We could find out.

Jim That might be one of the things they tell yer at the club.

Kate Oh, yeah, that and how to give yer profits back to Jesus.

Scene Seven

Fade to **Maggie** *and her mum,* **Eady,** *who is putting washing through a mangle.*

Maggie Evening, Mother. I brought you a bottle.

Eady Par, if it's not enough your father spending all his waking hours in the alehouse, now you're at it as well.

Maggie (*opening her own bottle and taking a swig*) You know you like one of an evening.

Eady Look at you supping that like you was a man or something. Put it down and give me a hand.

Maggie (*does so*) New girl started today.

Eady (*not at all interested*) Mmm.

Maggie (*trying to gain her interest*) Ellen's gone with her to find her somewhere to live.

Eady Mmm.

Maggie She was living in that place in Ashmead Road.

Eady She what? She's one of them sort then.

Maggie Suppose she must be.

Eady Disgusting.

Maggie She ain't brazen or nothing.

Eady What would you know, her sort seldom are brazen in front of women. Different story with the men though. That place where you work must be hell on earth. Come home stinking to high heaven, no wonder you can't get a man, no one could come within a mile of yer without keeling over.

Maggie I don't want no man.

Eady You what? What did you say?

Maggie I don't want to finish up like you, do I? Eleven children and half as many miscarriages.

Eady Shut your mouth.

Maggie What do I want with that, eh?

Eady Oh, you think when I was your age I thought I'd be spending the rest of me life being a drudge? That I wouldn't be able to have no sleep fer working, working, working, all day and half the night?

Maggie Why did you then?

Eady Did what?

Maggie Become a drudge.

Eady Because that's what's destined fer us, ain't it? Get married, have children, half kill yourself trying to mek ends meet, that's our lot. That's life and there's no denying it.

Maggie It's not going to be my life.

Eady Ha, that's what I used to say. You'll learn. Though I doubt if you'll learn too much off of them hussies down that hole where you work.

They continue to work in silence.

Maggie Why d'you do it then – have children? The whole thing don't seem to give you no pleasure, nor comfort or no joy as I see it.

Eady Because, because, there are no whys and wherefores, it's natural, it's what we was put here for, that's why. And if I'd dared to say to me Mother half of what you say to me I'd have been hit into next week.

Maggie But . . .

Eady Nothing else happen today then?

Maggie Oh yes, Lady Helena dropped in to see us.

Eady I know, don't I. Not that you'd ever tell me that. No, you relish your acquaintance with fallen women more. No, I heard it from Mrs Know-all-know-nothing in Czar Street. So what did she want?

Maggie For us to go to her silly club, to learn how to become decent wives and mothers, I suppose.

Eady If she's putting herself out for you, least you can do is show willing. God knows you could do with some lessons on those topics.

Maggie (*sweetly*) But I've learnt all I need to know about being a good Mother from you.

Scene Eight

Outside the shed, **Polly, Maggie, Ellen** *and* **Kate** *have finished their lunch.*

Polly At least we've been allowed to eat our sarnies outside, since old Helena graced us.

Ellen Oh, Gawd, if they told you lot to work eight days a week, standing on yer heads, I'm sure after a couple of months you'd be saying 'It ain't that bad really.'

Polly Pay attention everybody, the saviour of working girls is talking.

Kate Horrible though her birth-place was, a mere back room in Butchers Row, ridiculed and scorned by the world she taught us how to be free.

Ellen One day . . .

Maggie One day, we'll be queuing up to buy her latest book. 'My Life's Work Amongst the Gut Girls of the Gutter.'

Ellen You can laugh but – (*She is interrupted by* **Harry**.)

Harry Time to get back to work, girls. Not you Ellen. You can take over from Jim this afternoon.

Ellen That's not my job.

Harry He's needed in the slaughtering pens. (*To* **Ellen**.) Unless you don't want a job at all.

Ellen *goes.*

Kate What you made him do that for?

Harry Since when did I answer to you? 'Ere where's the other one?

Polly Gone to strain her greens, if you must know.

Harry It'll be such a relief when Lady Helena has finished with you lot. I can't wait till I've got a bunch of decent young ladies working for me.

Maggie She ain't even starting with us never mind finishing so you can forget it.

Harry Not if old Cuttle-Smythe gets his way with the Guvnors. She's bent his ear good and proper. And, if and when he wins through, you'll all be enticed to attend soirees at that club every Thursday evening.

Kate What you on about, Harry?

Harry That's for me to know and you to find out. (*He turns, prances off.*) Yes, I'd be delighted to help you, sir. Charmed to make your acquaintance, sir. Anything you say, sir. Your wish is my command, sir.

Annie *comes in.*

Annie What's he up to?

Polly Don't worry about him. He's just had a turn.

Annie Where's Ellen?

Kate She's doing Jim's job for the rest of today.

Annie That ain't right.

Maggie Oh, no, living in the same house as Ellen ain't done you no good at all girl. She's contaminated yer.

Annie She's got good ideas she has.

Polly Her trouble is she prefers shouting to laughing.

Maggie I mean who else d'you know who'd rather read a book than go to the Music Hall?

Kate Don't talk about her when she's not here.

Annie There is more to life than having a good time in the couple of hours they give you off at the end of a day.

Polly What you on about? You was only saying the other day how you was, now you're used to it like, happier than you been in yer life.

Annie I am. I can choose what I do in the evenings, I don't have to clear up after other people. I've got enough money to pay me rent and still buy a new hat, and I got friends . . .

Kate So, what you moaning about?

Annie It would be better, say, if we had a separate room to eat in, and wash our hands and a proper place to piss.

Maggie You can't have everything you want in life, girl.

Scene Nine

Outside **Lady Helena***'s house.* **Arthur** *is exasperated by* **Priscilla***'s reluctance of mind. He grabs hold of her elbow and turns her towards him.*

Arthur For God's sake Priscilla, anyone would think I was asking you to put your head in the lion's den. All I am asking is that you be nice to Lady Helena for my sake.

Priscilla It's just that I don't . . .

Arthur I know you don't feel like it. I know you'd prefer to sit and stare out of the window all day. I know you don't feel cheerful but please at least act cheerful in front of her, don't show me up.

Priscilla I don't want to let you down . . .

Arthur Then prove it. You're my wife, this is the chance to show your worth. I don't ask much of you, God knows. Just do this for me. She likes you. It's very important it stays that way. If we can become good friends of hers who knows where it will lead . . .

Priscilla But this club, I'm nervous Arthur, I don't think I'm cut out . . .

Arthur Just go along with her ideas, crackpot as they sound – for me.

Priscilla But, I . . .

Arthur Try, woman, try. Try to be charming, enthusiastic and even vivacious. Don't you understand there's a lot riding on this for us. Don't throw it away.

Priscilla I will try.

Arthur That's it, please just look the part for me. Smile – that's better. Smile.

Lady Helena Priscilla, Arthur, how good of you to come.

Arthur Priscilla is very excited at the prospect of helping you with your work.

Priscilla It's just that I . . .

Arthur On the other matter, I have spoken to the girls' direct employers who have voiced, unfortunately, some concern over allowing the girls to leave an hour earlier on a Thursday. Mainly that it might encourage a lapse of punctuality, that sort of thing.

Lady Helena I can assure you that my aim is to help them lead more responsible lives.

Arthur I know that. It's just if you were able to write to the employers yourself, telling them of your intentions, I'm sure they would comply.

Lady Helena Of, course. I shall do that today.

Arthur I'll leave you two ladies to plan your strategies in peace. Lady Helena. Priscilla. (*He kisses* **Priscilla** *on the cheek. He goes.*)

Lady Helena Such a charming man, your husband.

Priscilla Mmm.

Lady Helena And I'm delighted that you are as excited about my little venture as I am.

Priscilla It's just that . . .

Lady Helena Shall I ring for Emy and ask for tea?

Priscilla No. Please don't bother on my account. Emy? Do you call your servants by their pet names?

Lady Helena I've taken to it quite recently. I can't see it does any harm. After all they are people too.

Priscilla Do they not take liberties, become over-familiar?

Lady Helena Not at all. If I saw any sign of that, I should put a stop to it.

Priscilla We have a great deal of trouble keeping parlourmaids in particular. There are so many households with vacancies, it seems servants can pick and choose where they go or what they want to do these days.

Lady Helena Quite so. But whilst choice is there for them, there is very little choice for those young women in the gutting sheds and they are the object of my concern. In fact it's high time I spoke to the MP for Deptford about them.

Priscilla Ah, I was just about . . .

Lady Helena I thought with your husband's interest in the place you might know something about them.

Priscilla I have only one piece of information and I'm not sure how to impart it without giving offence.

Lady Helena Please speak freely. I need all the facts, however grimy.

Priscilla Apparently they wear no undergarments at all.

Lady Helena None at all? (*Then.*) But they have such expensively vulgar hats.

Priscilla Obviously they prefer to spend their money on outward frippery.

Lady Helena So that's something to be given priority on the club's agenda – sewing lessons.

Priscilla But where do I come in?

Lady Helena Do you play the piano?

Priscilla Why, yes.

Lady Helena Excellent. You shall be my right arm at the club.

Priscilla Are you going to run the club yourself?

Lady Helena Just until it gathers momentum as it were. It seems the presence of my personality will pull the crowds. (*Laughs.*) As I'm sure yours will too, Priscilla dear.

Priscilla Is that all you want of me? To play the piano?

Lady Helena Of course not. I wouldn't dream of patronising your capabilities. No, I have several other tasks allotted for you. One very important one you can do for me this evening.

Priscilla Well that's just it . . . I really don't feel . . .

Lady Helena I know, Priscilla. But sometimes, and please don't take this the wrong way, one needs help to overcome one's shyness.

Priscilla Please don't mention doctors, I have quite lost faith in them.

Lady Helena I couldn't agree more. My run-ins with them have left a lot to be desired. They might have intricate brains, but the other parts of them are, more often than not, ham-fisted. No, Priscilla, we have to learn to help ourselves. And, what better way than to find an interest outside the confines of domesticity?

Scene Ten

The Music Hall. The stage is occupied by **Madjacko.** **Annie,** **Polly, Kate** *and* **Maggie** *enter with drinks.*

Madjacko Thank you ladies and gentlemen, thank you very much for a warm welcome. I always look forward to coming back here to the Empire in Deptford.

Maggie Me mum didn't half kick up a stink about me going out again – (*Calls out in* **Madjacko**'s *direction.*) it'd better be worth it.

Kate Stop moaning.

Madjacko You're a friendly couple. You're honoured you are. You know the place you reside in is named after you – the people. Deptford. Everyone's in debt for things they can't afford. It's a hard life. Debt. Don't talk to me about debt. I'm up to here I am. (*Holds hand under chin.*) Wish I was a bit taller. That ferry service you got. Yes, that's right, what service? A man can go mad waiting for that to take him across the river. Saw this fella only yesterday. Given up, walking towards me down the High street going like this. (*Mimes rowing.*) I said 'Excuse me mate, but you ain't got no boat.' He says 'Haven't I? Jesus Christ' and he starts going like this. (*Mimes swimming.*) I said 'Don't worry mate, you'll soon be walking under the water.' He gave me an old-fashioned look. But yer soon to get a new foot tunnel at Greenwich. Isn't that right?

Anne What is he – a sort of speaking newspaper?

Polly Only less entertaining.

Madjacko But you'll be taking your picnics and your days out on the Isle of Dogs once the tunnel's built. And talking of dogs, you got your own isle of them up the top of the road here. Except none of 'em, to my knowledge, have ever walked up an aisle.

Kate Guess what's coming next?

Maggie Let him try . . .

Polly Shut up, Mag.

Annie What? What's coming next?

Madjacko The gut girls. Now if you take one of them home, boys . . . the dog sits in the corner biting its nails. You gotta watch them, fellas. Hard as nails they are, and drink? Drink, they ain't got hair on their chests they got twigs. Crack your ribs they could – with their eyelids. Oh, but they're being well looked after. Did you know they've even got their own patron saint – St Nickerless. He has to keep an eye on 'em on account of they don't wear none. And no one wants to marry a girl like that I can tell yer. But if that weren't enough, oh my, now the Duchess has taken 'em under her wing, going to give 'em all a new pedigree.

Priscilla *enters.*

Polly Bleedin' hell, that's old Cuttle-Smythe's wife.

Maggie Never mind her, fix yer eye on laughing Jacko there.

Madjacko (*turning his attention to* **Priscilla**) What's this then – a charity walk? (**Priscilla** *stops, like a frightened rabbit.*) You must have got the wrong address, lady. Don't you want the Temperance Society? (**Priscilla** *stands still.*) Where do you come from? (*No response.*) Don't keep us all in suspense, where you from?

Priscilla (*timidly*) Brockley.

Madjacko Brockley . . . umm nice place . . . bit like Lee Green with rigor mortis . . . No. No, nice place to come from . . . Not a nice place to go, mind. Do you do good works, lady? No need to be shy I bet you do. Well, see there was this Christian lady, this woman from the humanitarian league and this gut girl . . .

Polly (*shouts*) We can't hear yer.

Maggie (*shouts*) All we can feel is a draught.

Kate What's got four legs, a tail and barks?

Madjacko A dog.

Annie So you do know what dogs are then.

Madjacko You lot got a sister called Cinderella.

Maggie Just 'cos you look like someone sat on yer whilst you were still hot.

Kate You're so ugly, when you were born the midwife slapped yer mother.

Polly They warned us if we chopped up bacon a pig would come back an l haunt us – and it's here tonight.

Madjacko (*he can no longer be heard over the sound of the girls and decides to beat a retreat*) Thank you ladies and gentlemen, thank you very much. Goodnight.

Annie Good riddance.

Maggie Let's go round the back and get him.

Polly (*bringing her back*) Leave it Mag . . . Oh blimey don't look now.

Maggie What?

Kate Only Ma Cuttle-Smythe.

Annie She's coming over to us.

Kate What a show up.

Maggie Don't let her see us fer Christ's sake. We'll never live it down.

Priscilla *bravely picks her way towards them as they try to look away or hide under the table.*

Priscilla Good evening.

Maggie (*emerging awkwardly from under the table*) Evening miss.

Polly Can I get yer a drink?

Priscilla No err, thank you. It's just, I'm here . . .

Kate Why don't yer sit down and take the weight off yer pins.

Priscilla Again, thank you, but Lady Helena, has asked me to come here to let you know that she herself is at the club this evening, and to persuade you to come along.

Annie But we've paid to get in here.

Polly Now if Lady Helena were to come down here and do a turn up there on the stage we'd all be happy.

Priscilla Please say you will.

Maggie I'm sorry but look this is our time and surely we can spend it as we please?

Priscilla Yes, of course. But I'm sure that in the long run the club will be of more benefit to you.

Polly We're happy where we is, thanks.

Priscilla Well, if you change your mind, you know . . .

All Creek Road.

Priscilla Yes. (*She turns and walks away.*)

Kate What are we going to do?

Maggie What we always do when someone tells us what we should be doing – take no bleeding notice.

Kate What's so special about this place? At least Lady Helena won't stand around insulting us.

Maggie Par, she'll have to come up with better enticement than that if she wants me to go to her bleedin' club.

But **Kate** *stands up.*

Interval.

Act Two

Scene One

The club is in complete contrast to the shed. It is clean, clinical, sparse and quiet. **Polly, Kate, Annie** *and* **Maggie** *sit, sewing knickers for themselves.*

Lady Helena Quiet please. (*The room falls to hush.* **Lady Helena** *goes over to* **Priscilla**.)

Priscilla It was an excellent idea to allow them to leave work an hour early. The place is full to overflowing every week.

Lady Helena Unfortunately, the majority of them are still extremely unwilling to learn. Immediate gratification is the name of their game. Can't see the value of what they will achieve in the long run.

Priscilla Give them a few more weeks.

Lady Helena But in the meantime, I'm afraid of losing their interest so I've asked Edwin to pop in with a surprise.

Priscilla Oh?

While **Lady Helena** *and* **Priscilla** *have their backs turned the girls start to whisper to each other.*

Annie I can't understand Ellen. Still not coming here, even with an hour off.

Maggie Except that we have to stay for three hours in total and it's worse than school.

Kate It's not hard work though is it?

Maggie At least me Mum don't give me no aggravation 'bout coming here. She's well pleased me and Lady Helena are breathing the same air. What's the matter with you Pol, lost yer tongue?

Polly I'm trying to finish me fucking knickers ain't I?

Annie What's so special 'bout your fanny?

Maggie Annie, really. Try and remember you're a young lady.

Kate Here Polly, I dare you to call Lady Helena, Lena.

Polly I dare you to try her hat on.

Kate Call that a hat, looks more like a frozen cow turd.

Lady Helena Girls, girls, your attention please, you are here to learn not chatter.

Maggie (*to the others*) Wait for it, she's now going to make up a new rule.

Annie D'you remember the first time, when she said there'd be no rules.

Kate Yeah, now there's about twenty.

Lady Helena I will not tolerate talking whilst I'm talking, it is extremely bad manners.

Polly Look, miss, I've finished. (*She holds up an enormous pair of bloomers with about eight pockets, all shaped like pork chops or some recognisable piece of meat.*)

Maggie Creep.

Lady Helena (*walking over to her*) We usually wait till we're asked but (*Looking at the knickers.*) you have done well. I didn't expect anyone to finish until next week at least. Are you sure they're not a little on the large side? And, good gracious me, all these pockets. What on earth?

Polly Hankies, miss. We need a lot of them. Don't do ter go wiping yer nose on yer hand. Knife would slip right outta it.

Lady Helena Now where was I?

Polly Oh, Lena.

Lady Helena I beg your pardon.

Polly (*holds up the knickers*) You meant I was leaner. I've made these too big. Was that what you was meaning?

Lady Helena Oh I see. (*Looking at* **Polly**.) It is quite possible I was mistaken. Now I would like, with your consent of course, to introduce a new rule.

Kate (*to* **Polly**) Dare you to call her Hell then.

Polly Give over, you got to try her hat on first.

Lady Helena (*talking over them*) This new rule is that no loose women should be allowed to come to the club.

Kate We don't know what you mean, Mam.

Maggie (*to* **Annie**) Don't worry, we won't say nothing. Don't say nothing.

Polly I know I could be leaner but (*Holding up her arm.*) this is all muscle. May look loose but honest, miss, it's muscle.

Lady Helena Those who have strayed from the path of virtue.

Maggie Which side of Evelyn Street is that on?

Lady Helena I meant fallen women.

Polly (*trips and falls on the floor*) Oh blimey, what am I going to do, I've fallen.

The others slip off their chairs.

Maggie Oh no, we're all fallen women.

Lady Helena That's quite enough. All of you get up this instant, put your sewing away and sit, hands in laps. It's time for the Bible reading. (*She opens the Bible trying to find her place.*) Ah, here we are. Now I've found something very relevant and something I think you'll find very interesting because it's directly connected to St Nicholas's church which is the church just around the corner from where you work. Now who can tell me what it's got on its gate posts?

Maggie (*mutters*) Dog shit.

Kate (*calls out*) Two skulls.

Lady Helena Quite right. And does anyone know why?

Polly (*calls out*) Two heads is better than one, miss?

Lady Helena That's as may be, but these two have biblical significance. Can anyone tell me what it is?

Maggie (*calls out*) To remind us that there's more dead people in the world than live ones.

Lady Helena In fact not, no. They resemble a vision Ezekiel was given by God. And I'm going to read it to you. Now the language is rather antiquated and cumbersome so bear with me whilst I paraphrase for your benefit.

Annie (*mutters*) Wake me up when it's time to go to the pub.

Lady Helena *has to look down to do this. Consequently she can't see them all messing about.* **Kate** *immediately gets up, stands behind her, puts her hat on and starts mimicking.*

Lady Helena Ezekiel, Chapter 47. I felt the powerful presence of the Lord. He took me to the valley of dry bones. He said to me, 'Can these bones come back to life?' I replied, 'Lord only you can answer that.' He said, 'Tell these dry bones to listen to the work of God. Tell them I am the sovereign Lord,' and thus said the Lord God 'behold I will come, breathe life into you and you shall live. I will give you muscles and cover you with skin and cause your blood to flow.'

Kate *quickly replaces the hat, the girls applaud.*

Lady Helena I'm pleased you enjoyed that, but we don't usually clap at the Bible. Still I particularly like that passage myself.

Maggie Oh miss, excuse me, but where we come from 'passage' is a rude word.

Lady Helena Can anyone tell me what it means.

Kate Well, it's like your 'underneath': yer privates.

Lady Helena No. The reading from the Bible, can anyone tell me what they think the significance is.

Polly Hell?

Lady Helena What did you say?

Polly Isn't it like a vision of hell, everything dried up and that.

Lady Helena Oh I see. Yes, well done, Polly. It is sort of but with a happy ending and shall I tell you why I like it?

Maggie (*mumbles*) Do we have the power to stop you?

Lady Helena Because it's what I see today in Deptford. Young people like yourselves, all dried up without hope and future. But it doesn't have to be like that.

Maggie (*to the others*) Bleedin' arrogance of the silly mare.

Polly Maybe she means the sheep girls.

Maggie I don't care who she means. If anybody needs to dry up should be her.

Lady Helena Now next week is Holy Week.

Kate (*to Maggie*) No such luck.

Lady Helena Who knows what Holy Week is about?

Maggie Having a good time.

Lady Helena It is not. It is remembering that Jesus died and suffered for each and everyone of us. But . . .

Polly Who?

Lady Helena Our Lord, Jesus Christ.

Maggie Never heard of him.

Chorus of 'No'.

Kate Yes, you have. They're being silly miss. We learnt it at school, he was the one what gave someone a kiss.

Lady Helena Well, I can't quite recall.

Polly Nelson, that's right.

Lady Helena Goodness me, that's. . . . Come on now you

must know who. (*She sees* **Edwin** *come in.*) Excuse me a moment.

Annie (*to the others*) Don't keep this up. Now we'll get the life story of Jesus.

Maggie (*to* **Annie**) I wouldn't fret. We was going to get it anyway.

Lady Helena Listen, listen. This evening we have a special treat. Something that I'm sure will amaze you. Lord Tartaden very kindly agreed to come along with a lantern slide and we will be able to see details from our Lord's life with the aid of magic.

Edwin *sets it up. The girls show genuine interest for the first time, never having seen a lantern show before, it must seem like magic to them.*

Edwin All set.

Lady Helena Perhaps you'd be so good as to take us through.

Edwin (*decides to charm the girls by being skittish*) Right ho. (*Picture of Jesus in the manger.*) Here we have a picture of Jesus in the first perambulator ever invented. It wasn't until some years later that they decided to put wheels on it.

Lady Helena (*hisses*) This is supposed to be educational, Edwin. (*Then to the girls.*) This picture shows that the Son of God started life in very humble surroundings.

Edwin Here we have spouting – er – teaching in the temple, aged twelve. Then a little gap in the story 'til we find him here on the cross. (*Picture of the crucifixion.*) What a way to spend Easter eh?

Lady Helena He died so that we might know too of the life hereafter, to let us know that we all have a choice here on earth to be born again, a fresh start. Lord Tartaden, do you have the picture of the stone being rolled away?

Edwin Umm, let's see now. Oh yes, well, there's one of him making his first public appearance after the crucifixion to old Mary Magdalene.

Lady Helena Ah, now she is a very important character, and one of my favourites amongst the women in the New Testament. This Mary, unlike the mother of God, was shunned by those around her. She was coarse and led a heathen, contemptuous way of life, but Jesus didn't judge her. He went out of His way to get to know her and through Him her life was completely transformed.

Maggie (*to others*) What's she getting at?

Annie Search me.

Lady Helena Now please dismiss quietly, and remember to behave with social manners, not only whilst in this room but in the street, and in your work. This week I want you to take our Lord Jesus home with you. I'll see you all next week at eight o'clock prompt.

They start to put their hats and coats on. **Edwin** *goes over to* **Helena** *and helps her on with her coat.*

Polly (*unseen, except by* **Maggie**, *carefully takes the slide of Jesus and puts it in her coat pocket*) Come on Jesus.

Maggie (*hisses*) What you doing?

Polly (*shrugs*) She said we had to tek Jesus home with us.

Maggie C'mon, let's get outta here.

They all rush out laughing, screaming and shouting.

Lady Helena (*sighs*) Little more than riotous beasts.

Edwin (*with enthusiasm*) Rather. (*Then.*) I mean high-spirited coltishness.

Lady Helena Magic lantern was a great success. Many thanks, Tarty.

Edwin Don't mention it. I must be off. (*He kisses her on the cheek.*)

Lady Helena Edwin.

Edwin Wishful thinking, wishful thinking. (*He goes.*)

Lady Helena Well, Priscilla, we certainly have our work cut out.

Priscilla (*collects the undergarments*) There's one pair missing.

Lady Helena That one, Polly, finished hers. I was quite astounded. She shows precious little interest in anything else.

Priscilla But she hasn't paid for them.

Lady Helena We'll see her next week. Don't worry. Maybe we should try and extend the activities of the sewing class. Poor children have such disgusting clothes.

Priscilla That awful, gaudy jewellery and those hideous hats.

Scene Two

In the street.

Maggie What I can't understand is them having all that money and wearing such awful clothes.

Polly That hat. Fancy wearing it. I wouldn't be caught dead being seen in something like that in the street.

Kate If she'd'ave caught me wearing it I'd only be half alive.

Annie I ain't going next week.

Maggie Listen Annie, don't take it to heart, that rubbish about fallen women. She don't know anything 'bout yer and she ain't going ter find out neither.

Annie But that ain't the point is it. Anyway, I can't work out what she's bothering with us for in the first place.

Polly She wants to turn us into real ladies, don't she.

Maggie You lot are getting as bad as old po-faced Ellen, you are. And I've got to get home, otherwise I'll get it off old misery chops.

Polly She ain't that bad, yer Mum.

Maggie You don't know her like I do.

Annie We'll walk yer to the bottom of Evelyn Street.

Maggie Don't worry, I'm not so much of a lady yet to be worried about a few drunks. See yer tomorrow.

Polly Night.

Maggie *walks on alone. She thinks she can hear something. Looks back. Nothing there. Walks on.* **Edwin** *suddenly steps out of the shadows blocking her path.*

Edwin Good evening, young lady.

Maggie (*levelly*) Evening, sir. (*She steps to one side. He steps in front of her. She looks at him.*) Mind if I get on me way?

Edwin You've got time to stop and talk with a gentleman, just for a while, haven't you?

Maggie No, please let me pass.

Edwin (*takes her arm*) How would you like to earn a shilling?

Maggie (*removes his hand. Nervous*) Don't touch what you can't afford, sir.

Edwin Oh, but I can afford anything I want.

Maggie I just want to get home. Please get out of my way.

Edwin I only want a few moments of your time.

Maggie I said no sir, now.

Edwin (*pushing her. Suddenly produces a small pocket knife and points it at her*) Now this is not the way I normally like to conduct business, but you leave me very little option.

Maggie (*steps back. Looks at him*) I work all day with these. (*She gracefully pulls out a large knife from her skirts.*) So don't make me laugh wiv that plaything. (*She brings her knife down and knocks it from his hand.*) And if you don't want ter see yer wedding tackle on sale in Wellbeloved's tomorrow — fer less than a shilling no doubt – I'd scarper and sharpish (*Prods him.*) mate.

Edwin (*backing off*) I'll get you for this, you slut. Don't think I don't know who you are, where you work. I'll find you. Next time darling, next time.

He goes. She watches him. He breaks into a run. She into a sweat.

Scene Three

Lady Helena *at the club.* **Priscilla** *enters, she has a bruise on her face which she has tried to conceal with powder.* **Helena** *doesn't notice until. She looks closely.*

Lady Helena Priscilla, so prompt, as always. Lovely to see you. I have just finished the revised agenda for next Thursday. Have you brought your music?

Priscilla Yes. (*She takes out a pile of sheet music.*)

Lady Helena Your face. Goodness what on earth's happened?

Priscilla Oh nothing. Really. It looks worse than it is. I thought I'd try. (*She shows the music to* **Helena**.)

Lady Helena It looks frightful.

Priscilla Sorry?

Lady Helena Not the music. Your face.

Priscilla Oh, Helena, I walked into a door. Very clumsy and very stupid. Serves me right for wandering round in the dark, tripped and banged myself. I'm quite all right, thank you.

Lady Helena Are you sure?

Priscilla Perfectly. Now let me . . .

Lady Helena I hope Arthur has been looking after you.

Priscilla Yes, yes, he has.

Lady Helena He is such a thoughtful man.

Priscilla Yes, he is, he is. He's a good man. He is.

Lady Helena Without his help and concern we wouldn't have such a success on our hands.

Priscilla He's tried his best, it's been very difficult for him. You have to try and see his point of view. (*She starts to cry.*)

Lady Helena (*both concerned and embarrassed by this display of emotion*) I'm sure, I'm sure. Please, Priscilla, don't upset yourself.

Priscilla It's not for me I'm upset you understand, it's for him really. He's quite distraught and I've been no help whatsoever.

Lady Helena He's distraught? Because you bump into things?

Priscilla No, no I'm afraid it's all come as rather a shock to him.

Lady Helena Priscilla dear, please take a deep breath and tell me what all this is about.

Priscilla Arthur is displeased about the girls.

Lady Helena But he seemed so agreeable to the idea of the club. Why he even . . .

Priscilla Not that, no, about them having to be laid off next month.

Lady Helena What? Why?

Priscilla Because a large amount of his capital is tied up in those sheds.

Lady Helena Yes, yes. But why are they being laid off?

Priscilla Oh something to do with the Corporation of London. Stopping imports. I'm afraid I didn't fully understand.

Lady Helena This is absolutely terrible.

Priscilla But I thought, we both did, that it was your doing. I mean didn't you say that you thought it should be made illegal for girls to work there?

Lady Helena But this is too soon. Much too soon. Those girls are unemployable elsewhere. Besides I haven't even had time to take tea with the MP of Deptford, never mind chivvy legislation.

Priscilla You didn't know anything about it?

Lady Helena This is the first I'd heard of it. It's disastrous. Those girls have no skills whatsoever. I must go to the Corporation today and beg them, yes, beg them if necessary, to reverse their decision.

Priscilla But I think it's all cut and dried.

Lady Helena At the very least I will request an extension of time.

Priscilla Would you like me to come with you?

Lady Helena No, you go home and rest, and set poor Arthur's mind at rest too.

Scene Four

The sheds. There seems very little work for them.

Maggie Makes me bleedin' laugh it does. All that gab about fallen women. And then that bastard starts on me in the street. Threatening me and all sorts. That's it, I ain't going near that poxy club again.

Kate You should tell her, Lady Helena, what happened. Don't let him get away with it.

Polly And who's she going to believe? Between Maggie and him? It'll be him every time.

Annie You know what they should do, don't yer – pull their cocks off. They'd only have to do it to one. That would make all the others stop and think 'Now do I really want to rape this woman or do I want my cock pulled off.'

Kate Blimey, you've changed.

Maggie And I'm sick to the back teeth of these toffs waltzing through here, saying how awful it is – it's them by calling it awful made it seem so awful.

Kate It's always been awful. It's not just them saying it. This is an awful job whoever has to do it.

Annie But one thing's for sure. It'll never be the likes of Lady Helena, doing it.

Polly (*picks up some sheeps ribs and puts them round her waist*) And the sovereign lord said unto me 'Lady Hell, gather up them dead bones and put 'em round yer body so they squash the living daylights outta yer.'

Annie Watch it, Pol. Don't let Harry catch yer.

Polly I just had a vision. I was in the valley of dry bones. Make haste and take me . . .

Ellen *comes in.*

Maggie Carry on, Pol. It's only Ellen.

Annie (*to* **Ellen**) What are you doing here? I thought Harry put you on unloading again.

Ellen He has. Listen. Listen . . . I just sneaked back . . . I just heard we're all going to be laid off.

Polly (*picks her up swings her around*) Oh, you just had a vision an' all?

Ellen (*angry*) No, no. This isn't a joke.

Kate How d'you know then?

Maggie Probably something Jasper found out from his father's friends in the city.

Annie When?

Ellen I don't exactly know. But I overheard these two chaps.

Polly Ellen, you should know by now they'd do anything to wind us up.

Harry *comes in.*

Harry Ellen, what in hell's name are you doing in here? Get back up to the river end and count yerself lucky I've not fired you. (**Ellen** *goes.*) Which one of you ain't going to the club tonight to play pretty miss with Lady Helena?

Maggie Rest assured, Harry, I ain't setting foot in that place ever again.

Harry Right, you go out there and help Ellen. We need all the help we can get this evening.

Maggie *goes.*

Annie What's going on, Harry?

Harry (*sincerely*) I don't know, girls, really I don't. They don't tell me anything. (**Harry** *goes.*)

Polly Scaremongering again. The same happened two years back, when all the cattle got ill on the voyage over here but we're still here ain't we.

Annie Why, then did Harry . . .?

Polly 'Cos he likes to wind us up. Here why don't we get our own back on him – I've still got that Jesus picture. Let's shine it up on the wall an' Harry will believe Jesus has come to take him off to heaven.

Annie What good would that do?

Polly I dunno. Be a laugh though.

Kate You gotta put it in that special light box and you ain't got one, you dozy gizzard.

Annie Ellen's telling us that we ain't going to have no jobs and all you can think about is having a laugh.

Polly How can we not have any jobs? They've even taken some of us away to unload the ships, there are that many beasts.

Annie So how come the sheds are so empty?

Kate 'Cos there's always a delay – getting them slaughtered and that before they come into the sheds.

Polly And they need us to clean out the innards. Now all animals have got insides whatever Lady Helena or Ellen may think. So until they find a beast without none, we'll always have a job.

Kate You're right. But I reckon we'd be best keeping in with Lady Helena just to be on the safe side.

Polly Let's stop off at yours first Annie, and have a quick supper.

Annie But we ain't got nothing.

Polly (*lifting up her skirts to reveal the pockets stuffed with cuts of meat*) The Lord will provide.

Scene Five

The club. **Helena** *and* **Nora** (*one of* **Helena***'s servants who works below stairs*).

Lady Helena Nora, would you get the caps and aprons ready?

Nora Very good, madam. (*She proceeds to take a collection of caps and aprons from a bag, smooth them out and put them over the chair.*)

Priscilla *comes in.*

Lady Helena Priscilla, you got my message, how good of you to come a bit earlier.

Priscilla Have you heard anything from the Corporation?

Lady Helena Oh, your face. It's better.

Priscilla Yes, it was nothing.

Lady Helena No joy at all I'm afraid. From the Corporation. Nothing I could do or say would change their minds.

Priscilla Oh, but that's terrible.

Lady Helena I thought so too. But then, when I really sat down and thought it through I said to myself 'It doesn't have to look so bleak.' Isn't this the Godsent opportunity we were waiting for? There isn't time for despondency, we must use the time we have got to the full.

Priscilla But they . . .

Lady Helena They will have to work hard and be pushed for their own benefit.

Kate, Annie *and* **Polly** *arrive, chatting and laughing.*

Priscilla I've brought the music you . . .

Lady Helena I don't think we'll be needing it. From now on Priscilla, it's got to be work and not much play. Otherwise these girls will be on the street. (*Raising her voice to be heard.*) Settle down girls please. There isn't room for slackers, it isn't fair on those who want to learn.

Kate (*pointing at* **Nora**) Here, who's her?

Lady Helena. Who can tell me what was wrong with that statement? (*Silence.*) Firstly we never point. It is extremely rude. Secondly, the correct way of phrasing the question is 'Excuse me, but who is that young lady?'

Kate Well, who is she then?

Lady Helena Thirdly, one doesn't speak until one is spoken to. (*Then.*) Nora is what's called an undermaid, in my household.

Polly Under the thumb.

Lady Helena If you want to mumble or pass comments under your breath then you'd better go outside and do it. I have brought Nora along as an example of what you might aspire to if you listen carefully and learn quickly. If you don't want to, there are plenty of others willing to take your place. Nora will you stand here next to me.

Nora *stands, legs together, back straight, looking impassively in front of her.*

Kate (*to* **Annie**) Do you think she knows something we don't?

Annie Best not to fall out with her now, that's what I think.

Lady Helena All of you separate yourselves, so you don't feel tempted to chat. Now what do you notice about Nora?

Polly She ain't said nothing.

Lady Helena She hasn't said anything. Repeat after me. She hasn't said anything.

Polly (*begrudgingly*) She hasn't said anything.

Lady Helena You see you can talk properly when you want to. Why hasn't she said anything? No, don't answer that, it's a rhetorical question. She hasn't said anything because we do not speak until we are spoken to. And when we do answer, we do so as precisely and politely as possible.

Kate Do what?

Lady Helena What have I just said?

Polly She don't know, that's why she's asking.

Lady Helena No one speaks until they are spoken to, isn't that correct, Nora?

Nora Yes, madam.

Lady Helena Thank you. Now I want you to look at Nora very carefully. She is extremely well groomed. Her cap and apron, impeccably starched and stain free. You do not wipe dirty hands on your apron. Your appearance is all important. Nora would you please show these young ladies how to enter a room correctly. Mrs Cuttle-Smythe and I shall pretend to take afternoon tea.

She and **Priscilla** *sit down.*

Lady Helena Would you care to take tea with me this afternoon, Mrs Cuttle-Smythe?

Priscilla I should be delighted Lady Helena.

Lady Helena I shall ring for Nora. (*Ringing the hand bell.*)

Nora *enters.*

Lady Helena Ah, Nora, would you bring tea for Mrs Cuttle-Smythe and myself. (*She hands* **Nora** *a tray.*)

Nora Very good, madam.

Nora *goes out, comes back in with the tray, puts it on the table and pours tea from a pretend pot into pretend cups.* **Polly, Kate** *and* **Annie** *make appropriate noises 'tea pouring,' sugar lumps plopping, and an enormous slurping sound as* **Lady Helena** *and* **Priscilla** *pretend to take a sip.*

Lady Helena That will be all.

Nora Thank you, madam.

Lady Helena (*coming out of the charade*) Now, what did you notice about Nora? (*Silence.*) That she carried herself in a ladylike manner, she took small steps not large strides, she stood with her back straight, didn't slouch her shoulders. She was alert and attentive at all times without being intrusive. Nora would you sit in this chair for me?

Nora *does so.*

Lady Helena Rarely will you be required to sit in your employer's presence but nevertheless it is important to sit in a ladylike manner at all times, even when you are alone. You sit with your back straight, your legs firmly together and your hands in your lap. Is that understood? Excellent Nora, well done. In real life, Nora has probably never seen inside my drawing room, certainly she has never served tea. That's because she works downstairs. But what is your ambition Nora?

Nora To be head maid, madam.

Lady Helena And one day, I think, you're likely to achieve it. (*To the girls.*) Although you'll all be required to start at the bottom, it is worth remembering that domestic service gives you the chance to learn and improve so that when someone in a position above yours leaves to get married, there is every chance these days for promotion from within a household. Now that's enough talking. Please take your positions in a dignified manner, whilst Mrs Cuttle-Smythe finds caps and aprons for you to try on and let's get down to the real work.

Polly (*to* **Annie**) Oh my Gawd, she's going to dress us up as dollies.

Lady Helena In silence please. The next young lady I hear blaspheming, cursing or swearing, can leave. If you want to behave like street urchins then perhaps the street is the best place for you.

Priscilla *fits them with caps and aprons.*

Lady Helena What do you think Mrs Cuttle-Smythe?

Priscilla Well (*Straightening* **Polly**'s *cap*) with one or two adjustments.

Lady Helena (*to the girls*) Take a look at Nora and then at yourselves. A tidy appearance denotes a tidy mind. A slovenly appearance is the outward sign of a slovenly mind. Walk across the room now in a ladylike manner, turn, come back to me and say 'You rang, madam?' and remember all of you are capable of being young ladies, it is up to you.

They set off across the room.

Lady Helena (*to* **Priscilla**) What do you think?

Priscilla Well . . .

Lady Helena Don't forget, they all start with the most menial jobs. The sort they probably have to do at home for themselves now. It's the manner, appearance and attitude we have to break them into. (*Calls to the girls.*) Don't rush. Keep your heads up. No, not your noses in the air. Look ahead not down. Good, now turn round and come back to me.

They do so.

Girls (*loudly*) You rang, madam?

Lady Helena Not so loud. Don't drawl. Now one at a time. You.

Annie You rang, madam?

Lady Helena Good.

Annie I have been in service before.

Lady Helena (*interrupting*) No, no. I've not asked you a question. That'll be all. Go back and do it again. You.

Polly You rang, madam?

Lady Helena (*pleasantly*) There's a hint of impatience in your voice. Again.

Polly You rang, madam?

Lady Helena Better, you.

Kate You rang, madam?

Lady Helena That sounds downright impertinent, again.

Kate You rang, madam.

Lady Helena Again.

Kate You rang, madam.

Lady Helena Not quite, go back and do it again. Don't look at one another. Don't frown. You don't want lines on your faces before you're thirty. No, well, come on. No, don't skip. All right, now Nora would you take the tray and mime bringing it in, pretending to open the door, set it on the table, and say 'Will that be all, madam?'

Nora Very good, madam.

She proceeds to do as she's told.

Lady Helena Now please would you follow Nora's example.

Helena *and* **Priscilla** *proceed to have their own private conversation punctuated by* **Helena** *calling out instructions to the girls.*

Lady Helena (*to* **Priscilla**) Now, we're only going to put ourselves out for those girls who have attended the club regularly.

Nora (*having completed the mime*) Will that be all, madam?

Lady Helena Thank you, Nora. Right, first one, off you go.

Kate *goes first.*

Lady Helena No, I don't think so. The tea service would have fallen from the tray by now, go back and start again. (**Kate** *does so.* **Helena** *turns to* **Priscilla.**) Otherwise we're going to be inundated with requests for work and we must be seen to reward those girls who have made the club priority for Thursday evenings.

Priscilla What about those absent because of sickness?

Kate Will that be all, madam?

Lady Helena (*to* **Kate**) Don't fidget, when you've poured the tea, stand up straight. Go back and do it once more. (**Kate** *passes the tray to* **Polly**. **Helena** *to* **Priscilla**.) If they are going to be sick then they won't make good employees. I've put the word out about finding work and I'm fairly confident that we'll only be left with a minority of disobedient, insolent girls that nobody with the best will in the world could do anything with. (*She sees* **Polly** *bending over the tea table.*) Bend your knees slightly. Nobody wants the sight of your rear end taking up space in their drawing rooms.

Polly (*straightening herself*) Will that be all, madam?

Lady Helena Try again.

Annie *takes her turn.*

Annie Will that be all, madam?

Lady Helena Very good. The rest of you would do well to follow this example.

Priscilla It's quite extraordinary the amount of households now needing more servants.

Annie (*to* **Polly**) The sheep girls who work nights have been laid off. Pass it on.

Lady Helena You still need a maid yourself, don't you?

Priscilla True.

Lady Helena Well, my dear, take your pick, if you can't have first choice after all the work you've put in I don't know who can. That last one was very good.

Priscilla Do you know I rather like that one, Polly.

Lady Helena The girl who was so deft with the underwear? She's a bit dense. Not to mention ungainly.

Priscilla But pleasingly gentle of temperament. Not like the others. She's very slow to take offence.

Lady Helena Right girls, let's do it again. (*To* **Priscilla**.) I think the coffee and cake will be well earned this evening.

The girls go through the routine again.

Polly (*whispers to* **Kate**) The Sheep Girls have been laid off.

Priscilla I'll go and put the kettle on. (*She goes.*)

Lady Helena Hands by your sides, backs straight. Try at all times to look pleasant.

The girls go through the routine again.

Polly Will that be all, madam?

Annie Very good, madam.

Kate Thank you, madam.

Scene Six

Harry, *having given* **Jim** *his cards, sees him off the premises.*

Jim I thought I was going to be all right. I mean I thought it was just the girls what was laid off.

Harry I'm sorry, son. I am really. But nobody told me they was going to slaughter and gut the beasts before they even got here. Started to make them ice-cold an' all. That's progress for yer. It's lucky they decided to keep the older chaps on. At least you younger ones have a better chance of finding another job.

Jim What chance have I got, Harry? I don't know no other work.

Harry There's no shortage of butchers' shops round here boy. Go and ask 'em if they're looking for a delivery boy.

Jim But that wouldn't pay half of what I was getting. Besides, I don't know how to ride a bicycle.

Harry Oh, blimey, don't look now but there's Ellen the ever red. I'd best get back in ter work. Good luck, son.

He goes. **Ellen** *comes up to* **Jim.**

Ellen Harry? (*He doesn't look at her.*) You got the push and all, Jim?

Jim Yeah. Do you know where Kate is?

Ellen They've all gone running up to Creek Road to put themselves at Lady Helena's mercy.

Jim Oh, maybe she'll be able to do something for me.

Ellen She'd have her work cut out then, wouldn't she – trying to turn you into the shining ideal of christian womanhood.

Jim Eh?

Ellen She ain't offering a service for men because she don't care how they carry on. It's women's behaviour she wants to change.

Fade to **Polly** *and* **Annie.**

Polly Here Annie, what's it like? I mean how many days d'you get off? When do they pay yer? Do they give yer enough money to get home on yer day off?

Annie Depends. They set the rules. Might get one Sunday afternoon off a month. I dunno. Seeing as it's the Cuttle-Smythes yer might get more.

Polly Do you get yer own room or do you have ter share?

Annie Depends. You'll have to see when you gets there.

Polly S'pose they ask me to do something I've never heard of? What will I say?

Annie You've heard of peeling potatoes, polishing floors, cleaning steps, washing curtains, washing pots, making tea, making a fire. They ain't going to ask you to fly in the air.

Polly No, I s'pose it's just common sense at the end of the day.

Annie It's all the things yer hate doing when they're for yerself. Only you're going to have to do them for other people with a smile on yer chops.

Polly Yeah. I ain't looking forward to it.

Fade to **Ellen** *and* **Annie**.

Ellen What'd she say?

Annie She's fixed me up in service.

Ellen Annie what the hell are you doing? You know what it's like. I mean to the others it might be some sort of novelty but, Christ, surely you don't want to go back to that sorta life? Bowing and scraping and . . .

Annie Ellen shut it will yer. I feel nervous enough. Don't make it worse. They can't all be the same, can they?

Ellen But . . .

Annie I can't fall foul of Lady Helena now can I? I mean how can I say ter her 'thank you very much but no thank you very much'? 'Cos there ain't no other work, and by the time I finds that out I can't then go on me hands and knees back to her 'cos by then she'll have plenty more deserving cases than me to place.

Ellen It's worth a try, honest it is.

Annie You forget Ellen I've been on the streets once before. And, I can tell you, anything, yeah virtually anything, is better than that. I'm going to give this a try 'cos at the end of the day mate, what choice have I?

Fade to **Ellen** *and* **Maggie**.

Ellen Mag, what's happened to the others?

Maggie I dunno, there was so many asking fer help we lost each other. Polly got fixed up, straight off, I know that much. She starts work in the Cuttle-Smythe household.

Ellen But that bastard don't know her from Eve.

Maggie No, but his wife does.

Ellen What about you?

Maggie I didn't get no help at all, and what's more I ain't going to get none in the future 'cos I stopped going to her flaming club. So, Ellen, it looks like I'll have to come with you and try the jam factory.

Ellen They wouldn't take me on. I've been to every factory round here. They all say the same, only taking on girls with a reference from Lady Helena. I'm going to try down Southwark. Maybe her influence won't have travelled that far. Coming . . .

Maggie It's me Mum. She needs me at home.

Ellen She wouldn't have yer at home if you were in service.

Maggie No, but she'd have the satisfaction of thinking I'd made something of meself. I'd better get back and let her know what's happened.

Ellen *goes. Fade to:* **Kate** *comes up to* **Jim***.*

Kate What you doing here?

Jim They decided to kick out the youngest chaps an' all.

Kate What you going to do?

Jim Harry says I should try for a job in a butcher's. What about you, how did you get on with Lady Helena?

Kate She's fixed me up to see this family tomorrow for the position of general maid.

Jim So much for our idea of getting a shop.

Kate Them's dreams, Jim. Children's dreams.

Jim We're nothing we are. If we live or die tomorrow

nobody would care. Suppose this household don't want yer tomorrow?

Kate Any girl what won't find work through no fault of her own is to be given seven shillings a week.

Jim She's going to give money away?

Kate Yeah, I'll say this for her, she's really putting herself out.

Fade to **Maggie** *and her* **Mum**.

Eady You're telling me that even that dozy doe Polly got herself into a household with one of them joined together names. And you ain't got nothing.

Maggie Yes, that's the long and the short of it.

Eady Go back and ask her again – Lady Helena.

Maggie I won't, I got more bloody pride.

Eady Pride? Pride? You think you're a man you do.

Maggie I don't.

Eady What you got against being in service? Most normal, decent girls would jump at the chance.

Maggie I don't want to . . .

Eady It's only 'til yer get wed.

Maggie I don't want to get married.

Eady What are you going ter do then?

Maggie Oh, I don't know, maybe I'll follow wonderful Helena's example, live on me own, devoting my life to the good of others.

Eady At least she's got the respectability of widowhood. I tell you one thing, you ain't going to stop under this roof unless yer earns yer keep.

Maggie See you in hell.

Eady Not fer much longer, girl. Not unless yer get off yer backside.

Fade to **Ellen**, **Annie**, **Kate**, **Polly**.

Ellen D'you need any hands? No, I ain't had any experience of factory work but I worked down the gutting sheds in Deptford. I ain't had a day off sick ever. I'm a hard worker, honest, you only got to show me what to do, I'll pick it up, I'm a fast learner. Please take me on. Give me a chance. (*Pause.*) Oh no, I wouldn't have nothing to do with Trade Unions.

Annie (*at the front door*) Good morning madam, my name's . . .

Kate (*at the front door*) Good morning madam, my name's . . .

Polly (*at the front door*) Good morning, Mrs Cuttle-Smythe. Err, I'm not really sure like, should I have used the back door . . .?

Scene Seven

Lady Helena's *drawing room.* **Lady Helena** *and* **Edwin** *sit sorting through papers.*

Edwin The apprentice fund is growing fatter by the day, Helena. By my reckoning you'll be able to admit another ten girls to your school of Domestic Economy.

Lady Helena (*not listening*) Priscilla should have been here half an hour ago.

Edwin Oh, I doubt if you'll see her again.

Lady Helena Why ever not?

Edwin She's got her pick of servants, what does she need you for?

Lady Helena She's not like that, we've become good friends.

Edwin But she's such a sickly creature.

Lady Helena She was, but over the last few weeks, well, she's really come out of herself.

Edwin Helena, you can be so naive about people.

Lady Helena In what way?

Edwin The Cuttle-Smythes are after status. If enthusing about your hobby horse was part of the game, then so be it.

Lady Helena I don't agree with you at all. She's probably been laid up. Less gossip and more work is required. (*A knock at the door.*) See, that'll be her. Come in.

Emily *enters*.

Emily There's a lady . . .

Lady Helena Show her in Emily, you know there's no need for formalities with Mrs Cuttle-Smythe.

Emily Madam, it's not Mrs Cuttle-Smythe. It's a, er, lady, woman, one of them girls from the club.

Lady Helena Here?

Edwin The audacity.

Lady Helena Show her in Emily, please.

Maggie *enters.* **Helena** *stands to greet her.*

Maggie I'm sorry to trouble you Lady Helena, but I've come to ask for your help.

Lady Helena I remember you. You used to come to the club didn't you? And (*Trying to remember.*) it's Maggie isn't it?

Maggie Yes it is, madam. You see since the sheds closed down, I haven't been able to get work.

Edwin Only those who attended the club regularly can now avail themselves of help.

Maggie *jumps, recognising* **Edwin**.

Lady Helena Quite so. Otherwise it wouldn't be fair on those who did attend and are still looking for work. Can I ask why you stopped coming?

Pause, **Maggie** *sees* **Edwin** *stare at her. She looks from him to* **Helena** *and back to him.*

Maggie Me brother weren't well, madam. Me Mother 'ad ter work evenings and I had to look after him.

Lady Helena Well . . . I don't know.

Maggie Please madam, me Mother can't afford ter keep me. I have ter earn my way. I'll do any . . . any reasonable work.

Lady Helena I was going to suggest my apprenticeship fund where you work for nothing but the fund pays you a small allowance.

Maggie Would yer?

Edwin She's far too old Helena, the scheme's for thirteen to fifteen-year-olds. It would make a nonsense of it.

Lady Helena *(turns to look at* **Edwin** *then back at* **Maggie***)* Yes, I suppose that's right. There doesn't really seem much I can do at the moment but I will bear you in mind.

She pulls the bell cord for **Emily** *who enters promptly.*

Lady Helena Emily, please show this young lady out and take her address.

Emily *and* **Maggie** *walk out.*

Maggie *(to* **Emily***)* Don't trouble yerself I ain't got one, me Mum threw me out.

Lady Helena *(to* **Edwin***)* You were a bit hard on her, Edwin. I didn't like to contradict you but . . .

Edwin Oh Helena, she was a trouble maker, she'll have to learn. You can't be too soft on that sort.

Fade to **Ellen** *alone.*

Ellen I pawned all my books today, but it doesn't matter. It wouldn't have mattered in the end what I'd said or done. It wouldn't have made a shred of difference what five hundred of us had done. We'd still have been out of work. They'd still have got their way – those people with their schemes

and funds and clubs and allowances – all thought up out of
fear – out of a fear that we, the ones who made their wealth
might get out of hand. So we need to be tamed and trained
to succumb to their values and orders. What's the point of
kicking against it when all you damage is your foot. And
I'm left trying to explain myself to, yes, even to Jasper and
Sebastian who reply, 'But Ellen, at least she found them all
work.' Yes, but in service – in service. I could tell by the
look on their faces that they couldn't see anything wrong.
Why should they? After all isn't that what we're here for?
You service your husband and your children. What's wrong
with servicing those deemed better than you – at least you
get paid for it. I don't want to keep arguing and kicking
against it. I don't want to stick out like a sore thumb and be
seen as odd. Who am I to call the others fools, when I am
the biggest laughing stock of the lot – actually believing that
I had any say over what happened to me or anyone else.
(*She tears the pawn ticket into pieces and throws it on the floor.*)

Fade to **Lady Helena** *and* **Arthur**.

Lady Helena Please sit down, Arthur. I'm most terribly
sorry – about the loss of income. Priscilla did explain that it
wasn't my doing?

Arthur Oh yes. And in fact when the word got out that
you'd gone to plead personally with the Corporation for a
reversal of their decision I was able to sell, not as
handsomely as I'd have wished, but not at a loss, as I'd
originally feared. So I am quite satisfied with the outcome.
Thank you.

Lady Helena Well, now, that is a relief.

Arthur I have come to see you on a more delicate matter.
That of my wife's health.

Lady Helena Goodness me. What's happened?

Arthur Nothing. But, and I must come straight to the
point, it is not doing her any good at all, participating in the
club, and I have come to ask, now you have so many other
capable volunteers, if my wife might be excused her duties
and allowed to recuperate fully at home.

Lady Helena It seemed, if anything, that her interest in the club was boosting her self-esteem.

Arthur Quite the opposite I fear.

Lady Helena Well, she does still seem a bit edgy. I'm saddened. But Priscilla's well-being is of the utmost concern.

Arthur Thank you for being so understanding.

Lady Helena Promise me one thing Arthur.

Arthur Yes?

Lady Helena That you both won't desert me socially.

Arthur I will promise you that with pleasure, Helena.

Lady Helena Good. You will be top of the invitation list for the forthcoming fête.

Scene Eight

Priscilla's drawing room.

Polly They got a beautiful looking-glass in this room. As a special treat, I bring me old hat down here, only when I'm sure he's out and she's still a kip like, and I put it on and pretend all the girls are coming round for tea. (*She puts her hat on and straightens it. Whirls round to face the door. Putting on an upper class voice.*) Ellen, Maggie, Kate, Annie, lovies. So pleased you could come. Isn't this just splendid?

Priscilla *walks in*, **Polly** *stops*. **Priscilla** *stares at her.*

Polly Sorry, madam.

Priscilla Are you all right Polly?

Polly Yes, thank you, madam.

Priscilla Did you buy that hat for your mother?

Polly Yes, madam, sorry, madam.

Priscilla How is she?

Polly Very good, madam.

Priscilla Oh? Cook told me, that she wasn't well?

Polly No, madam.

Priscilla Why did you say 'very good' then?

Polly Beggin' your pardon, madam.

Priscilla Polly? Are you also trying to convince me that I'm mad?

Polly (*blurts out*) I'm sorry, madam, I am really but you know we only had time to learn how to say, 'Yes, madam,' 'No, madam,' 'Begging your pardon,' and 'Very good, madam.' I'm afraid if I start talking normally you'll get offended.

Priscilla Of course, that's good and proper in front of the master but you don't have to worry when it's just you and me. What were you doing just now?

Polly Trying me old hat on – to cheer meself up a bit like – (*Offering the hat.*) D'you wanna go?

Priscilla (*shakes her head but smiles*) There is a quote . . . a proverb, oh, I can't think . . .

Polly Blessed are the pure in hat?

Priscilla No, it's not in the Bible. 'Don't tame the wild God' that's it.

Polly Never heard that one. Are you all right, madam?

Priscilla I'm sorry. It's a pagan sentiment – it means don't squash the spirit out of someone. Christianity can be a rather stifling ideology, don't you think?

Polly If you say so, madam.

Arthur *comes in. They both freeze.*

Arthur Haven't you finished this room yet, girl?

Priscilla Polly has scrubbed the kitchen from top to bottom. I have been supervising her.

Arthur You got up at the appropriate time then? That's much better. I am pleased. (*To* **Polly**.) What on earth is that, girl? (*Meaning the hat.*)

Priscilla We found it on the top shelf of the larder. The previous cook must have left it – if you remember she disappeared very abruptly.

Arthur (*to* **Polly**) Get rid of it.

Priscilla Polly, please take that hat and dispose of it as you will.

Polly Yes, madam.

Arthur (*to* **Priscilla**) I'm pleased to see that you are learning to assert your authority with the servants at last.

Scene Nine

Lady Helena *and* **Emily**.

Lady Helena Emily, would you mind putting my hair back up. It seems to be all awry.

Emily Very good, madam. (**Emily** *stands behind* **Helena** *and does her hair*.)

Lady Helena Do you believe God answers prayer, Emily?

Emily Of course I do, madam.

Lady Helena When they are for ourselves only, of course. He is a little slow on the uptake. Rightly so, because selfishness should never be rewarded.

Emily No, madam.

Lady Helena But my prayers for those girls have been answered. As a species, they have been totally transformed. That is my reward. Do you remember the day I visited those sheds. You were very cynical about what could be achieved.

Emily Me? Why madam I'd never dream of being so presumptuous.

Fade to the Pub. **Maggie** *behind the bar. Sees* **Ellen** *walk past in the street.*

Maggie (*calls out*) Ellen, Ellen.

Ellen (*puts her head round the door, then sees* **Maggie**) Maggie, what you doing in here?

Maggie It's good ter see yer. I thought you'd have been in before now.

Ellen Times have changed ain't they? Lady can't go fer a drink on her own these days.

Maggie I called at your place but seems you moved.

Ellen Had to didn't I? Toff bought up all the places round Watergate Street, done 'em up with rents to match. I had to take lodgings with a family.

Maggie Are you working?

Ellen I'm going for a job down the new button factory in Rotherhithe.

Maggie (*teasing*) Got a union has it?

Ellen I don't know, do I. Fancy you working here. Still living at home are yer?

Maggie Na, me mum threw me out.

Ellen So where yer living?

Maggie Here.

Ellen Here? What happened to Len, then?

Maggie I married him.

Ellen *looks stunned.*

Maggie Don't look like that, Ellen. (*Then.*) He don't trouble me often.

Ellen (*aghast*) You married Len?

Maggie What bleedin' choices did I have, Ellen?

Ellen But what did you marry that great clod for?

Len *comes in.*

Len Hello, Ellen, how are you?

Ellen (*nicely embarrassed*) Oh, hello Len, we was just talking about . . . the weather.

Len Chilly out, ain't it. (*To* **Maggie**.) Can you give us a hand in the yard, sweetheart? (*Kisses her on the cheek and goes.*)

Maggie Be with you in a moment, dear. (*Wiping her cheek with her hand.*)

Ellen Sorry.

Maggie What for, ain't your fault.

Fade to **Kate** *and* **Jim, Kate** *is scrubbing the steps.*

Kate What are you doing here?

Jim I thought I'd call by on my round and say hello.

Kate Do you want to get me into trouble?

Jim (*grins*) Chance would be a fine thing.

Kate Don't you dare talk to me like that.

Jim Sorry.

Kate Can't you read? What does that notice say? There, in letters three inches high: 'NO GENTLEMEN CALLERS.'

Jim But, I ain't a gentleman, I'm a bleedin' butcher's boy.

Kate Jim, there is absolutely no need to swear. (*Pause.*) Listen, I'll try and slip out and meet yer tonight.

Jim You said that last week, but you never turned up.

Kate I can't help it if they've got eyes in their nightcaps. I'll try the best I can – now please go away.

Scene Ten

Arthur and **Priscilla**'s *drawing room.*

Arthur My dear, all I am asking of you is that you make

the effort and accompany me to the fête. It is not as if we are invited as guests of honour every day of the week, now is it?

Priscilla (*timidly*) Please, you go dear. I don't feel well enough.

Arthur You are my wife. It's your duty to come with me. Besides I promised Helena you'd be there. Stop this reclining nonsense. I thought that wretched club had knocked that sort of malingering out of you once and for all. Come and get your outdoor things on before it recurs.

Priscilla She's bound to ask why you put a stop to me helping her.

Arthur (*patiently*) I didn't put a stop to anything. We agreed, that you weren't suited to it. Besides she's far too well-mannered to bring the subject up.

Priscilla She'll only feel obliged to ask how Polly's getting on. And I won't know how to explain that you want to get rid of her.

Arthur You stupid woman, the girl's clumsy, incompetent and hopeless. Helena won't care a damn what I say about her and probably arrange to get us another. Christ, servants are two a penny, they're nothing. Fancy worrying over a trifle like that. Your soft heart has contaminated your brain.

Priscilla But she makes me laugh.

Arthur All the more reason to come then – I never see you laugh.

Priscilla Not Helena – Polly.

Arthur (*explodes*) A servant is not supposed to make you laugh. They are to be seen and not heard, to know their place. How d'you expect to maintain any kind of discipline if you converse with them, as if they were part of your social circle?

Priscilla Please, please, you go dear. I've plenty to be getting on with.

Arthur (*exasperated*) The whole point of having servants in the first place is so women of your social standing don't have anything to get on with. (*More reasonable.*) My dear, if you carry on like this I shall be left without excuse or option but to call the doctor in, for there is plainly something wrong with your head.

Priscilla It is not my head but my heart.

Arthur Healthier looking women than you are filling up the asylums today.

Priscilla (*panics*) No, I'm perfectly sane. Perfectly.

Arthur Of course you're not, and I shall vouch for that fact, why would a sane woman refuse to see her friends?

Priscilla They're not my friends, merely acquaintances of yours.

Arthur Refuses to go out with her husband, refuses to leave the house, preferring instead the servants for entertainment. My dear, these are the values of a mad woman.

Priscilla I am not mad, I am not mad, I am not mad.

Arthur (*very roughly, taking hold of her arm*) You're ranting, you're raving.

Priscilla Leave me be, leave me be.

Arthur Now you, up. Come on. I'll get you outside the door if it kills me.

Priscilla No, no, please, leave me alone.

Polly *enters carrying a full coal scuttle.*

Polly Did you call me, sir?

Priscilla Oh, Polly. (*She runs to her.*)

Arthur No I didn't. Get out.

Polly, *shaken, as* **Priscilla** *almost knocks her over, drops the scuttle on the floor and the coal spills out over the carpet.*

Arthur (*rounds on her*) You stupid, clumsy, oaf.

Polly I am sorry, sir. (*She starts to pick up the pieces of coal.*)

Arthur You are? You will be. Don't think you're taking this Sunday afternoon off or any other Sunday afternoon until you've made up the time to pay for it.

Polly Please. I will.

Priscilla No, Arthur, her mother's not well, she must be allowed . . .

Arthur (*to* **Priscilla**) Have you not a shred of loyalty to me?

Arthur *picks up the coal shovel.* **Polly**, *having put all the coal back in the scuttle, stands.*

Arthur I'll teach you a lesson you'll not forget.

Priscilla No, no, please calm down dear, it was an accident.

Polly Er, no, look sir, say what you like, I'm sorry. But don't hit me.

Arthur I can do what I like to you, I'm paying for you. Some men I know box their servants' ears for putting cutlery in the wrong drawer. Come here.

Polly (*holds up her hands. Says placatingly*) No one has ever hit me sir. Not me Mother, not me Father, not me Guv'nor, not no one. I've taken a lot of abuse and no mistake but I won't be hit. (*Stronger.*) I'm warning you – I won't be hit.

Arthur We'll see about that.

He takes a swipe at her with the shovel. She brings her fist up and hits him with an almighty punch in the face. He lands on the floor. **Priscilla** *lets out a little cry. Her husband lies still.* **Polly** *looks, then after a moment tentatively goes over to him, half expecting him to leap up at any minute.*

Polly Oh, my God, Oh, Jesus, Jesus Christ. I think I've done for him, miss.

Priscilla Go to the kitchen Polly, get me some lard.

Polly Madam?

Priscilla I'll grease his shoe and the floor.

Polly (*swallows*) Madam?

Priscilla (*shaking*) It's worth a try.

Arthur, *having only been knocked unconscious, lifts his arm to his head and groans.* **Polly** *steps back in fright,* **Priscilla** *sits down.*

Priscilla Will you go and fetch the doctor, Polly.

Polly Me??

Priscilla (*gets up*) No, I'll go . . .

Polly I can't be here not when . . . he comes to his senses.

Priscilla No.

Polly *runs off.*

Scene Eleven

Annie *sits alone on Blackheath.*

Annie They has their tea early on Sunday – three o'clock. And then I'm allowed to do what I want, as long as I'm back for six-thirty. And I come up here for some fresh air and I gulps it down. I sit here on me own, and I think, 'It's me. I'm here and I'm breathing.'

Some distance away she sees **Kate**, *pushing a pram.*

Annie (*squinting*) That looks like . . . It is . . . I don't believe it. (*She gets up, calls.*) Kate. (*Runs up to* **Kate,** *calling.* **Kate** *doesn't turn but continues to push the pram. Breathless,* **Annie** *catches up with her.*) Kate, it's me.

Kate *looks at her, then around, nervously.*

Annie Kate. It's me Annie.

Kate (*hisses*) I know. I should think every soul on Blackheath knows.

Annie Well, how are you, ain't you pleased to see me? (*To the pram.*) Is it a boy or a girl?

Kate I'm well thank you. This is Master John. I'm allowed to look after him on Nanny's day off.

Annie (*sarcastically*) Ain't that nice for you.

Kate (*seriously*) Yes, they say I've the potential to become a Nanny. (*She continues to look around her.*)

Annie They would wouldn't they. 'Ere what d'you keep looking over yer shoulder for?

Kate It won't do us any good if they see us talking together.

Annie You what? What, they got a spy glass from their windows then, that can see round corners and through houses?

Kate *starts walking on.* **Annie** *has to catch up with her.*

Annie What you walking away from me for? Kate, it's me. Annie.

Kate Annie, look. It's no good hankering after what was. We've got to try and make the best of what we've got, and I, for one am trying to better myself. If you've got any sense you'll try and do the same. (*She turns.*)

Annie (*catches hold of* **Kate**'s *arm*) What you frightened of? That I'll snatch the son and heir and hold him to ransom?

Kate That's just it – isn't it. Some of us are trying to forget who we are, where we come from and put the past behind us, but no, Polly goes and bangs her fist in her employer's face. And it's like we're all under suspicion.

Annie You're telling me? Suspicion. You know what mine have taken to doing, eh? Only locking me in me room at night. They think I don't know but I hear the key go. Then they have to unlock it really early so I can get up and do all the chores before they get up proper. Bet if there was a fire they'd forget to unlock the bloody door at all.

Kate Thanks to Polly.

Annie Poor Polly.

Kate She could have killed him.

Annie I don't see that by talking to me you'll get into trouble. What's that got to do with anything.

Kate She ain't been seen of since – they might think we've got something to do with her, or we're hiding her, or anything. We got to prove to them we aren't all like that.

Annie Let me put your mind at rest Kate. They caught her, the police, she's in Holloway.

Kate How do you know?

Annie Oh, don't they allow you to read the papers then – this household where they're so keen for advancement of general maids to nannies?

Kate Actually, I don't have to lay out the fires, they have another maid to do that. So I don't get to see the old newspapers. (*Pause.*) And, I'm sorry, but I really do have to go. (*She does so.*)

Annie (*shouts after her. Not caring who hears*) You want to know how I get to read them? Because them what I works for are so bleedin' mean. They make me put newspaper all over the carpet so it don't wear, then when they know company's coming they make me take it all up. I gets to know all the news that way. Everything they got is for show. They're so tight, that when they walk their arses squeak.

Fade to **Maggie** *and* **Priscilla**.

Maggie I know what she done like weren't right.

Priscilla Please, please could you sit down and keep your voice down. My husband's upstairs and the doctor says he's to stay in bed and have plenty of rest.

Maggie I'm sorry about that, I mean I know how you must feel. (*Gulps down the insincerity.*) I have got a husband of me own like. But, me and Polly worked together fer years. She weren't the sort to start a fight or nothing – even if there was an argument she'd be the one to smooth things over.

Priscilla *doesn't respond.*

Maggie Couldn't you like give her a good character? I mean I could, but it don't mean nothing coming from me.

Priscilla I can't give evidence against my husband in a Court of Law.

Maggie Well, can't you have a word with him? I mean I ain't suggesting you take Polly back, just drop the charges.

Priscilla You don't understand . . .

Maggie I know it ain't on. To go round smacking people on the jaw. It ain't right, and I know it, but I'm sure she never meant to kill him. (*Pause.*) And let's face it, if it was the other way round and he'd'ave hit her, no one would even have heard about it.

Priscilla It isn't that simple.

Maggie (*angry*) Oh, but it is. To your sort everything is. Bet you had one of them real pretty dolls' houses when you was a little girl and you grew up to live in one of your own, except it's got real people in it not dolls. When you don't like one of 'em for whatever reason you just get rid of 'em, throw them away . . .

Priscilla That's not fair.

Maggie No, it's not. You got a responsibility, Mrs Cuttle-Smythe, not only to yourself, but to Polly.

Scene Twelve

Len *and* **Jim** *in the pub.*

Len D'you reckon they'll hang her then?

Jim Dunno. He's claiming she intended to murder him.

Len You'd think he'd have more vanity than ter stand in the Old Bailey and admit that slip of a maid chinned and floored him.

Jim A slip of a girl? Polly? It's your memory what's slipping.

Len Yeah, but she's still only a woman, when all's said and done. Unless you know something I don't.

Jim But, you never know though what folks are capable of, do yer?

Len True. (*Pause.*) Hope your Kate ain't like that.

Jim Na, different girl she is, being so close to her betters has changed her for the better I can tell you.

Len A lady.

Jim Yes I s'pose she is. Treats me with courtesy and respect these days . . .

Len You lucky bleeder . . . Mag could do with that sort of training I can tell yer . . .

Jim Where is she?

Len You may well ask . . . said she needed some fresh air . . . said she weren't feeling too good . . . If you ask me I think it was too much helping herself to the profits last night. Here, (*He beckons* **Jim** *closer.*) she err, your Kate, did she ever bring anything up in conversation about um, sausage skins?

Jim Take no notice, Len. I never. I told her straight and she ain't likely to bring it up again . . . she's too well spoken these days to refer to sausages in any conversation except one concerning breakfast.

Len I don't know where they all think it up from, do you?

Jim Don't bear thinking about does it.

Pause.

Len We could take a tip off them toffs, Jim and no mistake. Look at what our women get away with, eh?

Jim How d'you mean?

Len When we're boys we have to bring our wages straight

home to our mothers, right? And she gives us pocket money out of it. And what happens when we're men? We give our wages to our wives and they give us our beer money. Now, you don't get that sorta behaviour from ladies do yer? It's all 'please could I have some housekeeping money, my darling.' See we've got it wrong all these years, boy.

Jim You got a point there Len, and no mistake.

Len Still, I can't stand round here discussing how to change the world all day. What you got for me this week, Jim?

Jim Sorry, I was forgetting . . . (*Taking out a package and giving it to* **Len**.)

Len (*looking inside*) Bleedin' hell. Sausages! What you trying to do to me boy?

Scene Thirteen

Lady Helena *sits, writing in her journal.* **Ellen** *talks to the audience.* **Annie**, **Kate**, **Maggie** *and* **Polly** *stand, separately alone.*

Lady Helena This morning I woke up and I felt like hugging myself.

Ellen It's hardly what you'd call a rewarding job.

Lady Helena The careful planning and hard work has been of benefit to so many.

Ellen You put a button on a metal plate, then cover it with material.

Annie This morning I woke up and I realised that I hadn't dreamed about running away for a whole week. It's much better not to hold on to your dreams. I suppose it's natural to let go of them as you get older.

Lady Helena It was of course a blow, when the girls were unexpectedly thrown out of work.

Ellen You bring the lever down.

Lady Helena But even that turned to our advantage, giving the coarsest girl a sense of urgency.

Maggie I wanted something more for myself, but me Mother was right. You got to make the best of what you got. It's easier to be ordinary, ter do what's expected of yer. It's just I wanted something more.

Ellen And there you have a perfectly covered button.

Lady Helena Through diligence and persistence even the rawest of material has been transformed into a servant of lower middle class acceptability.

Kate I've been admired for looking nice and dressing nice, I feel really special when men catch my eye. No one would dream of calling me common now. I know what to expect of them and they know what to expect of me. If a man swore in front of me today, he'd be mortified. I've earned that sort of respect.

Ellen At the end of the day you have a whole box full.

Lady Helena Two hundred and fifty of them placed to date in good households.

Ellen The conditions are cleaner but the whole place is very hot and noisy.

Lady Helena One tale of woe, Polly, an aberration.

Polly It struck me this morning that I've always been at someone's mercy . . . We all are when we're born an' that. It's after that, things unequal out a bit. I was at the mercy of the guv'nors in the sheds. I was at the mercy of the master in the house. And now I'm at the mercy of the law.

Ellen It makes it impossible to talk.

Lady Helena And one regret, namely Priscilla, who I've not seen since the incident.

Ellen The only variety in the work is when they change the quality of the material.

Lady Helena But I cannot help but marvel, modesty permitting, at the accomplishment.

Ellen But they have a works canteen here, thanks to the union.

Lady Helena Even the doubting Thomases have had to eat their words. ·

Ellen (*referring to a woman she works with, not any of the characters in the play*) See that woman – over there? She started it; she even gives speeches in public – you'd never think it would yer – People think she's mad.

Lady Helena (*turns*) Priscilla, what an unexpected surprise. (*She gets up and goes.*)

Ellen But she ain't . . . She says to me, 'Ellen, we got a right, and a responsibility to speak out.' I looked at her just like Maggie used to look at me an' I says, 'Good job we're only here once.' 'So,' she says, 'you just going to sit there and let it happen again, then?' –

BESIDE HERSELF

Beside Herself was first performed by the Women's Playhouse Trust at the Royal Court, London on 29 March 1990, with the following cast:

George/Dave	Tenniel Evans
Evelyn	Dinah Stabb
Eve	Marion Bailey
Shirley/Gaynor	Julia Hills
Lil	June Watson
Teddy	Mark Tandy
Greg/Richard	Nick Dunning
Roy/Tony	Des McAleer
Nicola	Lizzy McInnerny

Members of the cast double in the prelude to the play.

Directed by Jules Wright
Designed by Jenny Tiramani
Lighting by Jenny Cane

The play is set in London in the present.

Prelude

The Power and the Story

A dream. A supermarket.

Delilah *is cutting* **Jezebel**'s *hair.* **Mrs Lot** *is reading a copy of* Family Circle. She looks up as **Eve** *approaches.*

Mrs Lot Oh no, that's all we need.

Jezebel Ignore her, then she'll go away.

Delilah You can't do that, Jezebel. Hello, Eve.

Eve How lovely to see you, Delilah.

Delilah This is Jezebel and, er, Lot's wife, sorry I don't know your name.

Mrs Lot Hello, Eve. Where've you bin?

Eve What do you mean, where've I been? I've been here, Hell.

Jezebel (*to* **Mrs Lot**) If we're stuck here, I hardly think Eve would have gone to the other place – use your loaf.

Delilah (*to* **Eve**) Did you want a haircut then?

Eve Not just now, thank you, Delilah. I'm supposed to be taking a tutorial group on 'The burden of guilt and two thousand years of misrepresentation'.

Jezebel Oh Lor, who to?

Eve You, Jezebel, well all of you.

Jezebel Me? I only came over here for a trim.

Eve Only I've been stood on my tod for half a millennium and nobody turned up.

Jezebel Surprise, surprise.

Delilah Most seemed to have opted for Mrs Noah's seminar on 'How to survive a barbecue in a storm'.

Mrs Lot The others are clustered round 'Obedience and the dire consequences thereof' — to the right of frozen veg. Hey, Delilah, do you think you could make any headway with this frowzy brillo-pad?

Delilah (*examines* **Mrs Lot***'s hair*) Tut tut, too much conditioning too often. Very bad for your natural body, Lottie love.

Mrs Lot Oh, just chop the lot off, Delilah.

Delilah To tell the truth, I ain't really got the nerve for that any more, lost me bottle. I'll get rid of the split ends if you like.

Eve We spend an eternity condemned to wander these aisles alone and the first chance we get to meet, the only thing you want to highlight is your vanity.

Mrs Lot No need to get all hairiated, Eve. It was her profession. Even if her credibility was undermined before she was fully qualified.

Eve That's what we're here to sort out. How we've —

Jezebel Oh, what's the point. Let sleeping mud puddles lie.

Eve I hardly think you can refer to a series of violent deaths and twenty centuries of trivialisation as a mud puddle, Jezebel.

Jezebel And I don't need you to tell me to what I can or can't refer.

Delilah Keep your hair on. What d'yer want to know, Eve? That I was damned for being an evil castrating bitch. Because that's what everybody believes I am. But do they ever bother to try and imagine what it was like for me being married to a man for whom an afternoon's work was killing a few hundred people with the jaw-bone of a donkey?

Mrs Lot Come on, you must have done something.

Delilah It was his hair, weren't it. To cut a long story short — I did.

Jezebel You didn't ask his permission, did you?

Delilah Don't you start. It really got on his nerves. It come half-way down his bum and it was always getting tangled up in his armpit when he was asleep. He was so strong, see, that if he woke up with a jerk he nearly yanked his own bloody head off. I done him a favour really. Not that you'd know it.

Mrs Lot At least you've got a name. All I'm known as is the wife of Lot, the stupid slag who deserved all she got.

Eve See, that's what we're here to put right.

Mrs Lot Oh, Eve, it weren't that bad really. Na, see we had to abandon our house in a hurry. I only had the shoes I stood up in. Well, when one's home town suffers an arson attack from God, one doesn't exactly dither around pondering on which worldly possessions to pack. So there I was right, running hell for leather, molten brimstone spurting and squirting on my heels when me left shoe got caught in the rubble. So the choice was turn round and retrieve the shoe or hop to the Promised Land. I turned. A mere revolution for which I got metamorphosed into a pillar of salt.

Jezebel That's justice for you.

Mrs Lot Oh, it could be worse. I know people make jokes about 'pass Lot's wife' but they'll get their come-uppance cos I can tell you for a fact salt does for the blood pressure.

Martha *comes over.*

Martha Sorry to bother you. I'm Martha and –

Eve You're in the wrong place, dear. New Testament workshops are over there. (*Pointing.*) Mugs and kitchen tools.

Jezebel And I can still see Mary Mag wandering around the toiletries like a lost sheep.

Eve Probably trying to locate the corn plasters.

Martha For your information I've not had time to sit and listen to everyone's life story, muggins here has had to prepare lunch.

Delilah Oh, I thought Salome was giving you a hand.

Martha She's got a lot on her plate.

Jezebel Just so long as it doesn't end up on ours.

Martha So, how many of you are vegetarians?

Jezebel None.

Eve Speak for yourself.

Delilah Apart from Eve here, who'd die for an Eden Vale yoghurt.

Eve Not one with fruit in, I wouldn't.

Martha So, that's one. Thanks. Sorry for interrupting.

Mrs Lot So useless that Lot.

Jezebel Silly little po-faced domestic.

Mrs Lot I weren't alluding to her, Jezebel. I meant my husband.

Jezebel Ho. You think you had problems. As far as my old man was concerned moral fibre was a brand of breakfast cereal. Weak? You could've knocked him over with a Shredded Wheat.

Eve I wish we could just get on.

Mrs Lot We are, we are. Let's face it, none of us will see two thousand and one again.

Delilah So what happened to you?

Jezebel Me? Dear, I was eaten up by mad dogs.

Mrs Lot Isn't it funny what gets remembered and what gets forgotten.

Delilah Hilarious.

Mrs Lot Because I never did anything when all's said and done. One evening we was all sat down like a happy family, looking forward to a game of Scrabble.

Delilah Don't you mean squabble?

Eve Shush, Delilah, you've had your turn.

Delilah Was that it? Thanks a million.

Mrs Lot Two strangers came to our home. And a mob of pimps and rapists gathered outside demanding access to them. Rather than offend the two guests who Lot had never laid eyes on before, he shouted out of the window to the mob that they could have our daughters instead, using as sales patter, the fact that they were both virgins. This is all totally forgotten. But s'pose Lot had got his own way, I'd have been powerless to stop them.

Delilah Maybe that's why you got turned into a pillar of salt.

Mrs Lot No, that was because I turned back.

Eve At least you did something to be judged for.

Delilah So did you Eve. I mean all credit to you. You climbed the tree of knowledge even if it did fall into your lap in the shape of a manky bit of fruit.

Jezebel I've always meant to ask, was it actually an apple?

Eve No, it was a ripe avocado.

Jezebel Did it taste nice?

Eve Horrible – why d'you think I only took one bite.

Mrs Lot They perk up with a bit of salt.

Eve I caused your downfall and all you care about is a mouldy avocado.

Mrs Lot Don't take on, Eve. We all know you was talked into it.

Eve A red herring.

Jezebel Oh? I always thought it was a serpent. Still, I've never claimed oral history was my strong point.

Eve It was a snake but it didn't talk. Just being. That was my crime. When mankind gets found out he points at me. Her fault – seducer. Made from Adam, for Adam. His wife and his daughter – legitimizer of his will.

Jezebel Listen, we're getting fed up of being harangued by your homilies, Eve.

Delilah Speak for yourself.

Mrs Lot Shush.

They stop, as a **Woman***, pushing a trolley full of shopping, walks between them. She hasn't noticed that her* **Younger Child** *has climbed out of the seat and is now clinging to the side of the trolley. She is more concerned with the whereabouts of the other child,* **Jack***, who is nowhere to be seen.*

Woman (*letting go of the trolley, without looking at* **Younger Child**) Wait there. (*Walks back.*) Jack, where are you? Please, Jack. (*Then sees him clutching bags of crisps.*) Oh, there you are.

She takes the crisps from him, throws them back on the shelves and takes his hand.

You mustn't wander off or I might lose you. No, this way. Now, quickly. Why? Because this isn't a theme park. It's a bloody boring supermarket and we have to get to the post office before lunchtime. Because if we get there too late the queue will be outside the door and we'll get stuck behind someone who wants a stamp of every denomination, an airmail sticker without the rest of the letter and a padded envelope of a size they eventually won't have, by which time I'll be asking for a padded cell. So, please. Come on, take my hand.

Back at the trolley she lets go of **Jack**'s *hand to retrieve the* **Younger Child**. **Jack** *uses the opportunity to grab more crisps.*

You wanted to sit there so sit still. Jack, put those . . . (*Struggle of the crisps ensues.*) Because we can't afford them, that's why. Put them back. Jack? Because they're all full of animal fat – yuck, horrible.

She takes them from him, throws them back on the shelf. **Jack** *throws himself down in front of the trolley.*

Woman Come on, Jack, get up. Please come on. There's no need to make this noise. Don't say I didn't warn you.

Mrs Lot What the bleedin' heaven is she on about?

Jezebel Take no notice, she's lost her trolley.

The **Woman** *pushes the trolley forward.* **Jack** *rolls out of the way and the three of them disappear round the corner.*

Eve Where was I – Oh, yes, if it wasn't for me –

Mrs Lot Can we get back to having our hair cut, Eve. This is getting a bit depressing.

Eve Wait till Lilith gets here. She'll tell you.

Mrs Lot Who?

Eve Adam's first wife who refused to lie beneath him and got the big E.

Jezebel Nobody believes she's anybody. You're crazy.

Eve Oh, am I? I didn't take a bite out of the friggin' forbidden fruit for the good of my health.

Delilah Yeah, I know who she means. Lilith. The one who let us cop for the lot.

Mrs Lot Why do you have to keep dragging his name into it.

Eve Only she got away.

Jezebel She's hardly likely to turn up in here then, is she?

Thunder and lightning.

Man (*VO*) Would those women causing absolute havoc please put a sock in it. Yes, you in the biscuit aisle. Some poor devil has collapsed by fresh fruit and we're holding you responsible.

Mrs Lot Oh, crumbs.

Eve Oh, Christ.

Delilah What's new?

Part One

Scene One

In her father's house

George *hears the front door shut. He pours water from the kettle into the teapot.*

Eve *is by the fridge.*

George (*by table, calls*) Hello?

Evelyn (*calls*) It's only me.

George (*calls*) In here.

Evelyn, *carrying four bags of shopping, comes in. She sees* **Eve** *slouched against a cupboard.*

George *stirs the tea with a spoon, his back to* **Evelyn.**

Evelyn *is visibly shaken by* **Eve***'s presence. She looks at her. Hesitates. Makes a decision to focus on* **George** *as he turns to face her and puts the teapot on the table.*

George (*laughingly*) You're just on time. (*He sits down.*)

Evelyn Yes, yes. (*Smiling politely*) I can't stop, I'm very busy.

George (*pouring the tea*) I thought you'd like a cup of tea.

Eve *watches* **George** *and* **Evelyn. Evelyn** *is aware of this. She doesn't look at* **Eve.**

Evelyn No. (*Nicely.*) I've already had one thanks, Dad.

She puts the contents of the bag on a work surface where she can see **George,** *but he has to turn round to see her. Throughout the scene she calmly and methodically places each item in the appropriate place, be it cupboard, freezer or fridge.*

Eve Thanks, Dad. Only me. Nobody. Nothing.

George There's no rule about not having another one. Come on. It's getting cold.

Evelyn I've only just had my breakfast.

George Leave that, Evelyn, I can do that when you've gone.

Evelyn The sooner it's done, the better; it's out of the way.

George Sit down for a few minutes. You look quite pale.

Eve *stands.*

Evelyn Oh, I'm fine. Nothing that a good night's sleep won't put right.

George Noises in the house that have always been there take on a loud significance when you're on your own, don't they?

Eve I was never on my own.

Evelyn (*vaguely*) Umm.

George Phillip? Still away?

Evelyn Yes.

George It's very kind of him to always bring you over with the shopping but it's also nice to see you on your own for once.

Eve *smirks.*

Evelyn It's quite a trek though.

George And I really do appreciate it. How's things otherwise?

Evelyn Oh, you know, busy.

George Keeping busy is the wicket keeper of coping, that I do know.

Eve *mimes lifting a cricket bat in the air.*

George We had so many plans your mother and I for when I retired. But, now, well, it's not the same when you're on your own.

Evelyn (*goes to fridge*) No.

Eve *follows her and stands behind her.*

George (*jovially*) Evelyn, will you please stop fussing.

Evelyn (*putting things in the fridge*) It's no good leaving things uncovered in there, they just rot.

Eve *laughs softly.*

George Oh, I'll have a clear out when you've gone. Please sit down, how am I supposed to talk to you when you've got your head in the ruddy fridge.

Evelyn The microwavable dinners are arranged in order of their sell-by date. And, oh, you've still got some left . . .

George I still get invited out from time to time, dinner parties and do's of one sort or another. Besides, I don't like a lot of that goo under ruptured cellophane.

Evelyn Why didn't you tell me? (*Turns to face him.*) What do you like, and I'll make sure I get it next time?

Eve *kicks the fridge.*

Eve *walks away from* **Evelyn**, *stands back but between* **Evelyn** *and* **George**.

George What I'd really like is for you to sit down and talk to me.

Evelyn (*continues with putting the shopping away*) It's just that I have a meeting to go to and I'm running a bit late.

George I was going to suggest that you might like to come with me to one of these do's and what not. I'm often asked to bring a guest. It would do you good, to get out in the evenings with Phillip away so often. After all, what's good for the gander is good for the goose.

Evelyn (*unguarded*) What do you mean by that?

Eve You're thick.

George Nothing. Just that –

Evelyn What?

George If he's out enjoying himself I don't see why –

Evelyn You know I want to finish redecorating the house and with my daytimes rather full . . .

George You take on too much, Evelyn. Being the wife of an MP doesn't mean you have to spend every waking hour in voluntary work.

Evelyn It's important to practise what you preach.

George And charity begins at home.

Evelyn Dad, I do your shopping every fortnight. (*Goes to the cupboard and puts the tins away.*)

George (*hurt rather than angry*) I don't care about the shopping. I'd prefer a bit more of your company.

Evelyn I know.

George I'm not asking much.

Eve (*sarcastic*) You've never given much.

George We never asked much. When your mother was alive we hardly ever saw you. Now it's just me and you.

Eve (*sneers*) It's the least you can do.

George It's just putting the poor old man's shopping away with a 'yes', 'no', 'thank you for asking' and you're off. (*Turning round angry.*) For God's sake, Evelyn. Look at me when I'm talking to you.

He stands suddenly, accidentally knocking his cup and saucer on the floor. They smash. The noise makes **Evelyn** *and* **Eve** *jump in fright.*

Eve *covers her face and drops to the floor.*

George (*pathetically*) Damn! Damn!

Evelyn (*shakily*) It's all right. It was only an accident. No real damage done.

George (*sits down again, miserably*) Oh, God. I can't bear getting old.

Eve Then drop dead.

Evelyn (*shocked, responds to* **Eve**) I'm sorry, I didn't mean that.

George What?

Evelyn To make you angry.

George (*apologetically*) I didn't mean to lose my temper – it's the last thing (*He reaches out to put his hand reassuringly on hers. She avoids him.*) I wanted to happen.

Evelyn (*picking up the broken china*) Don't worry, I'll get you a replacement next time I'm in town. (*She goes over to the bin and throws it away.*)

George God knows I don't want to turn into one of those pathetic old goats who constantly makes demands on his family. What with your brothers so far away, it would be nice to see you and Phillip and Joanna a bit more often.

Evelyn We always spend Christmas.

George But darling, Christmas.

Evelyn Yes, I know it was months ago. But, you know, Phillip has a lot on and with Joanna away at school . . .

George I got a letter from her the other day.

Eve *and* **Evelyn** *are both unnerved.*

Eve *is closer to* **Evelyn** *at this point than at any other point in the scene.*

Evelyn (*coldly*) She didn't mention it.

George Thanking me for her birthday present. At least she keeps in touch. Many youngsters of her age can't be bothered to sit down and write a word unless it's to scrawl doggerel over tube train doors. It was a really chatty, almost witty piece of prose. She's really quite intelligent, you know. I've often wondered if we should have paid for your education. But at the time . . . Still, Joanna's a real credit to you.

Evelyn Which is more than you can say of me.

Eve Dunce.

George Oh, come on. I'm very proud of you, you know that.

Evelyn (*surprised*) Are you?

Eve (*jeers*) You're pathetic.

George Yes, of course.

Eve *moves away in disgust.*

Joanna said that she'd come and see me in the summer holidays.

Eve *turns back. Her concentration now strongly focused on* **George.**

Evelyn She can't. Not on her own.

George Nonsense.

Evelyn She's not old enough.

George She's old enough to get on the tube.

Evelyn It's too far.

George I'd meet her at the station.

Evelyn No. (*Then.*) I'll bring her over.

George Would you? That would be nice. Thank you.

Evelyn (*hurriedly*) And I'll see you in a fortnight. I must dash now. Sorry, I really do have to go. Sorry. 'Bye.

Evelyn *walks towards the door.* **Eve** *follows her.*

Eve (*jeeringly*) Sorry, sorry, sorry.

Evelyn (*turns*) 'Bye.

Eve Sorry.

Scene Two
St Dymphna's

The living room of a Community Group Home.

Along the back wall is a door which leads to a walk-in cupboard. To the left a door which leads to the rest of the house. To the right a door which leads to the hallway and front door.

The room has been vandalised. The recently emulsioned walls have been daubed with paint. The only decipherable word 'Loonies' has pride of place between the picture rail and frame of the mirror over the fireplace. The mirror is smashed. The fragments lie scattered over the floor.

Lil *enters. She carries a shopping bag containing cleaning materials and her overall. She puts the bag down and surveys the room with pragmatic dismay.*

Shirley (*VO from the cupboard*) Is that you, Lil?

Lil (*looks round*) Shirley? Where are you?

Shirley (*VO*) Won't be a sec. I'm just getting changed for the meeting.

Lil *puts bag by fireplace.*

Teddy, *complete with dog collar, enters right.*

Teddy (*blithely*) Front door open. Sorry. Shirley about?

Lil (*whirls round. Anxious to protect **Shirley** from being caught in a state of undress by a clergyman*) Cup of tea, Father? (*Turning back momentarily to check the cupboard door is still shut.*)

Teddy (*magnanimously*) Oh, Teddy, please.

Lil (*distractedly*) Eh? Oh, you want the Day Centre. They do a nice line in soft toys.

Teddy (*perturbed. Calls out*) Shirley?

Shirley (*VO from cupboard*) Coming.

Shirley *emerges smartly dressed. Track suit over her arm.*

Teddy Ah, there you are.

Shirley Good morning, Teddy. You're nice and early. (*She watches him as he looks at the state of the room.*) Not a pretty picture. I've made a start in the kitchen, Lil.

Teddy Were you here when it happened?

Shirley No. Oh, I'm so sorry, you've not been introduced. Lil, this is the Reverend Kegwin.

Teddy Teddy. I've recently been co-opted on to the Management Committee. (*Holds out his hand.*) Pleased to meet you, Lil.

Lil (*letting him shake her hand robustly*) How d'you do.

Pause.

Teddy (*brightly*) Where are the other residents?

Shirley (*short embarrassed laugh*) Oh, Lil isn't a resident. She works for the Local Authority. Twelve of her working hours a week are allotted to us here at St Dymphna's.

Teddy Mea culpa. Mea culpa. You're a Home Help.

Lil In a glorified manner of speaking. I actually work for the EDT.

Shirley (*in response to* **Teddy**'s *bewildered look*) The Early Discharge Team – to support those recently discharged from psychiatric hospitals into Group Homes like this – by way of daily living skills.

Lil Yeah, we used to be called 'Aides' but that word don't exactly inspire confidence in the public imagination. (*She starts to tidy the room.*)

Teddy Umm 'discharge' doesn't exactly roll off the tongue either. Still, I expect you're an old hand at this now.

Slight pause.

Shirley (*quickly*) I've made a list of the items missing and the damage. It's –

Teddy You know my feeling is that we should have a plaque or something on the outside with 'St Dymphna's' embossed on it.

Shirley (*mildly*) Would that do any good? I mean do churches named after saints get less vandalised than ones that aren't?

Teddy (*vaguely*) No idea. I've never thought about it. (*Then enthusiastically*.) But. I've been mugging up on St Dymphna.

Shirley (*smiling*) Oh, Teddy, I didn't know you had ecumenical tendencies.

Teddy (*seriously*) Only towards Anglo-Catholicism I hasten to reassure you. My views on Evangelical Liberalism are, I imagine, akin to the Romanian layman's on Stalin.

Shirley (*unreassured*) I see, (*Gestures towards the door*.) I've just got to . . .

Teddy (*he follows her towards the door. Then stops. Looks at the graffiti*) Remarkable. Seems like Community Mental Health is popular with everybody except the community. One thing's for sure, if I were psychologically disturbed I wouldn't want to sit and stare at the word 'Loonies' all day.

Shirley Yes, no, me neither. I don't know how we're going to manage to get them repainted.

Teddy The insurance?

Shirley These things take time.

Teddy No time like the present. Where did you say the details were?

Shirley On my desk.

Teddy Why don't I go and give them the once over and get on the blower to the insurance company?

He goes.

Shirley *sighs. Shakes her head.*

Lil *kneels on the floor and picks up the broken pieces of mirror.*

Shirley (*to* **Lil**) Remind me to order a new mirror. (*She bends down to help* **Lil**.)

Lil (*holding a piece of mirror*) Unnerving, ain't it – how you can only see a piece of yourself in a shard of mirror. It's sort of like trying to recollect a dream when you can only visualise the bit that woke you up.

Shirley (*not knowing what to say*) Oh?

Lil (*smiles*) I don't know what come over me. I must have read it in a book.

Shirley Are you a big reader then?

Lil Never used to be. Just took it up to pass the time. Now that, well now that I have more time.

Shirley How is your husband?

Lil Oh, he's home. They're all very pleased with him.

Shirley I don't imagine you get much time for reading at the moment or does your daughter help out?

Lil My . . .

Shirley You do have a daughter, or am I mixing you up with someone else? No, I'm sure . . .

Lil Yes, yes, but it's difficult. She's away a lot.

Shirley What does she do?

Lil (*hasn't seen her daughter for eight years and has no idea what she does. Lies*) She's er, an air hostess.

Shirley Really? Does . . .

Lil I get postcards from all over the place. Well, this won't buy the baby new shoes. I'd better get the Hoover. There is still a Hoover?

Shirley I forgot to check. If we haven't it's not on his list.

As they go towards the door left, conscious of the awkwardness, **Lil** *changes the subject.*

Lil Fancy calling something in a dog collar Teddy. I ask you. Jesus. (*Then.*) You know I thought this place was called 77 Headsend Road. That's what it says on my work sheet. Who the hell is St Dymphna when she's at home?

Shirley Don't look at me, the funding body christened it.

Lil Wretched Voluntary Sector. Cluttered with born-agains.

Shirley I better go and see what he's doing.

Lil Well at least he put his frock on before he got here.

They go out.

Evelyn *comes in. She carries a framed print of Breughel's* Icarus.

Evelyn I knew it was supposed to be unlucky to have a mirror over a fireplace but – (*Pause.*) I look good.

Eve Stupid.

Evelyn (*to Eve*) I feel okay.

Eve Dirty.

Evelyn (*to Eve*) I'm all right.

Eve Worthless.

Evelyn Now, best place for the picture.

Eve You shouldn't talk to yourself. Not here of all places.

Evelyn (*holding the picture against the wall*) No.

Lil *comes in with the vacuum cleaner.*

Lil Talking to yourself, Evelyn?

Evelyn Merely reflecting on my sanity out loud, Lil.

Lil Oh, really?

Evelyn Yes, haven't you heard that expression?

Lil No. What is it? Ascot blank verse?

Evelyn I brought this. I thought it might disguise some of the mess until you've had time to clean up.

Lil That's nice.

Evelyn Oh, it's not mine. I borrowed it from the library. Not the one round here. That's closed. Crying shame and in a Labour borough.

Lil *sighs audibly and switches on the vacuum cleaner.*

Pause.

Lil *vacuums round the fireplace.*

Evelyn (*shouts over the noise of the vacuum cleaner*) Shall I hang it over the fireplace?

Lil (*switches the vacuum cleaner off*) Why not? (*She gets a cloth and a bottle of white spirit from her bag.*)

Evelyn *stands on a chair, takes a picture hook from her pocket and hangs the picture so that it neatly covers the word 'Loonies'.*

Eve She's laughing at you.

Lil *isn't taking any notice. She concentrates on removing the paint that's been daubed on the fire surround.*

Evelyn *steps down and puts the chair back.*

Shirley *enters left, unseen by* **Lil** *or* **Evelyn**.

Evelyn (*looking at the picture*) There. (*Pompously.*) I know some people don't like Breughel but then some people do.

Lil (*casually without looking up*) And, there's every probability his wife painted it anyway.

Evelyn Really? He wasn't a homosexual then.

Shirley What a cost-effective idea.

Evelyn Thank you. Though I don't imagine that even the Tate has got enough stock to cover this doggerel.

Eve One of Daddy's words.

Shirley The? Oh, yes, the graffiti. It's not just this room. Teddy's upstairs now trying to evaluate the extent of the damage.

Evelyn Bless him. I'd better follow suit if I'm going to be in the picture for this meeting.

She goes.

Shirley Did his wife really paint it?

Lil (*still working*) No idea. I just said it.

Shirley Oh, d'you think he was gay then?

Lil (*lightly*) I really don't know. I suppose it's possible. Most talented people seem to have been. (*Starts to rub at the paint with a vengeance.*) Typical of her to try and get one over on me like that. (*Calmer.*) It was all because of her I took up reading in the first place.

Shirley Of her?

Lil Yeah. Them sort. All the same. Always casually relating real life to make-believe. To show off their education.

Shirley How do you mean?

Lil Oh, you know, something ordinary happens, some trivial everyday occurrence and they'll pipe up (*Mimicking.*) 'Oh, that's so reminiscent of so and so when that happens in that book so and so . . .'

Shirley Which book?

Lil Could be anything, who knows. The usual trick is to refer to a character and not the book's title. So if you ain't read the right book you're all at sea and if you have you have to be thinking on your feet.

Shirley Oh, I see what you mean. I always feel sorry for them not being able to relate anything to real life.

Lil Pah, I keep running up against her. I tell yer, Shirley, she's sat on more committees that I have buses. And she's always looked down her nose at me right from the time I used to clean for the old people in Swans' Walk.

Shirley She doesn't strike me as the sort of woman to be conversing chapter and verse with the cleaner.

Lil That's just it, Shirley. I had her down as one of them types but I'm telling yer she don't know the difference between a Trollope and a Tolstoy. All I can think is she must have spent all her time at school reading *Wish for a Pony* under the desk.

Shirley You've ploughed through loads of classics for her benefit to find she hasn't read one of them?

Lil (*laughs*) Yeah. (*She stands, wipes over the fire surround.*) Aw, don't look at me like that. I don't bother to try and catch her out no more. I do it for meself now. Oh, hark at me, I don't know what I'm going on about, take no notice.

Shirley What sort of books?

Lil Stories. You know. Fiction. The sort you can be absorbed in knowing the only responsibility you've got is to turn the page and it will all be resolved.

Shirley You only read novels with happy endings?

Lil Oh, no. Take Thomas Hardy for instance. He's so depressing that when the main character dies it's a relief to know they've been put out of their misery.

Greg *enters right.* **Greg** *is the Acting Team Leader in the hospital Psychiatric Social Work Department.*

Greg Morning, Lil, Shirley. How's things?

Shirley (*looking at the room*) Could be better.

Lil It'll be clean by the time I'm finished here today. Apart from the writing on the walls, I don't know what to do about that.

Greg (*looking through his papers in his bag*) I'm sure we'll be able to sort something out. I hope. I must say it was good of you to offer us coffee and sandwiches for lunch, Lil.

Lil (*unseen by* **Shirley** *or* **Greg**, *looks quite shocked, this being the first time she's heard of it*) Oh. Right. Fine. I'd better go out and get some bread.

Greg Where is everybody?

Shirley The charity cases are still upstairs marvelling over how the actual plumbing got actually nicked.

Greg (*looks up*) Now, Shirley.

Shirley They can't hear us.

Greg Still. Teddy's redeemable, isn't he? He's a bit of a liberal at heart.

Shirley I hope so. He's supposed to be shouldering some of my work balancing the books. (*Sighs.*) When I first started work, I never thought about money. I mean not the responsibility to find money to make the thing work.

Greg I find myself increasingly thinking about money, in respect of how little I get paid, weighed against mounting responsibility, crumbling resources and negligible job satisfaction.

Shirley That good?

Greg (*wearily*) Twenty-three unallocated cases, twelve case conferences so far this month, and to top it all, my motor got pranged in the rear. Moan. Moan. Some well-oiled nut behind the wheel. Oops. Sorry. There's another euphemism for your research. Where the bloody hell is Roy?

Shirley Do you call him Roy to his face?

Greg Only when I feel supremely confident. Usually I feel the weight of his status bearing down compelling me to address him as Dr Freeman. Ideally, I try to manage to converse with him without bringing his name into the conversation at all.

Shirley It will be interesting to see how you introduce him – what's he really like?

Greg Heavy drugs merchant. He views psychotherapy with the disdain most men reserve for male ballet dancers. You know that breed of psychiatrist whose only recollection from childhood is some distant memory of a grandfather clock ticking in a great aunt's house. On balance they aren't too keen to examine others' early experiences in case it triggers off some long forgotten trauma in their own past. (*Then.*) Don't mind me, I've just come back from a course in 'Burn Out' – I reckon I've caught it.

Evelyn/Eve *and* **Teddy** *enter left as* **Roy,** *followed by* **Nicola,** *enters right.*

Greg (*hurriedly mouths to* **Shirley**) Did he hear me?

Shirley *shakes her head*.

Roy A quick start, Greg, please.

Greg Okay.

Roy Hello, Evelyn.

Evelyn Hello, Roy.

Greg Please take a seat, everyone. I'd like to thank you all for being able to get here at such short notice. I know we're running to tight schedules and meeting in our lunch hour. However, we will be provided with a sandwich and coffee shortly. I'd like to welcome the Reverend Teddy Kegwin officially to our Management Committee. I think we all know each other. (*Then seeing* **Nicola**.) Oh, I'm sorry, I don't . . .

Roy (*offhand*) Oh, this is Nurse Cretsley.

Nicola (*self-consciously*) Adams.

Roy (*without a hint of apology*) Nurse sorry Adams, is training to be a CPN, temporarily on placement with me. She's here as an observer. Good experience. She comes from that Godforsaken place.

Nicola Cretsley. And it's Nicola.

Evelyn Hello, I'm Evelyn.

Eve Hello, I'm Evelyn.

Shirley (*writing, looks up*) Sorry, it's just for the minutes. It's not Nicola Cretsley, is it? It's Adams.

Nicola Yes. No. Cretsley's where I've been working.

Shirley (*writing*) I thought so. Thanks. (*Looks up.*) Oh, that's a coincidence. (*Stops herself, then more formally.*) I'm Shirley, by the way. House Manager. Part-time. Because the post is funded part-time.

Roy (*sighs*) This isn't a full blown case conference. It's an emergency ad hoc allocation meeting. Do we need bother with minutes?

Shirley Not formally, no. But it's always useful to have a record.

Greg (*to* **Nicola**) Teddy and Evelyn are part of the Management Committee and we have a worker from the EDT for a total of, umm . . .

Teddy Twelve hours a week.

Greg Yes, sorry, my brain's not in gear. Thank you, Teddy. Oh, and I'm Greg, acting Team Manager for the Psychiatric Social Work team based in the hospital. So, if we bump into each other in the corridors we'll know who we are.

Nicola (*self-consciously*) Hello, hello, hello.

Teddy I think I'm supposed to ask which budget lunch is coming out of.

Greg We'll get to the budget soon enough, Teddy. First, any smokers?

Nicola, *rather embarrassed, raises her hand.*

Teddy Tut, tut, a nurse as well.

Evelyn I've given up.

Shirley I didn't know you smoked.

Evelyn Only socially, but I've stopped altogether . . .

Roy *puts his pen down on his file impatiently.*

Evelyn . . . now.

Greg (*gathering pace*) Fine, fine. Well, the rule is only one cigarette to be smoked at a time. (*To* **Nicola**.) So, as long as you don't put two in your mouth at once you're laughing. Shirley, would you like to summarise the events of last week?

Roy We all know what happened last week. It's next week I'm concerned about.

Shirley It's just that . . .

Roy It's just that I've got wards due to close which are still chock-a-block. This home has six beds, only four of which are useable at the present time which represents approximately four per cent of patients already waiting to be rehabilitated into the community. And, although these places are supposed to be half-way hostels, as we all know the turnover is very slow because of the housing situation. They are also, for the record, supposed to offer an alternative to the dreaded Victorian asylum. But, what sort of asylum they offer when they get vandalised every other week, I don't know.

Shirley It's only been vandalised once before.

Roy It's only been open six months.

Teddy (to **Shirley**) At least I managed to pin the insurance rep down.

Evelyn Is that why there are so many ill-looking people begging on the underground?

Roy No, it's because we don't have the resources to start with, but let's not allow ourselves to get side-tracked.

Greg I would just like to point out, that because child protection is very much in the public eye, it demands, and rightly, more and more time and necessary statutory work, but its very urgency relegates the support given to those recovering from mental illness, who are out of the picture as far as the public eye and sympathy are concerned, to the bottom of the priority pile.

Roy Now we've all aired our sociological grievances, perhaps you could enlighten me to the relevance, if any, of what you're saying.

Greg Bluntly, that new residents we take on must be those most able to cope, because in person-hours alone, the support is just not available.

Shirley I agree and I would also like it minuted that we do have an Equal Opps policy and should be mindful of that. Also, when things get back to normal, residents should have a say in who lives here.

Teddy As you've got the pen I think you're at liberty to write anything you like.

This uncalled for interruption is coldly ignored.

Sorry.

Roy This EOP rigmarole is all very well except the majority of those needing places are men. Quite incongruous really because statistics show many more women suffer from mental illness.

Shirley That's another thing. The women in this place end up skivvying for the chaps. I mean, very little is done to challenge traditional roles and values.

Greg Yes, well, a lot of men we're trying to place have had nervous breakdowns after their mothers, wives or girlfriends have left them or died and they just can't cope.

Teddy Forgive me, but I can't see anything wrong with that, surely the family is something to aspire to not challenge – isn't that the whole purpose of this project – to create a happy family home as opposed to an institutionalised regime.

Shirley For an awful lot of people 'happy', 'home' and 'family' are not synonyms.

Evelyn If home is where the heart is, I'd live in John Lewis.

Greg Point taken, Shirley.

Teddy (*to* **Shirley**) I would like to take issue with you there.

Roy I am concerned with emptying beds, getting people out of hospital and well again and preferably not left to their own devices under railway arches.

Evelyn Surely, none of us want to see anyone on the streets.

Teddy Absolutely.

Greg Eric and Steve will be returning. They're both understandably apprehensive but both expressed a wish to come back.

Roy Would it be possible for some effort to be made to stop them returning to the hospital so much?

Shirley It's been their home, they feel secure there. Besides the canteen food is reasonably cheap.

Greg I was trying to explain earlier, er, Dr Freeman, about how hard pressed we were for putting in that sort of support. Besides, even if we could, it's not our job to police people like that.

Roy I thought that was part of the Management Committee's volunteer role.

Teddy Oh, rightho.

Evelyn Yes.

Eve Policing people?

Shirley Steve has actually found a job at the market and Eric will hopefully get a place on a rehabilitation work skills course.

Greg (*to* **Roy**) Mary, I understand, is not yet ready to be discharged in the near future.

Roy No.

Evelyn All this must really have taken its toll.

Roy Yes.

Greg That leaves us with two spaces. When the radiator, wash basin and carpet are restored in the top room, we'll have two more.

Teddy But who knows when that will be.

Greg I have selected a few applicants from a considerable pile, two of whom we must choose. Would you like to talk about them Dr Freeman, or shall I?

Roy Carry on.

Greg (*referring to his notes*) Rohima is twenty. She had a nervous breakdown during the first year at university and had to abandon the course. She was re-admitted to hospital six months after discharge following a suicide attempt. She returned to her bedsit and was re-admitted to hospital after being evicted owing to her refusal to claim DSS. She is depressed and can still be withdrawn and uncommunicative. However, she has not made any subsequent attempts to take her life.

Roy Everything is exacerbated by her refusal to take the prescribed medication. However, living in some kind of supportive set-up will undoubtedly be beneficial. She needs jollying along a bit and certainly does not warrant a place in hospital. It all seems very straightforward. Can we have a nod of assent on this one?

Greg (*looks round*) Any questions?

Roy No.

Evelyn I was just going to say. No, it's all right.

Greg Fine, good. That's Rohima settled. (*Picking next application.*) Dawn is twenty-two. She has a very severe hearing loss. Her speech is indistinct, often incoherent. She relies heavily on lip reading and doesn't mix with deaf people who use sign language. Because of her lack of communication skills, she finds it difficult to make friends and is very isolated. Five years ago, her child, then aged three months, was taken into care.

Shirley What were you going to say, Evelyn?

Evelyn It doesn't matter. Only that she will have to claim benefit while she's here. No one can expect to live rent free.

Teddy Quite right.

Greg Yes, they all do. (*To* **Roy**.) So far, I think I'm correct in saying she has been difficult to diagnose.

Roy Who are we talking about now?

Greg Dawn.

Roy Yes, yes, she has a personality disorder certainly. It's difficult to tell if she has learning difficulties or if it's the hearing loss.

Shirley Not being able to hear doesn't impair one's brain.

Roy In this game people's prognoses are supposed to be arrived at after talking to them. If you can't understand what they say, it does complicate things somewhat.

Shirley So she could be talking perfectly rationally. Just that others aren't tuned in to the enunciation.

Roy That's what I said.

Evelyn Suppose someone's so depressed they don't talk at all?

Roy I have a foolproof method, Evelyn, for spotting depression, in women at least. If it gets past four o'clock in the afternoon on the day they're admitted and they still haven't asked for a cup of tea – they're depressed.

Teddy (*laughs*) Oh, that's good. (*Stops, aware that this isn't appropriate behaviour.*)

Evelyn Suppose they don't like tea. (*Pause.*) I know I don't very much.

Greg (*anxious to continue*) Anyway, from time to time Dawn appears in the Self-Harm Unit. She has a history of violent outbursts and has not come to terms with the baby's adoption.

Evelyn Why was the baby adopted?

Greg Oh, that's rather a sad story which I hasten to add I wasn't involved in.

Roy And one we don't need to hear right now, with due respect, Evelyn. Dawn is on medication which has put a stop to the violent outbursts.

Evelyn Roy, we are supposed to be actively involved with the residents' welfare. It does help –

Roy Very well, but a potted precis please, Greg.

Greg (*condensing as he talks*) Dawn ran away from home when she got pregnant. Got a flat and was living alone with the baby. She went out leaving the baby alone. The police got involved when the baby was admitted to hospital with bad burns. Dawn was charged with negligence, put on probation and the baby was taken into care.

Teddy Oh, that's sad.

Greg However, the real story has since emerged. The baby became ill one evening. Dawn wrapped it in a blanket and left it in front of the fire for warmth while she went out to try and persuade someone to phone the doctor for her. When she came back the edge of the blanket had caught alight. From then on it seems the system became 'deaf' to the truth.

Teddy Shame.

Greg (*to* **Teddy**) Yes, it is. But, the only effective work that can be done now is trying to get her to accept it.

Roy Adoption is irreversible and she didn't help matters much by physically attacking her Probation Officer. Doesn't like men. Apparently she was sexually messed about with as a child.

Eve You started this. Don't just look out the window.

Nicola (*deep breath*) Actually, I do think it's important –

Greg To be fair, I think it was more that the Probation Officer had rather a profusion of beard and was quite impossible to lip read, although, it is suspected that the father of the child could have been her own father.

Eve Let's go. Come on. Who wants to hear all this?

Nicola I was just about –

Roy (*to* **Greg**) Have you got Dave's application there?

Greg (*surprised*) Yes.

Roy Well, do you think we could move on to it. He has been waiting rather a long while and I was hoping we'd cover him first.

Nicola *takes out a cigarette and lights it.*

Greg Oh, I'm sorry.

Roy Perhaps we could do that now?

Greg As you wish. (*He puts* **Dawn***'s application down and picks up* **Dave***'s.*) Dave is an intelligent man. He's fifty-four and been in institutions for years. Consequently his physical health has suffered. Twenty odd years ago he was sent to Broadmoor when . . .

Teddy (*before he can stop himself*) Broadmoor??!!

Nicola, *conscious of everyone's disapproval of the smoke, stubs the cigarette out.*

Roy (*drearily*) It was policy to send a quota of non-criminal patients there in the late sixties to eradicate the stigma of the name. Unfortunately, it had the opposite effect, taking Dave and many others with it.

Evelyn Poor man.

Shirley They'd have done better to change the name like they did with Sellafield. By the time people remember it used to be called Windscale they've forgotten to remember why it was changed.

Greg He has no history of violence to himself or others.

Roy Although when deluded he believes he did kill his father.

Eve With a look? With a word? With a wish? With a thought?

Greg (*flicking through the notes*) Throughout the years no diagnoses seem to have escaped him but (*Looking at the top page. Reading.*) at the beginning of this year, he is schizophrenic and stability is maintained with Modecate. (*Turns over.*) Oh, I see you've put homosexual under diagnosis.

Roy (*flatly*) Well, he is.

Greg (*very politely*) With all respect Dr Freeman, as you know better than me, homosexuality was removed from the ICD-9 over twenty years ago.

Roy (*blithely*) Oh, cross it off then.

Teddy (*unable to completely conceal his panic*) But I take it he has had a test?

Greg (*to* **Roy**) It's just that he might not want everyone to know.

Roy (*to* **Teddy** *mildly*) He's been in an institution for twenty years, man. (*To* **Greg**.) Well, it's you who told everybody, not me.

Teddy Still, hold on. You can't put people at risk. Don't you agree Evelyn?

Eve Just smile.

Greg I hope I don't need to remind everybody that this meeting is confidential.

Roy So are my notes.

Teddy Evelyn and I are rather worried. Am I speaking out of turn Evelyn?

Evelyn No, I'm quite all right. Thanks for asking.

Roy I think Dave fits the bill exactly. Time methinks for the promised cup of coffee. (*He looks at* **Shirley**.)

Shirley Refreshment, I assure you, is on its way. However, I would like to point out that if we leave it at that, we'll have three male residents and one female. As the second applicant is a woman I would like to reconsider her application.

Evelyn I thought it was settled.

Roy It's quite preposterous to suggest we start juggling with age, sex, class and race now. I for one am too busy.

Eve Run now.

Greg Shirley does have a point Dr Freeman.

Teddy (*grasping at straws*) And, maybe a 'she' will be more suitable. I mean who are we to set Dawn asunder. Given of course Shirley's criteria. (*Quickly*.) Where does she come from?

Eve You could try and say you've got to go.

Greg (*trying to read the writing notes*) Shropshire would it be?

Teddy Ah.

Greg (*peering closely at the paper*) No could be Southshield or Stratford. I can't make it out.

Nicola (*to* **Teddy**) Excuse me but what's so relevant about where she comes from?

Teddy Well, it's a well-known supposedly regular occurrence in some rural pockets – incest, that is. Not to me – to us. Our values. But isn't that what tolerance is all about – not imposing our own brand of morals?

Shirley Isn't that what the church is there for though?

Eve Think of something else.

Teddy For example . . .

Eve Don't think about it.

Teddy I have recently been enlightened about the impact of the imposition of Anglican missionaries on other countries' modus vivendi.

Greg I agree with Nicola. It's not an activity confined by geography or social class Teddy. (*To* **Nicola**.) That is what you were driving at I take it?

Roy (*before* **Nicola** *can reply*) That's not my experience.

Greg Could be because middle class crises don't often cross our path on the NHS these days.

Eve The bathroom. Think about re-decorating the bathroom.

Nicola (*quickly/nervously*) But, statistics show, don't they that a large proportion of female patients in mental institutions were sexually abused by a father figure?

Eve It has got dirty, filthy.

Roy (*scoffs*) I can't imagine where you got that so-called statistic from. (*Then severely*.) And it's not very helpful to use the term 'mental institution' in this day and age.

Eve Pink. Paint it pink?

Greg (*courteously to* **Nicola**) I think it's misleading and potentially dangerous to suggest that abused girls end up as women on psychiatric wards.

Nicola But I weren't saying –

Roy 'Weren't' you now.

Nicola No, it's a small per cent admitted to hospital, it would have to be. There isn't room for a quarter of the female population.

Roy In all my years of experience I could count on one hand the number of patients who've admitted that to me. And they were naughty precocious girls who certainly had no doubts about their attractiveness to men.

Eve Count on one hand. Dirty white, blue grey . . . blue grey . . . blue grey . . .

Greg We do have to be careful in the present climate not to make unfounded or rash judgements based on partial information.

Nicola I do know.

Eve Try and remember the names of the pencils in the box. Ivory, black, gunmetal, terracotta.

Nicola GP's have always pleaded ignorance. Now with the present backlash their ability to avoid the fact is frightening. Without medical evidence no one is believed. They come up with the most unlikely explanations rather than put their necks on the line. Their ability to avoid the facts unless haemorrhaging is actually occurring is frightening.

Eve Count on the other hand. Copper beech, golden brown, raw sienna.

Roy That is grossly inaccurate. If not libellous. You are speaking out of turn Nurse. You are here as an observer.

Eve Olive green, cedar green.

Greg (*wanting to take the heat out of the situation*) What would you put the figure at Shirley? (*To the others.*) Shirley's done quite a lot of research into mental illness for her M Phil.

Shirley Not really. I mean I am doing an M Phil but on how our language is obsessed by turning everything into a noun. Naming it thereby distancing it from personal experience, er, making it safe – er, well, er, there's a chapter on labelling and social behaviour but that's about it.

Greg It's not an original idea you know.

Shirley Of course it's not. If it was, my thesis wouldn't have a bibliography and I wouldn't pass.

Roy Goodo. So you can all feel sorry for me – labelled psychiatrist and subject to all the jokes that go with it. Is that what you mean?

Shirley Yes, no, sort of.

Roy Well is it or isn't it?

Shirley Not really, although I do take your point it's very valid. I . . .

Nicola (*helping her out*) Do you mean loaded words like 'precocious'?

Eve Again. Cedar green, may green, grass green, emerald green.

Shirley Yes, no, sort of.

Roy For your information Nurse, 'precocious' is not a noun. I was merely pointing out that adult women I'd –

Nicola (*very unconfidently*) I know Dr Freeman. It's just that, I'd been told that psychiatrists see the adult as the product of the child not the other way round.

Greg 'Product' now that's an interesting word for you Shirley.

Eve Mineral green, jade green, kingfisher blue.

Teddy Nouns by their nature often necessitate gender – boy, girl, husband, wife, mother, daughter –

Roy And where was Dawn's mother in all this. Two safe bets, either gadding about relinquishing her responsibilities or turning a blind eye.

Nicola *lights another cigarette.*

Eve Prussian blue, spectrum blue, ultramarine.

Greg (*consulting notes*) We don't know.

Roy Quite. Besides, it can often be a complex liaison of some duration, indicative of a caring relationship. (*To* **Nicola** *coldly.*) Children do have a sexuality you know.

Nicola I do . . .

Eve Blue violet, light violet, dark violet, imperial purple.

Nicola . . . and I didn't say they didn't, but . . .

Teddy How did she lose her hearing by the way?

Greg (*looking at notes*) Fell down the stairs. Query NAI.

Teddy NAI? CPN? ECT? EDT? ICD? Seems there's no time left for words (*To* **Shirley**.) never mind nouns. Maybe you should do your M Phil on acronyms.

Greg Sorry, Non-Accidental Injury.

Roy Really. What's this got to do with anything.

Nicola I think that's a good point.

Eve Imperial purple, crimson lake, scarlet lake.

Roy I'm gratified to see we agree on something Nurse.

Nicola No – about her hearing – (*With her last shred of confidence. Almost apologetically.*) In that, there can be, like we can tend to forget that physical bullying often goes hand in hand with these (*Coughs.*) nurturing so-called relationships.

Eve Deep vermilion, orange chrome.

Teddy I tell you one thing, that cough's an indication of two cancer sticks too many today.

Roy Your research is poor, Nurse, without any factual basis. Starting with the ludicrous notion of how many? Are you seriously suggesting that a quarter of the male population should be locked away?

Nicola No, I . . . (*She looks to* **Shirley** *to help her out.*)

Eve Deep cadmium, lemon cadmium.

Shirley I'll just see where the coffee's got to. (*She goes.*)

Greg No, that's not the answer. It's much more complex than that. The family –

Nicola But it's not really 'the family' that's to blame.

Greg On the contrary, it's part of a very intricate set of family dynamics and family therapy does work. Fathers I've seen, show considerable remorse.

Eve Straw yellow, copper beech, bronze.

Nicola But, I mean, does that surprise you? You know, in front of an authority figure.

Greg Okay. Maybe. But I don't feel blame per se is a very healthy approach to rebuilding lives. I agree it happens in all classes but is the product of a dysfunctional family where the man is looking for affection and nurturing, albeit inappropriately, and therefore the whole family, starting with the mother, need re-educating into their appropriate roles.

Teddy Tout comprendre est tout pardonner. (*Subtly waving the cigarette smoke away from him.*)

Roy (*agreeing with* **Teddy**) Absolutely.

Nicola If no one takes responsibility.

Greg That's just the point – everyone takes responsibility.

Nicola But then that surely only reinforces the girl's feeling of shame, self disgust and guilt.

Roy Which brings us back to why she felt like that in the first place.

Eve Magenta, brown ochre.

Roy (*sees* **Shirley** *come back into the room*) Ah coffee. Yes? No? Sort of?

Shirley Coffee will be upon us any second now.
And I'm sorry to interrupt but it's just occurred to me that we'd have to take advice about the fire regulations before Dawn could come here. Presumably she can't hear the alarm.

Nicola It's possible to get a flashing light system.

Shirley Fine, but that'll take time to organise.

Roy Well, that's solved that then.

Greg So that's Rohima and Dave. Okay, thanks very much everyone. Meeting over.

Shirley (*going over to* **Greg**) Can you catch me up on anything I missed that needs minuting? (*She sits next to him.*)

Roy (*putting his notes away in his case*) All that time wasted frittering on.

Eve As soon as they stand up just go.

Evelyn I thought it was a very good discussion. It's so difficult with so many people but very democratic. Only the same conclusion was reached half an hour ago of course. That's the disadvantage of everyone being allowed a say – the time it swallows up.

Roy Oh, Evelyn, I saw your father the other day.

Evelyn (*shocked*) He's retired.

Roy I know. But he gave a wonderful paper at a conference.

Evelyn Really?

Roy On bone cancer.

Evelyn Did he?

Roy He's a great man.

Evelyn Umm.

Roy I was very privileged to work under him as a houseman.

Eve Crimson lake, rose pink, flesh pink.

Roy (*inquiringly*) Evelyn? Are you all right?

Evelyn Oh, in the pink, absolutely. Absolutely miles away. (*Suddenly.*) Oh my goodness, is that the time? I'm due at another meeting.

Roy Oh?

Evelyn Working Party on Canine Control.

Roy Oh.

Evelyn Yes, did you know, there are four and a half million litres of dogs' urine floating daily on the surface of Britain?

Lil *enters with a tray of coffee which she puts down.*

Roy Really? You'll have time for a cup of coffee though. (*Turning to* **Nicola**.)

Eve No.

Evelyn Yes, I think so. Just.

Roy (*to* **Nicola**) I don't care what you say, we have statistics to prove mothers collude.

Nicola Unfortunately there aren't any which record the women who leave their homes taking their children with them.

Lil *brings two cups of coffee. She stands between* **Roy** *and* **Nicola**. *As* **Nicola** *looks up to take the cup they recognise each other. The cup meant for* **Roy** *accidentally slips from the saucer and into his lap.*

Roy Ah bloody Nora!

Eve *laughs.*

Evelyn Oops.

Lil I'm sorry, sorry. I'm sorry. Let me get you something to wipe it with. (*She goes.*)

Roy Jesus!

Eve Go. Get out.

Roy *follows* **Lil**, *trying to hold the front of his trousers away from his body.*

Evelyn *makes her way to the door.* **Teddy** *thwarts her escape.*

Teddy Very interesting to be let into this sort of world, a real eye-opener don't you find?

Eve Your brain, Teddy, is the dying throb of a tomcat with tertiary syphilis.

Evelyn (*pleasantly*) Yes. Yes. I suppose it is. I really must be off I'm afraid.

Teddy Thought-provoking question your husband asked the other week.

Evelyn Oh yes?

Teddy It's a great treat to be able to browse through Hansard. I don't often get the chance.

Evelyn Better make the best of it while you can. Before you become a fully fledged leader of the flock.

Teddy Pardon.

Evelyn Flock? Forgive me. How silly. I meant of course when you have your own parish.

Teddy Oh yes. You will come to my induction won't you?

Evelyn I'd love to. Thank you. How exciting.

Eve Will he have to kiss the bishop's ring?

Greg *goes over to* **Evelyn**.

Greg Thanks very much for coming Evelyn.

Evelyn I'm afraid I wasn't able to contribute very much, but anyway I'll see you soon.

Greg Could you just hang on a second. I know Shirley wanted a word with you.

Evelyn What about?

Greg Shirley will explain.

Eve Shirley is a pain in the arse.

Evelyn I'd better go and find her.

Teddy (*watching* **Evelyn** *go, muses*) Good egg, Evelyn. Good egg but absolutely barking mad. (*Then businesslike.*) Now Greg, about this chappie Dave . . .

Greg Teddy, I refuse to be drawn further on the matter. I'm a very old-fashioned fella I'm afraid. I still believe in civil liberties.

Teddy Look, I don't want you to get the impression that I'm a fuss-pot, but being a curate does give one a bit of a high profile. You know what the local press . . .

Shirley (*coming into the room*) Greg, it's Martha from your team. An emergency.

Greg (*calmly*) Excuse me. (*He walks out of the room.*)

Teddy (*to* **Shirley**) I suppose I'd better be making tracks, I've got to drop in on the Mothers' Union.

Shirley Pleased to have you on the team Teddy.

Teddy Good. Splendid. Pleased to be here. I'll give you a ring and arrange a time to go over the demon figures. (*He goes.*)

Shirley Fine. (*To* **Nicola**.) I'm sorry I had to go out for the coffee just then. I thought what you were saying was very thought-provoking.

Nicola (*coldly*) Thank you.

Shirley It's still a very difficult subject. And everyone's so subjective about it.

Nicola I thought you disagreed with objectivity – your dissertation.

Shirley Oh, my thesis – it's more complex than that.

Nicola Ah.

Shirley (*looks round*) Oh no, has Evelyn gone?

Nicola She went to look for you.

Shirley I must have a word with her. We can't have the residents moving into this. (*Gestures at the walls.*) I know she likes decorating. Keep your fingers crossed.

She goes. **Nicola** *is alone.* **Lil** *comes in.* **Nicola** *immediately turns her back, pretending to be intensely interested in the Breughel print.*

Lil Nicola?

Nicola *doesn't turn round.* **Roy** *comes in. The front of his trousers is very wet from where the stain has been sponged. He follows* **Nicola**'s *gaze, positioning himself between her and* **Lil**.

Roy Well I never, my grandmother used to have a reproduction of this in what she used to refer to as her back parlour. I haven't seen it for years.

Lil (*feeling she has to respond*) What a coincidence.

Roy Yes, I'd quite forgotten. My father explained it to me when I was knee-high to a grasshopper. (*Explaining to them, as though they were knee-high to grasshoppers. Pointing.*) You see this person here carries on ploughing the field while the other person, only one leg in view, drowns. (*Then more to himself.*) My father thought it wildly funny but it always made me shiver. Well, fancy remembering a thing . . . (*Then abruptly without warning.*) Are you ready Nurse?

Nicola Yes.

Greg *comes in.*

Greg (*apologetically*) Roy, that was the hospital on the 'phone. Are you available to come with me for a mental health assessment?

Roy (*looking at his trousers*) Now? I can just hear the Appeal Tribunal now 'our client claims that she was sectioned by an incontinent psychiatrist'.

Greg It's between here and the hospital. My car's in the garage. Can I cadge a lift?

Roy By all means. (*He and* **Greg** *walk towards the door. He turns.*) Sorry about this, er, Nurse. You'll be able to find your way back to the hospital on your own won't you?

Nicola Yes Doctor.

Roy *and* **Greg** *go.*

Lil So, you're a nurse.

Nicola (*gathering her things together*) Yes, what did you think I was, a singing telegram?

Lil I didn't know. You could have been anything for all I knew.

Nicola Or cared.

Lil That isn't true. I asked everyone. Even tried to find you – that friend of yours said you'd gone to Spain – to stay with that pen friend. I even . . .

Nicola Spain. Don't be so stupid. You can't go to Spain aged fifteen without a passport. Did you tell the police why I'd left?

Lil We didn't know what to say.

Nicola (*with disgust*) You're still with him?

Lil He's been very sick.

Nicola I could have told you that.

Lil Nicola please, listen.

Nicola Listen? To you? I don't want anything to do with you. Nothing, do you understand? Nothing at all.

Lil But I . . .

Nicola I work from the hospital not here. So it shouldn't be a problem.

Nicola *goes.*

Lil *turns and stares at the blank space where the mirror was and covers her face with her hands.*

Shirley *enters.*

Lil *quickly turns away and starts collecting the cups.*

Shirley (*brightly*) Oh, she's gone. That Nurse. I was going to say she has the same surname as you. Probably just a coincidence.

Lil (*putting the cups on the tray rather frantically*) Probably.

Shirley You're not related are you? Only I thought she looked quite like you.

Lil Was Jane related to Mrs Rochester or was Mrs Rochester part of herself which had to die before she could live happily ever after.

Shirley (*totally confused*) I'm sorry?

Lil Have you ever been in an aeroplane, Shirley?

Shirley (*laughs*) Why yes, of course.

Lil I have, just the once. Well, I tell a lie – I had to come back again. I couldn't get over it. Moving along the runway and the stewardess standing in the aisle demonstrating how to put a life jacket on and this taped voice coming over and nobody except me taking a blind bit of notice. And, then the voice says 'And once in the water, if the life jacket fails to inflate, blow into this tube!' And I'm thinking. In the water! Once I'm in the water! And I'm imagining myself struggling in the ocean with the duff life jacket but nobody else is even listening. They are too busy rooting out their credit cards for their duty frees.

Evelyn *and* **Eve** *re-enter.*

Shirley (*confused*) Oh, yes, of course, you said. Your daughter's an air hostess.

Lil (*picking up the tray*) Don't mind me, I read too much. (*She goes.*)

Evelyn She's gone up in the world then?

Shirley Lil?

Evelyn No, this mythical daughter. She told me once she was a hairdresser. What do you make of that?

Shirley I don't think it's any of our business.

Evelyn She's a liar.

Shirley Now what do you make of this? (*Meaning the room.*)

Eve What are you doing in this place?

Evelyn It's better to use gloss over this sort of paint than emulsion otherwise it will just show through. I don't mind doing it.

Eve Why do you have to open your big mouth.

Shirley (*pleased*) Would you? It would save a lot of time and money.

Evelyn Actually I'm always pleased to do practical things. In fact I'd rather . . . I'm not very good with people.

Shirley Oh, I wouldn't say that.

Scene Three

In sickness and in health

Lil's *kitchen diner. That evening.*

Tony, *her husband, sits in front of the TV.* **Lil** *puts* **Tony**'s *meal of steamed fish, broccoli and brown bread on a plate. She places it on a tray with a knife and fork and puts it on his lap.*

Tony (*appreciatively*) Thanks. (*He closes his eyes and takes a mouthful of fish.*)

Lil What are you doing?

Tony Pretending it's cod in batter.

Lil (*smiles*) Unfortunately it weren't on the diet sheet the doctor gave me. Did the District Nurse call today?

Tony I'll say. It wasn't the usual one, a slip of a girl. Highlight of my day.

Lil (*gently disapproving*) Tony.

Tony (*mildly*) Apart from you she's the only person I've seen all week. What's the matter? Jealous?

Lil (*sits down in an armchair*) No. It's just. I don't like you talking like that.

Tony Give over. It's the sort of thing any bloke would say.

Lil I suppose.

She picks up her book and starts to read. **Tony** *continues to eat and watch the telly. But she can't concentrate.*

Tony?

Tony Um. What?

Lil Nothing. (*Pause.*) You know when you went into hospital I was very frightened that I, that I might lose you.

Tony I know. (*Slight pause.*) But there's life in the old dog yet, don't you worry.

Lil I wanted. (*Deep breath.*) When Nicola left home.

Tony (*groans*) Oh Lil.

Lil Please. Don't get upset. What she said.

Tony (*tense*) Yes.

Lil (*almost apologetically*) Was there, (*Slight pause.*) I'm only asking, any truth in it?

Tony (*flatly*) No. Why bring that up now?

Lil I want to know. Now.

Tony You asked me then and I told you.

Lil Why d'you suppose she said things like that then?

Tony Why are you asking me all of a sudden? You seemed sure at the time.

Lil I didn't believe it. (*Pause.*) It's not the sort of thing you tackle someone you love about when you want to believe them, anyway. But . . . (*Hesitates.*)

Tony (*reasonably*) She did it out of spite – pure malice. She never liked me. Right from the beginning – remember the fuss when you changed her surname to mine.

Lil It seemed the best thing years ago. I didn't want her to face awkward questions at school. We hadn't had it easy.

Tony She resented me. She resented our relationship. She wanted to split us up – it's never been the same since – has it? Oh I know, it's all right but I catch you looking at me from time to time and I think, if it hadn't been for her vindictiveness. Still, what's done is done. (*Pause.*) There. You can get on with your novel now.

Lil (*pause*) It does go on, not that we ever used to hear about it. It's in all the papers.

Tony (*slowly*) And leaving some innocent couples with their lives in ruins.

Lil (*this is difficult*) What d'you s'pose the men who did do it say when their wives ask them?

Tony How the hell should I know? Unless of course you think that I do. Is that it?

Lil Sometimes people have affairs for years without their wives or husbands knowing.

Tony What are you saying; you've had an affair?

Lil No, no. That's not it.

Tony If it was true, why didn't she tell you?

Lil She did.

Tony Only as a garbled excuse when you caught her flying out of the door with her bag packed. Why not before?

Lil Maybe she was frightened.

Tony Frightened? Lil, have I ever raised my hand to you?

Lil No. That's why you were different. Why I couldn't believe my luck. But why?

Tony (*sighs*) You took her to the doctor once didn't you?

Lil (*surprised*) Yes, yes I did.

Tony What did he say?

Lil She said she was allergic to soap.

Tony And you believed the doctor?

Lil Yes.

Tony But you don't live with the doctor. Look Lil, you know everything about me. We don't have any secrets. I tried hard remember? She just didn't like me. Every Friday I'd buy her something on my way home from work.

Lil I know.

Tony I wasn't able to win her trust or affection.

Lil (*sighs*) No.

Tony Can we leave it? Arguing and open heart surgery don't go together as well as steamed fish and broccoli.

Lil Sorry.

Pause. She picks up her book.

Tony I can't imagine why you brought all this up.

Lil (*pause*) I saw her today.

Tony Who?

Lil (*pause*) Nicola.

Long pause.

Tony Where?

Lil At work. She's a nurse.

Tony What did she say?

Lil She wouldn't speak to me.

Tony Oh.

Scene Four

St Dymphna's

Ten days later.

The mirror has not yet been replaced but the walls have been repainted and the room looks 'homely'.

Lil *is cleaning the windows. The curtains lie on the back of the chair.*

Shirley *enters.*

Shirley (*surprised to see* **Lil** *alone*) Oh, I thought Dave was in here.

Lil I think he's gone to make a cup of tea.

Shirley (*lowering her voice a little*) How is he?

Lil He seems to be settling in okay.

Shirley Has he said anything?

Lil Not much. Yes and no. Please and thank you.

Shirley He's not said a word to me since he arrived. See if you can . . .

She stops as **Dave** *enters carrying two cups of tea and quickly changes the subject.*

The new mirror should arrive sometime today. Do you know where Rohima is? I'm supposed to be giving her a lift to the DSS.

Dave (*puts the two cups down on the coffee table next to the armchair and sits down*) She was here a few minutes ago. I've just made her a cup of tea.

Shirley *and* **Lil** *exchange a glance.*

Lil She went out to post a letter.

Dave *takes a mouthful of tea and appears to have some difficulty swallowing it.*

Shirley Are you okay, Dave?

Dave One of the disadvantages of being a state registered junkie is the side effects. Although one of the advantages admittedly is that I've never had to steal to support the habit. Don't look so surprised I can speak but it's just that until today I didn't want to.

Shirley Would you like me to suggest to Dr Freeman that he reduce your medication?

Dave I reckon it's the reduction in the tablets that's made me like this. Cold Turkey or is that a frightfully outmoded phrase? I'm a bit out of date with street jargon.

He laughs which causes some pain in his chest. He tries not to draw attention to this but **Shirley** *notices.*

Shirley Are you sure you're all right?

Dave If there's one thing experience has taught me, it's that once you have the label 'nutter' and you complain of physical ailments, they certify you before they operate.

Shirley Is something wrong then?

Dave Oh, take no notice, I'm being facetious. The tea was too hot, that's all. I'm fine. Honestly.

Shirley If you say so.

Dave I do. Thank you.

Shirley Okay. Well, I'd better see where Rohima is. (*To* **Lil**.) And then I've got to take some things to Greg's office. The number's on the list by the 'phone if you need me. (*To them both*.) See you later.

She goes. **Lil** *contiues to work. Silence.*

Lil That's the most I've ever heard you say Dave. Why haven't you spoken before?

Dave Under the scrutiny of the psychiatric profession each syllable is weighed, waiting to be labelled before it's even uttered. Such meaning is heaped upon the spoken word that one becomes too inhibited to perform the act. Humour – that's a no-go area. And as for flippancy, try that out on them and they look at you as if you're about to self-destruct.

Genuine emotion is so painful that it's reduced to self-conscious clichés.

Lil Well don't mind me, I'm not one of them. Wax as lyrical as you like.

Dave I'm sure half my life has been wonderful. I just can't remember it. All I can recall when I'm well is the minutiae of long-stay institutionalised existence. The intensity of feelings over such tiny discoveries like the far-reaching ecstasy of turning over the pillow to find the cooler side. The heartfelt relief of not getting the first or the last cup of tea out of that humungous pot. The throat-closing joy of knowing that the biscuits have three layers this week. All these petty but all the same deeply felt things take on a passionate poetry of their own. (*Slight pause.*) Very boring really.

Lil Carry on, it's nice to see you so chatty.

Dave But that's about all I know – institutions. Have you ever been in one?

Lil Butlins? (*They both laugh.*)

Dave I don't suppose you'd care to sit down and have this cup of tea which is going to waste?

Lil All right, if you don't mind me mending these. (*She takes the curtains and a sewing box. She sits down in the other chair and starts to repair the hem of the curtains.*) Now you've gone all quiet on me. Your life must have had a little more variety.

Dave Let me see. Oh yes, in 1961 I was put in prison for being an unneighbourly bugger.

Lil (*surprised*) Were you under 21 then?

Dave I'll take that as a compliment thank you. But no, the law wasn't changed till '67. We were both the same age, 30. He, Jon, had a so-called prestigious job in local government and had been paying a proportion of his salary to a person who threatened to go to the press. It happened quite a lot in those days. By the time Jon got round to telling me, we were living together by then, and I said, well I can't remember exactly what I said but the gist of it was to call this person's bluff and stop paying. (*Laughingly*.) I must have been mad. I don't know how I managed to delude myself that spite doesn't exist for spite's sake when it so obviously does.

Lil Do you really think so?

Dave Yes, don't you?

Lil I don't know.

Dave Take my word for it or do you think the world revolves on revenge?

Lil But hadn't you done something to this person?

Dave I don't even know who they were to this day. There was a scandal of course. Jon lost his job. We both did. We were sent to jail. You don't want to hear about this. Tell me about Butlins.

Lil Yes I do. What was your job?

Dave I worked in the soft furnishings department of a shop in the West End. My father nearly had an apoplectic fit. First throwing all his hopes of an army career away and then the downright disgrace and perversion of living with Jon. God, at least it took the abuse partially away from my mother. But Christ, have I paid for not opting into his world.

Lil What happened when you got out of prison?

Dave We were out of work. Jon felt the shame more than I did. He couldn't get a job, none of the people he'd worked with would speak to him. A year after our release he killed himself.

Lil Oh, I'm sorry.

Dave (*pragmatically*) Perhaps clichés are clichés because they happen too often.

Lil Is that, I mean after his death, is that when you became ill?

Dave I'd had a nervous breakdown before I met him. If you were privy to my medical records you'd see an entry which reads 'time of stability whilst living with friend'. After his death I had another breakdown, yes. And since, everything out there has got better but I've missed it. I've come out to be greeted by exactly the same climate as I left. And why should I feel so indignant? I haven't contributed anything to making it better. I haven't fought for anything, I've done nothing.

Lil You're not in the minority then are you? (*No response.*) Dave?

Dave If I was in the position to analyse myself I might conclude that I was struggling between dignity and despair. (*Pause. Then very cheerfully.*) But tomorrow is another day isn't that what they say and it's never too late and all those things. (*Slight pause.*) Lil, you look so sad.

Lil You don't tell happy stories.

Dave So now, holiday camps – is the excitement intense?

Lil No, it's in chalets.

Dave Go on then.

Lil Aw, there's nothing to say. Just, we had a lovely time.

Dave Who's we?

Lil Tony took me and my daughter there a few months after I'd met him. She was only six. I'd been married before. She was just old enough to go into shops on her own. And she bought me a birthday present that she'd chosen herself for the first time. Only she was so excited she couldn't wait till my birthday to give it to me. Silly the things you remember.

Dave What was it?

Lil A magnet.

Dave (*laughs*) I wonder what Dr Freeman would make of that.

Lil Actually it was a magnet tied to a piece of string wrapped up in a shoebox with ten paper fish that she'd drawn and cut out herself and put a paperclip on the end of their noses and she showed me how to play fishing. I don't know where she got the idea – school I suppose. For ages afterwards every Sunday after we'd had supper and washed up we used to sit together on the kitchen table, put the fish on the floor and take it in turns to reel them in.

Dave I don't remember my parents spending any time with us at all but then my memory isn't cracked up to much.

Lil You have brothers and sisters then?

Dave Two brothers. At least I started out with two brothers. I haven't seen them for years. Last I heard one of them was working for a bank in America and the other one was a naval officer.

Lil My first husband was in the Navy. He wasn't an officer or anything. Just an ordinary seaman.

Dave Rum lot was he?

Lil Oh yeah and he liked a drink an' all. When he came home on leave it was like, after the first day, he couldn't stand the sight of me. They got used to my face in the Casualty Department. I don't think there was a law against it then. Certainly there was nowhere to go. When he got out of the Navy altogether it was awful, my home was like a prison. At one time I thought we'd never get away.

Dave But you did. To Butlins with Tony.

Lil Yes. He taught me to dance while we were there. I was so het-up about making a mistake. He'd just laugh. He was like that about everything. Easy-going. 'What's the point of being so worried about getting it right that you can't enjoy yourself', he'd say to me. He never lost his temper over anything, big or small. (*Then.*) Oh dear, I don't know how you got me onto all this.

Dave Are you still married to him?

Lil Oh yes.

Dave Only you said 'was'.

Lil Oh he is. He's still like that. (*Slight pause.*) Dave? You know what you were saying about (**Teddy** *enters right.*) spite –

Teddy Is Shirley about? Sorry I didn't . . .

Lil I think she's gone to look for Rohima.

Dave (*winks at* **Lil**) Of course the hardware department was the most sought-after to work in but I preferred soft furnishings. Its allure is so theatrical. (*Picks up a curtain. Mimes ripping the curtain in a theatrical fashion.*) Three and a quarter yards for you modom? (*This exertion causes him some pain which he tries to conceal.*)

Teddy I'll just go and check. I think I've left my lights on anyway.

Dave (*to* **Lil**) Sorry about that. The devil got into me.

Lil (*laughs*) His lights may be on but there's no one at home. Sorry I didn't mean . . .

Dave (*laughs*) It's all right. What were you going to say? Before?

Lil Oh yes. Will casserole be all right for supper? (*She stands, starts folding the curtains.*)

Dave I thought we were supposed to get our own meals?

Lil One meal a week I prepare. And I'm running late.

Dave That wasn't what you wanted to ask.

Lil Some other time. I must get on.

Leaves curtains on chair and scissors.

Dave Okay.

Lil See you the day after tomorrow. (*She looks at him.*) Dave, do you feel all right?

Dave Just tired. Time for my afternoon kip I think.

Lil *goes off left,* **Teddy** *meets* **Shirley** *in the hallway right.*

Teddy (*urgently*) Oh Shirley, there you are. I've been wanting to have a quiet word with you all day.

Shirley Can't it wait Teddy? I'm just about . . .

Teddy This is urgent I'm afraid. I'll have to resign from the Management Committee.

Shirley Teddy, you can't do that. Well, I mean, I suppose you can but you've only just joined us. Why the change of heart?

Teddy News has reached my ears, actually someone told me, that a man called here wearing a frock. Don't you see? If this place attracts that sort of attention. It's my reputation. Well, it's not mine – the Church's. You know what the papers are like and it's not just the tabloids these days. Even the noun bachelor is all innuendo.

Shirley (*slight pause as she looks at* **Teddy** *who's wearing a cassock*) Words fail me. (*Then.*) Who told you a man wearing a dress came to the door?

Teddy The Churchwarden's wife heard it from the WI and they heard it from a member of the PCC. Sorry, Parochial Church Council. I can't name names you understand.

Shirley Please think it over. At least see this week out. I've been doing the accounts for last month and I'm only half-way through.

Teddy (*guiltily*) Oh, I know I shouldn't just up and leave you in the lurch.

Shirley I suppose I could ask Greg.

Teddy (*blasé*) What does he know, all he cares about is people. (*Decides.*) All right, point taken. I'll have a stab at totting up the figures. But we must find a time to discuss this more fully.

Shirley Thanks. They're in my office. The cleaning receipts are in the cupboard in the living room.

He goes. **Evelyn/Eve** *enter right.*

Ah, Evelyn. Just the person.

Eve Careful.

Evelyn Hello Shirley . . .

Shirley I've got to go out. I shouldn't be too long but we are destined to have a call from a couple on behalf of the local Ratepayers' Association. Would you see them and give them the benefit of your diplomacy?

Evelyn Me?

Shirley If you don't mind.

Eve I do mind.

Evelyn What about Teddy?

Shirley I, er, think you're eminently a better choice. Just listen to what they have to say and explain how necessary this place is.

Evelyn How?

Shirley (*curtly*) Try, if at all possible, to put the liberal point of view.

Eve She hates you.

Evelyn I resent that. My husband toyed quite sleeplessly with the SDP for a while.

Eve Liar.

Shirley Sorry. This is your afternoon here isn't it? It won't take long. All you have to do is make them a cup of tea. You can show them the living room and the kitchen but don't show them the residents' bedrooms. I'm sorry but I'm in a bit of a rush. Rohima's waiting for me in the car.

Evelyn But what about . . .?

Shirley Don't worry. Steve's at work, Eric is on a course and won't be back until late this evening and Dave usually takes himself off for a sleep in his room in the afternoon. Thanks very much.

Evelyn Shirley, I'd love to but I'm afraid –

Shirley (*not hearing*) And thanks very much for doing the decorating. You'll find your painting things in a carrier bag in the kitchen. See you later.

Shirley *goes out right.* **Evelyn** *goes to the kitchen left.* **Teddy** *enters the living room.* **Dave** *looks asleep in the chair. He opens his eyes as* **Teddy** *tiptoes in.*

Teddy All right? Didn't mean to disturb you. Sorry. Just got to get something from the cupboard.

Dave (*yawns*) Would . . . could you give me a hand to my room?

Teddy You're all right having a snooze there. Not to worry – it's your home after all.

Dave (*sighs*) Lil.

Teddy Pardon?

Dave Would you please tell Lil, I'm sorry about the seaman.

Teddy What? (*He quickly leaves the room.*)

Dave And say thanks.

Teddy *has already gone. He paces the hallway.*

Teddy (*calls*) Lil? Lil? Where are you?

Lil (*runs towards him onion and knife in hand. Worried*) What is it?

Teddy I don't know how to say it – it isn't a very pleasant task.

Lil Don't hold back. The gamut of my curriculum vitae runs from nappies to incontinence pads – only a few of us are left dealing with our own shit in the meantime. What is it? A dog turd through the letter box?

Teddy No, but something equally unpleasant.

Lil What? Where?

Teddy On the upholstery I think. Culpable emission – an accident I'm sure.

Lil (*impatiently*) You what?

Teddy (*very embarrassed*) Bodily fluid. Male.

Lil (*with disbelief*) Are you trying to tell me someone's wanked over my loose covers?

Teddy Brutally speaking, yes.

Lil Are you playing with a full deck?

Teddy (*lowering his voice*) Please try and be discreet about it.

Lil I can't do anything right this minute. I've only got one pair of hands unless of course you'd . . .

Teddy No, no, I've got plenty to be getting on with. (*He goes left.*)

Lil So've I.

Lil *raises her eyes to the ceiling. Sighs. She follows* **Teddy** *and meets* **Evelyn/Eve** *coming towards her.* **Evelyn** *is holding a carrier bag.*

Evelyn (*very friendly*) What's got into Teddy?

Lil Don't ask me. St Dymphna's. Huh. Tower of Babel more like.

Evelyn I'm sorry?

Lil You know, that story in the Bible where no one understands what anyone else is saying and the whole thing collapses.

Evelyn Lil, I'd like you to do me a big favour?

Lil (*not unkindly*) Depends what it is.

Evelyn Shirley wants me to see two people who are going to call this afternoon who want to know something about this place. Would you see them for me?

Lil If Shirley asked you that's who she wanted to meet them. If she'd wanted me to talk to them she'd have asked me.

Evelyn I wouldn't ask but –

Lil I'm sorry Evelyn but I probably couldn't answer their questions. You're on the Management Committee, you're the ideal person.

Evelyn It's just that I might not be able to wait all afternoon.

Lil You should have explained that to Shirley. I won't be here myself, I'm due at the Sparidae project in less than an hour. If you don't mind me saying I do think it's important that you hang on here. It's obviously a public relations exercise. I'll show you where the tea things are kept if you like.

Evelyn Please Lil –

Lil It's not my place it's yours.

Lil *goes leaving* **Evelyn** *alone.*

Evelyn *stands, looking out.* **Eve** *stands beside her looking out.*

Interval

Part Two

Scene Five

St Dymphna's

Richard *and* **Gaynor Brittain**, *the rate-payers, stand nervously in the hallway preparing their thoughts.*

Richard (*practising his speech*) I do understand and I'm very sympathetic. However, my wife and I, no, no, Gaynor and I, have been elected to speak for, no, no – on behalf of – a group of us who are concerned about the social problems in the area. I mean the safety of the residents is uppermost in our minds, no, no, not the community at large. I mean those in here. They're at risk from threats, general intimidation, riots – we had a riot only a couple of miles away in '81.

(*Lapsing into his own thoughts.*) It's not as if I'm one of those people who continually checks how much their house is worth. It would be too depressing, now the market's slumped and what with the threat of the Channel Tunnel Rail Link, the extension of the South Circular and Docklands Light Railway. A place like this, plonked in the same road is hardly likely to improve the situation, remove the blight. It doesn't bear thinking about. I've worked all my life to maintain my mortgage. It's not as if I'm able to earn thousands and thousands of pounds. I missed out on that band wagon. Not that I want to make a career lusting after money. I could do with a break as a matter of fact but whatever else my working life has been, it's been one long scramble to earn enough. Even now the kids are gone – and Gaynor wasn't able to cope as I thought she would. She told me she worked in a nursery. I'd got round to proposing before I discovered it was a flower sort but somehow my original idea that she must be good with children stuck. She now works three days a week in a Garden Centre in Lofton Park. Huh, and she had to settle long ago for the fact that I wasn't a climber. No, I wasn't going to reach the top and be able to sit on my laurels contemplating the view. I've just managed to reach a little ledge which now threatens to crumble beneath the weight of everyone else who's trying to cling on, pulling me down with them in the process. My wife's never been what you might call solid as a rock in the upstairs department. She's always been rather edgy. Living close to people who are really disturbed might tip the balance. She might go mad. My daughter might take drugs. My son might get AIDS and I've worked all my life to be a normal family man. (*Pulling himself together.*) Good afternoon, my name is Richard Brittain. It's not that I don't understand it's just that I can't see any alternative. Can you give me permission to feel less afraid?

Gaynor (*practising her speech*) I do understand and believe me we're very sympathetic but we have been asked. It's not that I've got anything against people who've had nervous breakdowns. (*Lapsing into her own thoughts.*) In fact I nearly had one myself once only the doctor got to me just in time and the Valium got to me sooner. I'd not thought about it until we did the fortnight's shopping. We do it together these days which is nice. Besides, they all seem to be built a car ride away. Sort of ranch-like places in the middle of open concrete.

It was a young woman with two toddlers, reminded me of myself. I thought, I should write a book I should. I stood racking my brains for a title when it struck me 'Let's Go Mad In Safeways'. I rather liked it. We were behind her you see, biscuits to the left of us, crisps and Hula Hoops to the right, when I sent Richard back. We'd picked up the unmicrowavable lasagne by mistake. Well, he had.

The elder one of these toddlers had just recovered from a tantrum at not being able to gain the enviable position of the shopping trolley seat which was now triumphantly occupied by the younger one. I couldn't swear to the gender, it's so difficult with these Benetton and what-not designer clothes, but the tantrum one was called Jack because the woman kept droning, 'Put those back, Jack' as he was busy collecting as many packets of crisps as his chubby fingers could grasp and she was automatically snatching them back, replacing them haphazardly on the top shelves amongst the gravy granules and the custard powder.

When it dawned on Jack that this was no longer a game, he threw himself flat on the floor in front of the trolley and screamed – in that way that goes right through you – she said so blankly, 'Come on Jack, get up' and a variety of matter-of-fact coaxing until with her teeth firmly gritted together she says, 'Don't say I didn't warn you' and pushes the trolley forward regardless. He just managed to roll out of the way unhurt but screamed even louder. It made my stomach lurch. I thought, Jesus God, let's hope there's not a Social Worker in the shop and my heart went out to her because I knew how she felt.

My children have grown up now. My eldest daughter's got a girl of her own. I didn't want to work when they were small, I wanted to make the most of them, you never get that time again do you? You don't bargain for the sleepless nights, snatching half a tin of apple puree for lunch and never going out in the evening, until it was me who insisted. My brother was at college in London and he'd come over to babysit.

It only came out at Christmas when my daughter refused to take the baby over to his house. Why didn't you tell me then? She said, 'Because he threatened me with ridiculous things but when you're small you believe them'. 'But', I said, 'Didn't you say no?' She virtually spat back, and she's not like that with me normally, 'Saying no to a grown man makes no difference unless you're trying to make me feel I said no in the wrong way'. 'Of course not', I said.

Oh I should have seen the signs. She used to wake up with bad dreams. Cling to me on the one evening a week we'd go out, but I thought it was because I'd never been out without her since she was born.

I said, 'But he's got kids of his own now.' She said, 'Yes. I don't want anything to do with him.' I said, 'But you used to go over there at Christmas.' She said, 'Yes but that was before the baby was born.' Then she said, 'Don't say anything. You won't tell Dad will you?' I said, 'I don't know what to do.' She said, 'I don't want any fuss, I don't want them looking at me thinking – whatever they will be thinking. I don't want anyone to know.'

And I haven't said anything. I blame myself. I shouldn't have been so selfish wanting to go out but I was desperate. I must have been a little crazy in those days. He was my own brother. After she told me I can't stop thinking about it. I don't want to. It drives me mad.

Evelyn *comes along the passageway to greet them.* **Richard** *gives* **Gaynor**'*s hand a reassuring squeeze.* **Eve** *sizes up* **Evelyn**'*s performance.*

Evelyn Hello, I'm sorry to have kept . . .

Richard Good afternoon my name is Richard.

Gaynor (*nervously*) And, I'm his wife, Gaynor.

Evelyn I'm Evelyn. I'm sorry but I'm afraid Shirley has been unavoidably called away but I'm on the Management Committee and I hope I'll do.

Richard Pleased to meet you.

Gaynor Pleased to meet you.

Evelyn I'm sure you'll understand but I can't show you all the way round (*She goes into the room.*) because people live here, it is their home – but I can show you the sitting room. Please come through.

They go into the living room. **Evelyn** *turns unconsciously obscuring their view of* **Dave** *who looks asleep in the chair, his cup of tea lies on its side, its contents spilt.* **Evelyn** *acts normally.* **Eve** *jumps back in fear.*

Gaynor (*to* **Richard** *pointing at the picture*) Oh look darling. Do you remember when we first moved, we borrowed that picture from the library. (*To* **Evelyn**.) Those were the days before you could buy reasonable prints.

Eve (*turns to look at* **Dave**) He's dead. He's dead!

Evelyn I'm afraid the mirror got broken and we're still waiting for a replacement.

Eve Stop being so polite, that man in that chair there has died.

Gaynor Not a very welcoming omen.

Richard (*tightly*) Dear? (*Then pleasantly to* **Evelyn**.) It's not that we're . . .

Gaynor (*ruefully*) Not for the first seven years at least.

Evelyn Can I get you a cup of coffee? (*Gesturing them towards the door left.*)

Eve Try and say excuse me but I think something's wrong and I can't cope.

Evelyn (*unnerved*) Please come through to the kitchen. The kettle's boiled and you can see what it looks like. (*Turns to go into the kitchen.*)

Eve Don't just pretend it's all right.

Gaynor (*follows*) Don't get me wrong, we always donate to charity. Despite any financial crisis that might occur I've never turned anyone away on the doorstep with an empty envelope or switched the telly off without ringing in our credit card number for that matter.

Richard No it's not for ourselves. (*Sees* **Dave**.) I say is that chap all right?

Evelyn (*takes two paces back but doesn't look at* **Dave**) Oh Dave. I didn't see him there. He often drops off in the afternoon.

Eve *starts to refer to herself in the third person.*

Eve Are you mad? Are you mad? You are mad!

Eve *weeps.*

Richard (*takes* **Dave**'s *hand and tries to find his pulse. Simply.*) He's dead.

Gaynor *instinctively turns away. Puts her hand in front of her mouth.*

Evelyn (*looks at* **Dave**) What? (*Shakes him.*) Oh God, wake up Dave! What shall I do? (*She goes.*)

Gaynor I'd 'phone for an ambulance if I were you.

Evelyn Yes . . . yes . . . (*Exits.*)

Richard (*after her*) That's no good. They'll refuse to budge him. He's cold.

Gaynor Come on Richard, come away. Don't touch him.

Richard Somehow I don't think it's appropriate to continue our visit.

They go to the door right and meet **Teddy** *coming in.*

Gaynor You're too late Father. He's passed over.

Teddy I beg your pardon.

Richard Gaynor. That's probably what he's here for. (*To* **Teddy**.) All in a day's work for you I expect. (*He puts his arm round* **Gaynor**'s *shoulders and they go.*) Rather you than me.

Teddy *stares at* **Dave**. *Immobilised by fear.* **Evelyn/Eve** *come back into the room.*

Teddy How?

Evelyn I don't know. But he is. We can't leave him here.

Teddy You should ring a doctor.

Evelyn I have rung the hospital. Roy. He's dealing with it. The ambulance. He's with my father.

Teddy Best not to touch him then.

Evelyn But he's dead.

Teddy How do you know?

Evelyn He's not breathing is he.

Teddy He should never have been let out of hospital.

Evelyn The others mustn't find him here. Please you must help me. We should put him in his own room.

Teddy I can't.

Evelyn Why not?

Teddy I can't touch him.

Evelyn Please.

Teddy He disgusts me. 'Men leaving the natural use of the woman, burn with lust for one another and are paid in their own persons the fitting wage for such provisions.' I can't do anything for him.

Evelyn Teddy.

Teddy Romans. We all have a choice Evelyn either to stick by what we believe in or distort it to suit our own ends.

Evelyn God. (*Calling to* **Eve**.) Please help me.

Teddy It's my faith Evelyn. I can't be shaken from it.

Lil (*VO*) Would somebody come to the door it's the mirror.

Teddy The Press!! (*Then to* **Evelyn**.) Don't let them know I'm here. They'll have a field day if they find me here.

He goes as **Lil** *comes in carrying the mirror.*

Lil I don't give much for his episcopal potential. (*Then seeing* **Dave**.) What happened?

Eve Don't let her blame you.

Lil (*goes over to* **Dave**) Dave? (*Tries to find his pulse.*) He's . . .

Evelyn I know.

She turns and walks away.

Scene Six

Three in one

Roy's *office.* **George** *flicks through some case notes.* **Roy** *enters,* *carrying two cups of tea. He gives one to* **George**.

George You were the last person I was expecting to bump into.

Roy The mother's on my admission ward. At first I thought it was a ploy to get into the same hospital. But our records show she was admitted once before, some years ago, obsessive personality. Seems she had psychotherapy in between. Now she thinks the child got cancer following her divorce – stress.

George Well she saw something, a review of my book or something in the paper and asked the child's consultant to get in touch with me. Very well educated I thought; and asked all the right questions. I'm only sorry to have had to confirm the original diagnosis. Such a pretty child.

Roy I was hoping, well, I was hoping if the child had a better prognosis so would Mrs Derwent. When she's not blaming herself she's compulsively reeling off lists of what they've eaten to me, all organically grown wholefoods.

George If the reports one reads every other day in the papers are anything to go by the only healthy way to die is to starve oneself. How's life treating you?

Roy Much the same. I'm very flattered that you remembered me after all this time.

George Never forgotten you dear boy. You're wasted in psychiatry, you know that don't you? Made the choice too young.

Roy It's very kind of you to say so but . . . (*The phone rings.*) Excuse me. (**Roy** *picks it up irritably.*) Freeman. Joan, I thought I said no calls. (*Pause.*) Oh, I see. Yes of course. Put her through. (*To* **George**.) It's Evelyn, your daughter. (*Offering the receiver.*)

George It can't be for me. She doesn't know I'm here.

Roy (*on the phone*) Evelyn. What a coincidence. Guess who's with me? Your father. Would you – (*Pause.*) Oh I see. (*Pause.*) Are you sure? (*Pause.*) Yes, of course. Don't worry.

I'll deal with it straight away. I'm sorry. It must have been a terrible shock. (*Pause.*) Thank you. 'Bye.

George Something happened?

Roy The group home where she does some voluntary work. One of the patients has died. She found the body.

George Oh dear. How did she sound?

Roy Very calm and competent. Excuse me. (*He presses the intercom on his telephone.*) Joan? Can you get on to ambulance control? One of my patients has died at Headsend Road. We're going to have to get him out quickly. Explain the set-up there and see if you can persuade the crew to take him – I don't want any nonsense. In the circumstances waiting around for undertakers is out of the question. Any problems please get straight back to me. (*To* **George**.) I am sorry about this.

George Not at all. I do remember what it's like.

Greg *knocks before entering.*

Greg The file you wanted on Ruth Derwent.

Roy You took your time. We've finished discussing her now.

Greg I'm sorry. I was in a meeting. I didn't get the message until . . .

Roy (*joking*) Well I hope you're not going back into one. (*To* **George**.) Social workers. The bane of our lives.

George And consciences.

Roy (*seriously*) I've just had a phone call Greg. Bad news. St Dymphna's. (*Gently.*) It seems Dave died this afternoon.

Greg (*genuinely*) Oh, I am sorry . . . How? . . .

Roy I think we should go over there. Unfortunately my wife's got the car today.

Greg Mine's still in the garage.

Roy Go and ask that Nurse Cretsley – she's on the ward.

She's got a car. It'll be good experience for her to come with us.

Greg All right. I've got supervision with Martha now. I'll just have to let her know. (*He goes.*)

George I'll leave you to it.

Roy Unless you'd like to come over to St Dymphna's and meet Evelyn?

George I think Evelyn sees quite enough of me as it is. Besides I said I'd drop in on Morpeth-Jones while I was here.

Roy Maybe I should get him to talk to Mrs Derwent. According to him we're all predetermined from the womb. He blames DNA for everything.

George St Dymphna's?

Roy The name of the hostel. Not my choosing. Patron saint of the insane apparently.

George What on earth did she do to deserve that?

Roy I didn't know either. It took the local curate to enlighten me. She's supposed to have left home after her mother died and her father turned his attentions to her, so the story goes. He caught up with her and proposed marriage. When she refused he cut her head off. And she became enshrined or whatever they call it in the thirteenth century.

George (*laughs*) God help us all.

Roy Quite.

Scene Seven

St Dymphna's

Shirley, Lil and **Evelyn/Eve. Lil** *picks up* **Dave**'s *tea-cup and wipes up the spilt tea.*

Shirley I should have taken more notice.

Lil Don't blame yourself. You weren't to know.

Shirley I had no idea.

Lil I can't believe it.

Shirley I should have done something.

Lil But he was so well, in himself, I mean. Talkative.

Shirley Tried to persuade him to see someone.

Lil (*cuts the string around the mirror*) I didn't know anything was wrong. I didn't expect.

Shirley You don't have to do that Lil.

Lil I've got to do something. I can't bear to think about it.

Shirley Evelyn, are you okay?

Roy, Greg *and* **Nicola** *arrive.* **Lil** *puts the scissors down on a chair.*

Roy We came over as soon as was humanly possible. Nurse, do you think you could organize a cup of tea for us all?

Lil I'll do it.

Roy Please be careful how you bring it in. (*To* **Shirley**.) Did the ambulance agree to take him?

Shirley Yes.

Roy Good. I had a word with them.

Eve Words.

Shirley There's something sadly final about a silent ambulance. The police took a short statement.

Greg And?

Shirley There wasn't much to say. (*To* **Roy**.) Why, I mean, how did he die?

Roy We won't know that until after the post mortem. I was rather hoping you'd be able to tell me.

Evelyn *sits down, first taking the scissors off the chair. She holds them in her hand.*

Shirley Me?

Roy You were here weren't you?

Shirley No I . . .

Greg Who was here?

Evelyn No one. No one.

Shirley Evelyn.

Roy What happened Evelyn?

Eve Careful.

Evelyn Nothing.

Greg (*to* **Shirley**) Where were you?

Roy (*to* **Evelyn**) Nothing?

Shirley (*to* **Greg**) I took Rohima to the DSS.

Eve In the counting house counting out the money.

Roy You're supposed to be a house manager not a taxi driver.

Shirley She agreed to claim benefit. I thought I'd give her a lift.

Roy And it had to be today?

Shirley It seemed too good an opportunity to miss.

Greg Where is she now?

Shirley She's still there. She's coming back on the bus. Oh God, what'll I tell her?

Evelyn Do you have to say anything?

Roy You saw him before you went out?

Shirley Yes of course. (*To* **Evelyn**.) Of course I do.

Roy And you couldn't see anything wrong? Fit as a fiddle one minute, drops dead the next.

Nicola (*to* **Roy**) He did complain of breathing problems and chest pains while he was on the ward.

Roy He felt claustrophobic, that's why I wanted him moved.

Greg (*to* **Shirley**) You left Evelyn to meet the ratepayers?

Shirley (*to* **Greg**) Yes, I'd just popped back to collect the papers and stuff I was supposed to give to you.

Greg Evelyn, what happened?

Roy (*to* **Shirley**) I can't believe no one suspected a thing.

Shirley When I saw him earlier he didn't look well.

Roy Why didn't you say anything?

Shirley I did. I asked him if he was all right. He said he was.

Roy Why didn't you do something?

Shirley I'm not a doctor. You discharged him from hospital.

Roy Yes, but I don't have day-to-day contact.

Greg Shirley wasn't to know, Dr Freeman.

Roy Presumably, you do know that the words psychic and psychiatrist are not synonymous?

Greg He was no longer on a section. If he didn't want a doctor, then Shirley had no right to call one against his wishes.

Roy If someone has a heart attack, even if the last words they spoke were, 'If I have a heart attack, don't call the doctor!' you jolly well do because we don't practise euthanasia in this country yet.

Greg I think you've misconstrued what I was trying to say Dr Freeman. (*To* **Evelyn**.) Evelyn, what exactly happened?

Lil *comes back in with the tea.*

Eve Tell them.

Evelyn Shirley asked me to see those people. I met them in the hall. I showed them in here like you said. I didn't see him there. Not at first. Well, I did. But, I didn't expect – I didn't think anything was wrong. Well, I sort of did but I didn't want to make a fuss, cause alarm.

Lil You didn't want to make a fuss?

Eve I did. I did.

Evelyn I couldn't.

Nicola (*to* **Lil**) I'm surprised you find that hard to believe.

Lil (*to* **Nicola**) You didn't know him like I did. (*To* **Evelyn**.) How could you carry on like nothing had happened?

Evelyn I don't know.

Roy Why didn't you check to see if he was all right when you first saw him?

Evelyn I don't know.

Greg You don't know?

Shirley Evelyn wasn't to know, she'd only just arrived.

Greg It was unfortunate that you had to go out.

Shirley Even if I did get paid for it, I don't have the metaphysical capacity to be in two places at once.

Evelyn Shirley said he often had a sleep in the afternoons.

Lil You must know the difference between being dead and asleep.

Evelyn How?

Roy I don't believe this, one of my patients has died and I've not had a straight answer since I arrived.

Shirley We don't know! We knew he'd been mentally ill, but we had precious little knowledge about his physical health.

Roy My God, the whole world can see in, where are the curtains.

Lil We took them down for the painting. I was talking to Dave when I was mending them.

Roy Do you think they could go back ASAP. No not now. When we've gone will do. So you were the last person to have seen him, is that right?

Lil Yes, I was the last person not to notice anything. The last person to mend the curtains, clean the kitchen, prepare the meal, use the phone to let the Sparidae project know I couldn't make it this afternoon. I was the last person to have talked to him and I couldn't feel any worse than I do now for not realizing.

Greg I realize it's been upsetting for all of us. Dave was –

Lil You don't know him like I do.

Nicola He's dead.

Greg Let's put the brakes on. There was nothing any of us could have done.

Shirley It's my responsibility. I wasn't there and I should have been.

Eve While they stand and point and tell each other you're to blame, I am smashing my fist, splitting my skull. Inside my head someone is wielding an axe. I am smashing all the things in my father's house. Everything is splintering around me. Every stick of furniture lies useless and broken. I am crashing my way through the brickwork and plaster, the rendering and the mortar until nothing, nothing is left of my father's house but rubble and dust. And it goes on and on and it will never stop.

Roy So he was on his own. When Evelyn came in he'd died?

Evelyn Are you blaming me?

Roy No, of course not.

Evelyn You think I'm to blame though, don't you.

Roy No I don't.

Lil If anyone's got stick, it's me.

Greg No one's to blame. It's not a question of blame.

Evelyn You think it's all my fault.

Shirley No one's implied that Evelyn.

Roy Are you all right Evelyn?

Evelyn Is that a real question or is it, what's the word Lil, you're so much better with words than me?

Lil Rhetorical?

Evelyn Rhetorical.

Roy Of course it's a real question. You're imagining . . .

Evelyn Yes, yes, I know all about imagining that I'm not here, I'm somewhere else.

Greg Evelyn, I think you're in a state of shock. Do you feel cold?

Roy Here. (*Offers his coat.*) Put this around you.

Evelyn Don't touch me.

Roy Now, I think we should all calm down and drink our tea.

Evelyn We? You mean me. That I need a cup of tea. I don't want a cup of tea, as though a cup of tea will make me better. I don't even like tea. How will that calm me down? You – you stride in here, pointing the finger, attacking me . . .

Roy Evelyn I don't know what you're talking about.

Lil Evelyn, it's all right.

Nicola No, it isn't. Evelyn, would you like me to drive you home? (*Takes scissors.*) Come on. You'll have to tell me how to get there.

Lil Nicola? What about me?

They go.

Roy What the hell does she think she's up to? Just who does that wretched Nurse Cretsley think she is?

Lil Adams.

Shirley She's your daughter isn't she?

Lil Not so as you'd think I'd notice.

Roy She's asking for trouble. Evelyn's obviously very perturbed and she's no idea how to handle it.

Shirley I can't understand why she was so upset. She never even spoke to Dave. (*To* **Lil**.) There's no love lost between you?

Lil Something's lost – that's for sure. Probably the stuff between my ears.

Shirley I don't think so.

Lil Well I'm not laughing.

Roy (*sighs*) 'The troubled world is sighing now. Death is at the door. And many folks are dying now, who've never died before.'

Lil, **Shirley** *and* **Greg** *look at him.*

Shirley She doesn't speak to you?

Lil We don't see eye to eye.

Roy I'm so sorry. I don't know what made me say that. Some childhood rhyme popped into my head for no reason at all. (*Then.*) There's no point in going over the top. This sort of thing happens all the time. It leaves a place and we should fill it as soon as we can. Did you get the fire alarm business sorted out?

Shirley Yes, that's the stuff I wanted Greg to authorize.

Roy Good. (*To* **Greg**.) Can you get the ball rolling and bring Dawn on a visit?

Greg Will do.

Roy Right. We'd better be getting back.

Greg It was Nicola's car.

Roy That's the final straw.

Lil The 23 bus will take you most of the way there.

Scene Eight

Exodus

A supermarket.

Evelyn *is throwing groceries into a shopping trolley.* **Eve** *is cowering against the shelves watching her.* **Nicola** *stands in front of* **Evelyn**.

Evelyn You don't understand, I have to shop for him, it's my duty. He doesn't ask much, never has.

Eve *laughs.*

Nicola Evelyn.

Evelyn It's the least I can do.

Eve Stop it, stop it.

Nicola It doesn't have to be done now.

Evelyn Soonest done least mended.

Eve You don't have to behave like this.

Evelyn I do have to do it you see otherwise –

Eve No, you don't.

Evelyn They might have to send him away.

Nicola Evelyn. I would like us to go now. Evelyn?

Evelyn Yes?

Nicola There's no need.

Evelyn But the shopping?

Nicola Leave it. I'll drive you home.

Eve No please. Not home.

Evelyn Ummm.

Nicola I said let's go home.

Evelyn Can we just walk?

Nicola Er –

Evelyn There's something I want to tell you.

They leave the supermarket. Open air. Early evening. They walk. Silence.

Scene Nine

Genesis

Nicola How are you feeling?

Evelyn Calmer. (*Then.*) Oh God, how am I ever going to face them again? (*She looks over her shoulder.*)

Nicola That doesn't matter now.

Evelyn I didn't want to go home.

Nicola It's all right.

Silence.

Evelyn Phillip might be there and if you have time I'd like to talk.

Nicola Fine.

Silence.

Evelyn Lil's your mother isn't she?

Nicola Only by birth.

Evelyn She told me you were a hairdresser.

Nicola I used to say I wanted to be one when I was small.

Evelyn She's never liked me. (*Pause.*) I don't like myself much.

Nicola Have you any children?

Evelyn A daughter. Still at school. Away at school. (*She looks behind her.*)

They cross the road and walk until they get to a bench on a piece of grass in the middle of a housing estate.

Evelyn *sits,* **Eve** *sits on one side of her,* **Nicola** *on the other.*

Evelyn This used to be an expanse of wasteland. Behind that block of flats there is the canal.

Nicola This estate must have been built about twenty years ago. Certainly council housing like this hasn't been built in the last ten years.

Evelyn People shouldn't be made to live like that.

Nicola No.

Evelyn There's something I want to tell you. Back there I felt an overwhelming urge to scream it in Roy Freeman's face. But something stopped me.

Nicola (*pause*) I'm listening.

Evelyn Now, I just want to go to sleep and not think about it.

Eve Just say it.

Evelyn It's about my father.

Eve It's about me.

Evelyn (*blurts out*) You see the first time it happened I thought it was my mistake. The bathroom. He came into the bathroom, which wasn't unusual in itself. He asked me for a cuddle, that wasn't unusual either but there was something in the way he touched me that made me feel uncomfortable. Even so, if it had never happened again I would have thought it was my mistake.

Nicola But it wasn't.

Evelyn No, you don't understand, he's such a well thought of man. Important, respected.

Eve What about me?

Nicola I believe you.

Evelyn Everyone admired him, being so busy and still managing to find time to spend with his children. He would take my brothers to cricket matches and he would make special time to do the things I wanted. I liked to go to the zoo. I'd been on a school trip there. I wasn't really interested in the animals. I found them boring but in a small corner was a wishing well. It seemed like magic to me.

Eve And?

Evelyn Actually, it was more of a small pond with a rockery around it and a little waterfall splashing onto a bed of coins. I was entranced by it and the first time we went together I took him straight over to see it. He seemed to understand. He said 'This'll be our secret'.

Eve There's more.

Evelyn But, on the way home he stopped the car and this time I knew it was not a mistake. (*Pause.*) From then on I would try and insist that I went to the cricket with my brothers. And my mother would chide me for being so ungrateful when I was lucky to have such a caring father. And I would walk around, lingering longer and longer, hoping that there wouldn't be enough time to stop the car and praying that this time would be different because I loved him and I wanted it to be all right.

Eve But it wasn't. It never has been.

Nicola I understand.

Evelyn Do you?

Nicola Yes.

Evelyn When he got wise to my time wasting, looking and looking into empty cages, pretending I was dying to see whatever creature it was that never appeared, he did it before. He stopped the car on the way to the zoo. Then I was supposed to walk round and enjoy myself. But, I would stop and look into the pond and refuse to move until it was time to go. He would grab my hand and squeeze his loose change into it and indicate that I could throw it in. And, I wanted to, but I couldn't. I held it so tightly I couldn't let go.

Eve I held it so tightly I couldn't let go.

Evelyn And the threats got worse. What would be done to me, to him, to my mother. And I wanted none of these things to happen. I just wanted it to stop.

Nicola And eventually it did?

Evelyn Yes.

Eve Just like it had never happened.

Evelyn *nods.*

Nicola You never told anyone?

Evelyn How could I?

Nicola What about your mother? Do you think she knew?

Eve No.

Evelyn No. I used to. But I don't any more.

Nicola What made you think she did?

Evelyn He did. Everything he did to me was carefully planned. At the time I thought she knew and didn't care because he planted that idea in my head.

Nicola How can you be sure?

Evelyn I can't. She's not here to ask. She's dead. But I can remember in front of her and other people that mattered, he'd use certain words, say things that were significant to me but of course not to them. Only at the time I didn't realize. I thought they all knew and found it endearing.

Nicola How do you mean?

Eve *pulls her knees up to her chin and holds herself tightly.*

Evelyn Things like. (*Deep breath.*) He would make a big fuss making me wipe myself. He always carried a new hankie, which he would then throw away. He would give it to me and say 'wipe, wipe' in a forced jolly way and move his arms back and forth like windscreen wipers. Then in front of other people, if something got spilt, like a drink, he would give me his hankie and laugh and go 'wipe, wipe'. And they'd smile at my obedience.

Nicola There are ways of knowing, suspecting, however carefully they've covered up.

Evelyn Are there?

Nicola Without a child needing to find the words to say it.

Evelyn My mother warned me as conscientiously, as her mother had warned her, to beware of strange men. But strange men live in twilight worlds, haunt open spaces. They do not have homes, families, children. They are not the men you marry, depend on, build your whole life around. Because if they were, there would be the words to say, 'Don't be alone with your father – he's . . . he's . . .' (*She cannot finish the sentence. She looks at the ground.*)

Nicola It's over . . .

Eve I'm still hurting.

Evelyn Is it? I still feel so ashamed. If only I'd been able to stop it when it first started.

Nicola If he did that to your daughter would you blame her?

Evelyn Of course not.

Nicola Well.

Evelyn It's not that simple.

Nicola No.

Scene Ten

House built on sand

Evelyn*'s father's house.*

Evelyn/Eve *enter the kitchen.* **Evelyn** *puts down the two bags of shopping she's carrying on the floor.* **George** *greets her smiling. He thrusts an envelope containing ten £10 notes in her hand.*

George Last time I saw you, you rushed off so suddenly I forgot to pay you for the shopping.

Evelyn (*looking in the envelope*) That's too much.

George Just a little pressie to say thank you – take it, what use is money to me at my age?

Eve (*moans*) Oh no, no.

George Would you like me to give you a hand with these? (*Lifting the bags and putting them down again.*)

Evelyn No, leave them. Sit down Dad I want to talk to you.

George (*pleased*) Right. I'll fill the kettle then shall I?

Evelyn No need. It's a long time 'til four o'clock.

George What's that?

Evelyn One of Roy Freeman's gems.

George (*filling the kettle all the same*) Oh, I saw him the other day. Nice chap. Did he tell you? Of course you rang while I was still there. Some poor blighter died in that home. It must have been terrible for you finding him like that.

Evelyn Yes it was.

Eve I've not come to talk about that.

Evelyn What did he want to see you about?

George (*sitting down*) He didn't. I bumped into him. It's a long story but I was asked to examine a little girl who was terminally ill.

Eve I feel cold. So cold.

Evelyn I've been thinking about my life.

George People usually do when someone they know dies.

Evelyn I didn't know him. Really.

George I can remember the first patient who died on me. I went through hell.

Evelyn Do you remember when I was young?

George Of course I do. You were what your grandmother always described as a bonny child.

Evelyn I wasn't very good at school.

George Well, in the fifties education wasn't considered very important for girls. A shame because of course it is.

Evelyn Do you remember taking me for days out?

George The cricket, yes. The boys wanted to move to Kennington so we could be near the Oval.

Eve He doesn't remember.

Evelyn No, me. Can you remember – taking me to the zoo?

George Well, of course, at my age, I can't remember every detail.

Eve You bastard. I can.

Evelyn You had a bloody season ticket.

George There's no need to be like that. Yes, yes I do, now you come to mention it, vaguely. You were very taken with all the money in that pond.

Evelyn I didn't like going.

George Yes, you did. Don't you remember that ghastly, ornamental rockery fascinated you.

Evelyn (*quietly*) I remember screaming in the back of your car.

George Bonny you might have been but you could also be wilful and obstinate.

Eve Just tell him. Tell him.

Evelyn I remember being raped by you.

George (*shocked*) Evelyn! What on earth made you say a thing like that?

Evelyn You know what I'm talking about.

George I don't.

Evelyn What do you call it then?

George Call what?

Evelyn What you did to me.

George I don't know what you're talking about.

Evelyn (*angry*) You're not talking to someone who wasn't there. You're talking to me.

George (*unbelieving*) What is all this? Evelyn, for God's sake. Are you mad?

Eve (*questioning herself*) Who's mad? Who's mad?

George If you're going to carry on in this silly way, you can just go. (*He turns away and starts to put the shopping away.*)

Evelyn I know I can now. (*Spits out.*) 'Our secret.' Do you remember? Do you remember when I bought bolts for my bedroom door?

George Yes.

Evelyn And why do you think I did that?

George To stop anyone coming into your room.

Evelyn No, not anyone.

George Me.

Evelyn And why?

George To stop me going into your room.

Evelyn But I didn't find a way to stop you, I was too stupid.

Eve I was too frightened.

George It never happened.

Evelyn It did.

George Evey, let me.

Eve Make yourself say it.

George Just go, get out.

Evelyn I remember pleading with you at first. Then I fought with you but you were stronger. Then later I remember, can still remember, every grain, every pattern, every mark on that car seat while I wished myself away. It was as though I was standing outside the car looking in, looking down on another me that I despised.

George (*wanting her to stop*) Stop it!

Evelyn That's how it was.

Eve That's how it was.

George (*turns to face her*) It wasn't. You were special, vulnerable. I wanted to keep you to me. It was the only way I knew to show love. It wasn't talked about then. The boys, cricket matches and all that, that was different. I was closer to you.

Eve You fucking liar.

Evelyn Special?

George (*upset*) Oh Evelyn, you don't understand. I loved you. You mustn't think for one moment I didn't love you. I never wanted to hurt you. Really I didn't. I just wanted you to love me.

Evelyn You didn't love me. You bullied me, despised me. I was always hurting.

George I didn't know how to love. Nobody ever taught me.

Evelyn And that's what I learnt from you. I have never trusted anyone. I have existed, got by, doing what was expected of me, a hollow performance, almost convincing. I dare say Phillip, as you hinted, does have affairs. It never occurred to me I've been too busy defending myself against being betrayed.

George You know, now you're grown up, how men are. We're all weak and we're all strong. I didn't know about children. I wanted to be part of it. I didn't want to spoil it.

Evelyn You were a grown man.

George You don't know what it was like for me. I didn't even know myself what I was doing.

Eve Everything was planned down to the last detail.

Evelyn I don't believe it, any of it. You're lying.

George Evey, I'm an old man now, please forgive me. You're all I've got. You, Phillip, Joanna.

Evelyn It's not our secret any more. I've told them. And I've written to Roy Freeman, as I will anyone else who might want a medical opinion of their daughter.

George How dare you? How dare you? You stupid bitch Evey, it wasn't all like that. You're making it into something more than it was. You had everything.

Evelyn Bribery.

George They won't believe you. They'll think you're mad.

Evelyn I wonder why. But I'm not protecting you any more.

George (*explodes*) Revenge, that's what you want – all these years you've stored it up. Waited till your mother was out of the way. Now you want your own back, is that it?

Evelyn (*calmly*) There was a child who was abused by her Father for many years. It hurt. She was in pain and humiliated and eventually robbed of herself. No, Father, I don't want revenge. What could I possibly do to you that would undo what you've done to me? I've lived with it and I don't want to any longer. You can live with it. (**Eve** *turns and looks at* **Evelyn** *and slips away*.) And I won't forgive you because what you've done is unforgivable.

Eve *holds out a large bath towel towards* **Evelyn. Evelyn** *takes it and slowly starts to wipe her hands and face and neck, carefully, taking pleasure in it. She repeats the action with* **Eve.**

Scene Eleven

St Dymphna's

A week later.

Shirley *helps* **Lil** *put the mirror on the wall.*

Shirley This isn't in our job description.

Lil These days people either have work or they don't. Job descriptions got thrown out with free enterprise. At least Teddy will be pleased that the chair covers got dry cleaned.

Shirley What a weird bloke. He seemed more frightened of newspapers than the wrath of God.

Lil S'pose it's only human really.

Shirley Evelyn's resigned from the Management Committee. I couldn't persuade her to change her mind. Though I did try.

Lil Oh.

Shirley I thought you'd be pleased.

Lil I don't know what I am.

Shirley Lil, you know what you told me.

Lil Forget it, Shirley. We were all overwrought.

Nicola *comes in.*

Nicola The front door's wide open.

Shirley It's about to get a coat of anti-graffiti paint. Is this an official visit?

Nicola Only in so much as Dr Freeman sent me to collect his coat.

Shirley Oh. Yes. It's . . . (*She goes to get it.*)

Lil I know where it is. I'll get it. (*She goes.*)

Shirley Do you have time for a cup of coffee?

Nicola No, I'm sorry, I'm afraid I don't.

Shirley Then I wonder if you'd mind giving me a lift back to the hospital. I have to see Greg. Hopefully, we'll be ready for Dawn to move in at the beginning of the month.

Lil *comes in with the coat.*

Pause.

Shirley *takes it from her and goes to give it to* **Nicola**.

Nicola I thought you wanted a lift.

Shirley I do.

Nicola Well you can carry the coat then.

Shirley If we go out the back we can collect the file on the way. See you later Lil.

Shirley *and* **Nicola** *go.* **Lil** *starts to polish the mirror.*

Evelyn *alone, comes in.* **Lil** *sees her in the mirror.*

Lil (*turns*) I thought you'd . . . Shirley said.

Evelyn I've come to take the picture back to the library.

Lil It's here. (*She gets it.*) Are you all right?

Evelyn (*taking the picture*) Thanks. No, but I will be.

Lil ⎱ I wanted . . .

Evelyn ⎰ Are you . . .

Lil Go on.

Evelyn Are you still frightened of flying?

Lil No. I never was. What I'm frightened of is crashing; sinking with the wreckage.

Evelyn So was I.

Scene Twelve

World without

Outside **Lil**'s *front door.* **Nicola** *hesitates before ringing the bell. She steps back as near to the balcony as she can, in case she decides to run.* **Lil** *opens the door, a book in her hand, her finger marking the page.*

Tony (*VO*) Who the hell is it?

Lil *looks behind her, then drops the book on the floor.*

Lil It's for me.

Steps over the threshold shutting the door behind her. The two women stand facing each other.

HEAD-ROT HOLIDAY

Head-Rot Holiday was first performed by Clean Break
Theatre Company at Battersea Arts Centre, on 13 October
1992, with the following cast:

Dee/Jackie/Chris	Natasha Alexander
Claudia/Sharon/Angel	Yonic Blackwood
Ruth/Barbara/Helen	Susan Gifford

Directed by Paulette Randall
Designed by Jenny Tiramani
Lighting by Jenny Cane

The action takes place in Penwell Special Hospital during
1991/2.

Characters

Dee	Patient aged 22
Jackie	Nurse
Chris	Claudia's Social Worker
Ruth	Patient aged 33
Barbara	Nurse
Helen	Ruth's Step-Mother
Claudia	Patient aged 29
Sharon	Nurse
Angel	

Note

Empty brackets – ( ) – are used in this play to denote
pauses of variable length. For example, when a character
waits for the reply from an unseen person, the actor can
then imagine what has been said and decide on the length of
the pause.

Part One

Scene One

Friday 20th December 1991. The ward. It is decorated, albeit sparsely, for Christmas. **Jackie** *stands behind an enormous dustbin which is overflowing with clean but often mis-shapen, shrunken and dye-run clothes. She is sporting a pair of protective glasses. She addresses the ward while* **Ruth** *meanders up and down behind her.*

Jackie Roll up, roll up. Your dirty laundry's back. Clean. Come on you lot settle down. Anyone would think that you couldn't care less whether you had washed clothes for the Christmas disco. All right, so now, are we all sitting comfort –

Patient Oh for fuck's sake –

Jackie Who said that? No one? No one very brave at any rate. Right, then. (*Taking a jumper out of the bin.*) Who's – ? (*Sees* **Ruth**.) What are you doing skulking behind me eh, Wanda?

Patient Her name ain't Wanda.

Jackie I know but it suits her. (*To* **Ruth**.) Go and sit with the rest of them Ruth. See I do know her real name. (**Ruth** *goes and sits down. Front row of the audience?*) Come on, you might have all day but I've –

Patient Got to get back to reading 'Bella' and chain smoking.

Jackie One more interruption and we'll have a few minutes silence for five minutes. (*Waving jumper in the air.*) Right, I'm getting arm ache. Who the hell does this belong to? (*Silence.*) Will you stop playing games. It's yours Margery isn't it? () Well I've seen you wear it. () You reckon? Shrunk? It's you that's put on weight. Like your food a bit too much.

Patient Ha. (*Pause.*) Ha.

Jackie (*decides to ignore this*) Either that or your PRN. Never occurs to you lot to ask how many calories there are in your medication. Still I mustn't go putting ideas into your heads. Just take hold of it Margery. (*Holds up blouse.*) This is yours isn't it whatsyername? () Yes, yes you'll all have plenty of time to do your ironing. (*Holds up dress.*) And this dress? () Yours? Good. (*Holds up a cardigan.*) This cardy? () Go on then, take it. (*Holds up dye-streaked shirt.*) () You what? () Look, I know it's the pantomime season but for your information my name is not Widow Twanky. And you know you're not encouraged to wear blokes' clothes anyway. Gawd.

She looks at her watch and starts distributing the clothes much faster. Unseen by **Jackie, Sharon** *enters.*

This? () Okay, catch. And these? Here you go. (*She starts throwing items of clothing across the room.*) Right, and finally. (*She dives into the bin and brings out a fist-full of bras.*) Whose is this? () Yes? Right, there you are Fiona. (*Throws it at her.*) This one? (*Looks at the label.*) 32B? Not worth burning that for Women's Lib, eh? Mind you, with your track record dear no one would have believed it was a political act. Just another arson offence. Ho. Just a joke. Come on what's the fricking matter with you? For Gawd's sake own up to these bras. () These two are Monica's? () Oh right, yeah she's in seclusion. Well, she won't be needing them for a couple of days then. Whose is this one? Jesus God, would you look at it? Next size is the scaffolding firm. (*Looks at the label.*) Thirty-eight double-D. It's yours isn't it Wanda, sorry I mean Ruth. (*She throws it at* **Ruth**.) You could make two nice lamp shades out of that in occupational therapy. Ha, ha.

Ruth (*holds out the bra to give it back.*) It's not mine.

Jackie Never mind. You have it. (*She goes over to* **Ruth** *and affectionately places the bra on* **Ruth**'s *head.*) I can't think who's it was originally then. You're the only one in this place big enough to fit it apart from Doctor Reed and I hardly think it would flatter him on the Rugby pitch do you? (*She turns and sees* **Sharon**.) Oh, I didn't see you there. Who are you?

Sharon I'm looking for the Ward Sister.

Jackie I'm not her. (*She takes off the glasses and puts them in her pocket.*)

Sharon No.

Jackie She'll be in the office. I'll show you. Are you the new Nurse, then?

Sharon Yes. Sharon.

Jackie I'm Jackie.

Sharon Hi.

Jackie Hello. (*Grins.*) With the emphasis on hell. Welcome to Head-rot Hotel.

Jackie *walks off.* **Sharon** *stands staring out at the ward a moment longer.*

Patient Hey you, Mary bloody Seacole, who d'you think you're bloody staring at, eh?

Sharon *follows* **Jackie** *off.*

Ruth (*looks at the bra*) Only men like big breasts. The women who have them never like them much. They get in the way. They attract attention and things happen you don't need. My life would have been different with small breasts. To be called 'Flat as a pancake' or 'fried eggs' would be honey to my ears. Honey don't you fool around. You just keep on pushing my love over the borderline. Sometimes I say things I think but sometimes I say lines from songs, they just slip out. It's here all day in the background, the music, like a mask with the emphasis on marshmallow and no features. So if I suddenly shout out 'Like a virgin', it doesn't mean anything except I like Madonna. As my RMO says it's like she has permanent house room in my head. Just as well my name isn't Donna or they'd call me Mad Donna.

Dee No they wouldn't. They'd call you mad slag.

Ruth What? What do you go and say that for?

Dee Take it easy. I didn't mean nothing personal by it. I was only mucking about. Whore and Madonna and that. Forget it.

Ruth That's what I like about her. She's both. Two in one. Like the Holy Trinity only with one missing because that had three.

Dee Why do you have to talk daft all the time?

Ruth I don't have to but it helps.

Dee It don't you silly mare. It just confirms them in their belief that you're round the bleeding S-bend, that you're not fucking sound upstairs.

Ruth Around. Round. Sound goes round. It never dies. It is connected to going round. And then there's a connection between words that rhyme. So sound and round –

Dee Why can't you just talk about the weather?

Ruth I can't see any. It goes round and round, bouncing round the universe because it can't get out. How can it get out? It can't. So that everything everyone has ever said is trapped inside forever. Every song that's ever been sung, every noise ever made for that matter. Is it matter, though? But it doesn't die but it does matter –

Dee That's a matter of opinion.

Ruth Every sound that was ever made is still somewhere around us.

Dee Put a bra in it will ya?

Ruth So what's so round the twist about hearing voices? Because they must all be boinging off the earth's crust ten-a-penny and echoing all around because even dead people's voices don't die. They might stop saying new names –

Dee Eh? Oh yeah. They might, yeah.

Ruth But the old ones go piling up and the babble must be like a big ball, a meteorite of sound with voices spattering off into orbit all over.

Dee (*offers* **Ruth** *a cigarette*) Here. Perhaps you should make a bit more room for them and shut up and have a fag.

Claudia *comes up to them.*

Claudia Did I just see you offer her a cigarette Dee, or am I going sane?

Dee Still speaking to us then Claudia? I thought Ward Workers were s'posed to behave more like staff.

Claudia You better make the most of me babe cos come the new year I'll be on the Parole Ward.

Dee Big deal. I'll come and visit yer –

Claudia You'll have to behave yerself then.

Dee From the outside.

Ruth They're not going to let you out, you intravenous drip.

Dee See? You can talk normally when you want to. She's been tormenting me Claud with sound goes round and round the bleeding round houses.

Ruth Just cos you've got no eye into the inner –

Dee Yeah, yeah. I know Ruth, I'm just a material girl.

Claudia Don't waste your intellect on her, Ruth. She's not worth it.

Dee Don't think I don't know what you're doing. You're trying to wind me up ain't yer? Trying to mess me up for me tribunal. Cos you'll miss me too much. Well, bad luck cos come the new year I'm off. You can keep your ambitions of parole wards. I'll be in me own bed-sit.

Claudia That's some delusion you're suffering from, girl.

Dee Fun-knee ha, ha.

Claudia Look around you.

Ruth Around and around this world you go. Spinning through the lives of the people you know –

Dee See? Now you've set her off again. The one woman karaoke machine.

Claudia Is there anyone here who has been here less than eight years? And all most of them did was fart in front of their Social Worker.

Dee What about you? You're on your way out.

Claudia I've been here seven years.

Dee Oh yeah. Course.

Claudia Ruth's been here twelve –

Dee Yeah, but I mean she's not . . . Shit, no offence but –

Ruth I'm crazy for you too –

Claudia If you're not mad when you come in here, you will be by the time you get out –

Dee Yeah, yeah, yeah.

Claudia Dee, listen. I know it's hard but it's better to prepare for disappointment believe me –

Dee Leave it out –

Ruth No one gets out of here in a year unless they top themselves. (*Laughs.*)

Dee You're sick, you are.

Claudia She's not far wrong though.

Dee That's obviously why it's taken you so long. Your negative attitude. And even now you're having to crawl your way out, doing their dirty work –

Claudia *starts to walk off.*

Dee Don't get like that Claudia. I didn't mean it. (*Offers cigarettes.*) Here, have one.

Claudia *turns back.*

Dee Don't look so surprised. It's Christmas ain't it? Go on take it. Anyway I'm going to give up. That'll go down well with the doctors.

Ruth You are mad. You are, burn my bra, you are, you are.

Dee *and* **Claudia** *look at her.*

You are. They won't want to know that. If you can give up fags then you might want to give up drugs. Then you'll be your old self and end up back in here. Round and round.

Dee Ruth, make my day why don't you, and go and see if you can get us both a light?

Ruth Okay. Seeing as you're making a big effort.

Dee Eh?

Ruth If I'd called you mad yesterday you'd have blocked my nostrils with your knuckles.

Dee I've turned over a new leaf.

Ruth Leaf it out. (*Laughs. Then.*) Leaf, beef, grief – no connection. There's no connection –

Dee (*pointing at* **Ruth**'s *cigarette*) Just connect the end of this snout to that lighter on the day room wall. Comprond? A light would be a might right sight, eh?

Ruth All right, all right, I'll be right back. I sound like Doctor Reed. Ha. When his bleeper goes off. (*She goes.*)

Dee D'you reckon she puts it on? One minute she's two fucking sheets to the wind, the next minute she's more with it than 'The Clothes Show.'

Claudia Let's see how long it takes her to come back with a light, if she does at all. (*Seeing* **Fiona**.) At least she's in a better mood than someone I could mention –

Dee What? Oh, hi Fiona, err all right?

Claudia I don't reckon she is. D'you?

Dee She won't do nothing, not today –

Claudia Why not? She's like you. She'd rather be banged up without fags than go to the disco.

Dee Ah, well, the thing is Claud, I've changed ain't I? I was wondering, hoping like, if you'd do us a favour . . .?

Claudia (*goes to give the cigarette back*) I knew it was too good to be true.

Dee Na. Listen. It's not anything that'll put the mockers on you going on the Parole Ward or nothing.

Claudia It bloody better not be.

Dee I was wondering –. It's . . . Right, don't laugh or nothing. Err, yer know this evening . . .

Claudia It will have been and gone at this rate.

Dee The disco. I was wondering if you'd help us out?

Claudia Out?!

Dee I mean pull the stops out.

Claudia They having an organist then?

Dee Are you trying to fuck me around or what?

Claudia I haven't a clue what you're talking about.

Dee I want to impress them.

Claudia Oh yeah? How?

Dee Get done up properly and that. You know, make-up, a dress. The works.

Claudia You do?

Dee Will you help us? Please? What you looking like that for?

Claudia This is some attitude change, Dee.

Dee It's like I woke up this morning, Claud. Why d'you think I didn't barrack Nurse Boggle-eyes when she was doling out the gear? Cos it's like it just finally sunk in that if I'm going to stand a chance at my tribunal I'm going to have to start doing what they want when they want –

Claudia Yeah, I'll give you a hand. Course I will Dee but –

Dee Don't you worry. I've got a feeling, a good feeling –

Claudia That someone's watching over you, eh?

Dee Crap. I don't need no one.

Claudia Dee –

Dee It's that sort of namby-pamby-someone-else-help me-behaviour that keeps most of them here so long. You got to help yourself cos if you don't sure as hell nobody else will.

Claudia Tell me about it.

Dee They can take away everything, they can strip you naked, but they can't take away your self, who you are, not inside. D'you know what I mean?

Claudia Sort – No.

Dee I mean your soul, don't I?

Claudia Well, Barb did confiscate my Motown Five album.

Dee You can take the piss all you want but you can't put me off you know.

Claudia Dee, I don't want to put you off. I just don't –

Dee You just watch me, Claud. You just watch me. (*She goes.*)

Claudia I don't want to watch you. I want to watch myself thanks very much.

Scene Two

The nurses' office. **Barbara** *has her back to us. She is pinning up a Christmas decoration which has fallen down. There is a breakfast tray for someone in seclusion on her desk. The phone rings. As she turns to answer it we see that she has a bruise on her face.*

Barbara (*picks up the phone*) White ward. Sister Barbara – () Oh, it's you. () No, no, of course I am. () Yes, I know, you said. () No, honestly it's all right. Look I have to go the new nurse will be here. () Sorry, look I'm going to have to – () Yes, Pete. Yes, I know you do. Me too. () I must go –

Jackie *and* **Sharon** *come in.*

Barbara Bye. (*Puts the phone down.*) Hi, you must be Sharon. (*Holds out her hand.*)

Sharon (*shaking hands*) Pleased to meet you Sister –

Barbara Barbara, please. I must say I was beginning to get rather worried about you.

Jackie I just took it on meself to show her some of our glorious facilities, Barb.

Barbara I'm afraid that there's not that many nor are they very glorious, not on the women's side anyway.

Sharon I wasn't shown round when I came for my interview. And when Jackie offered – I hope you don't mind.

Barbara No, not at all. Anyway, as you've no doubt discovered by now it must be very similar to where you've worked before –

Sharon Umm, quite.

Barbara But you've worked in a psychiatric hospital before?

Sharon Yes.

Barbara Of course you must have to be a RMN. You must have seen locked wards?

Sharon Yes, of course.

Barbara Well, this isn't that different surely?

Sharon No but –

Jackie Except for the patients. We've got the most dangerous people in the country in here yer know.

Barbara Jackie. I imagine Sharon is well acquainted with the function of a special hospital.

Jackie But some of them. Make your hair curl? I tell you they'd have yours running for cover.

Barbara It's a little early in the day to have to try and decipher your sense of humour, Jackie. Besides, you of all people should know full well that my policy is to let new staff get to know the patients, before allowing them to read anyone's notes. I don't agree with pre-judging or prejudice of any kind.

Sharon That's good.

Barbara I'm glad you approve.

Sharon Oh, I didn't mean to –

Barbara No, nor did I. Sit down. (*Offering cigarette.*) Do you want one?

Sharon (*taking one*) Thanks.

Barbara *lights* **Sharon**'s *then her own cigarette.* **Jackie** *has to smoke her own which she promptly does.*

Barbara What a week to start. Everything's a bit in the air but the day to day routine is pretty much the same. Roll on the start of next year. Oh, Jackie get a couple of the others out of the day room and take this to Monica. (*Hands her the tray.*)

Jackie Oh, shit. I just lit up.

Sharon (*taking the tray*) What is it?

Jackie Her breakfast. She's in seclusion.

Sharon But it's virtually stone –

Barbara We have to cater for the majority first. We can't allow the whole ward's meals go cold while we serve the one or two in seclusion –

Jackie Especially with that Monica. The other day right –

Barbara (*sees the protective glasses in* **Jackie**'s *pocket*) Jackie, what have you got those goggles for?

Jackie It's my right to wear them if I want to and after what happened to you I'm not taking any chances. (*To* **Sharon**.) See Sister's face, Monica done that.

Barbara Whatever, whatever, Jackie. She's still got to have her breakfast sometime.

Jackie I'm off, okay? (*She takes a drag of her fag and picks up the tray and saunters off with it.*)

Barbara This is Jackie's first nursing job.

Sharon Yes?

Barbara Hopefully I won't have to throw you in at the deep end, not this week. You'll need to spend the time just getting to know the ward. Observing. You'd do well to make observing the position of the emergency bells a priority. Any time you feel in physical danger ring it. Hesitation doesn't come into it. It will summon at least ten of your colleagues in the time it takes to say 'pass the Stellazine'. It isn't an empty threat either. It's amazing how many patients will actually stop what they are about to do if you threaten to ring the bell. But despite what Jackie says this is really a very safe place to work.

Sharon Except for your face.

Barbara Yes, but that was really silly –

Dee puts her head round the door.

Dee Sorry to trouble you Sister.

Barbara Yes, Dee? What do you want?

Dee There weren't no escorts sent over. Me and Ruth are still waiting to go to work.

Barbara Since when have you been so concerned about getting to work?

Dee I'm always concerned to do the right things these days. Haven't you noticed?

Barbara Yes, it's like waiting for the other shoe to drop.

Dee You've got no soul, Sis.

Barbara But you've got plenty of tongue.

Dee Ooh, thank you. I will be in demand.

Barbara I didn't mean –. Dee, meet Sharon who joined us today.

Dee Oh yeah. What you done then?

Barbara As a member of staff.

Dee I know that. I was just wondering what she'd done wrong to deserve to end up working here.

Sharon I'm not sure.

Dee You're not in the minority then.

Sharon I'm very much afraid that I am.

Dee Yeah, I see what you mean. Anyway nice to meet you.

Sharon Likewise.

Barbara (*to* **Sharon**) Don't speak too soon. (*To* **Dee**.) Go back to the day room while I check how many staff there are on the ward and then, all being well Sharon and I will take you over.

Dee Ta. Barb. (*She goes.*)

Barbara She's got a tribunal in the new year that's why she's trying to be pleasant. It might be quite good for you to go over to the workshop and spend some time there this morning seeing what goes on.

Sharon Okay.

Barbara A word of warning, charming though Dee is, she can also be quite volatile.

Sharon I can imagine.

Barbara Only two things to remember in this place. One, none of them are here for picking daisies. Two, give 'em an inch and they'll take a yard. Now let me –

She is interrupted by the sound of a plate glass window smashing.

Sharon (*jumps*) What –

Barbara (*starts to go,* **Sharon** *follows her*) No, no you stay here. I certainly don't expect you to have to deal with this on your first day.

Barbara *goes.* **Sharon** *watches her, trying to see what has happened. The phone rings.*

Sharon (*picks up the phone*) White ward. No, I'm afraid she's not here, she's busy at the moment. Can I take a message? () Has she got your number? () Oh, how nice to have your husband working in the same hospital. () Okay I will do, err, Pete. () Yes, that's right. Sharon. () Well, it's a bit early to say but yes, I hope it's going to be all right. Thanks. (*She puts the phone down.*)

Scene Three

The workshop. **Ruth** *and* **Dee** *sit next to one another, making teddy bears.* **Ruth**'s *is a rather haphazard shape and its head is hanging on by a few threads.* **Dee**'s *would be all right if it had a head.*

Dee Fuck. I don't seem to be able to get a head.

Ruth What is it with you? You moaned to come over here and you've done nothing but moan since you got here.

Dee We was late to start with and then that div-brain Fiona decides to bugger things up further. What the fuck does she think she's about, that's what I'd like to know.

Ruth She thinks she's the Antichrist, she does. He walked on water so she tries to walk through glass.

Dee Walk? She went at it like the fucking devil was behind her. And now thanks to her me bear aint got no bonce.

Ruth Go and ask for one, go on –

Dee Off of him? You're joking. I ain't asking him for nothing. Besides there ain't no more. Been a rush on heads ain't there. Look at them all, mindless plebs, breaking their necks to get teddy ready for Christmas.

Ruth Just cos you don't have anyone to give yours to.

Dee I do. That old whelk from the League of Friends.

Ruth In comparison to most stuff they make you do in here Teddy bears is a picnic. (*She puts her fingers inside her bear as though it were a glove puppet.*) If you go down to the woods today be –

Dee What the fuck are you doing? For Christsakes get your hand-out from up that bear's bum.

They both giggle.

Ruth (*to the teddy*) Oh dear. She said a rude word.

Dee There must be something seriously wrong with me, still laughing about bums, at my age. You know when I was little, there was this woman. I don't know who she was but she was quite posh and she had a little boy about my age and she used to take us out, for treats and that. One Christmas she took us to a museum.

Ruth She took you to a museum at Christmas?

Dee So?

Ruth Bloody cheap treat. They're free.

Dee Oh are they? Anyway. She always done educational stuff with us.

Ruth She'd be overjoyed to see how it's paid off wouldn't she?

Dee Here, they been messing about with your medication again? Cos when you woke up you was your usual head-the-ball self and now you're on the ball, almost.

Sharon *comes over*.

Sharon Are you two all right?

Dee Here you ain't s'posed to talk to us Nurse, you'll distract us from working.

Sharon I can't see much work being done.

Dee It's not her fault. They've upped her medication. She can't see straight.

Sharon I don't think they can have. The RMO hasn't been on the ward today.

Dee You won't take this as racial prejudice if I call you green.

Sharon Look, can I help you? Because you don't seem to be making any headway.

Dee My point exactly. I was just –

Sharon (*turns to see the Occupational Officer beckoning to her*) Excuse me a moment I'll just go and see what the Occupational Officer wants. (*She goes.*)

Dee He wants that you don't talk to us like we were human beings dear.

Ruth I thought you were going to be good.

Dee I was. I am. Bit of backchat don't do no harm though. Got to show you got your wits about yer.

Ruth You've got your work cut out then.

Dee Did you just not take your medication today? Is that it?

Ruth She never gave it to me.

Dee Who?

Ruth Barb, the barbed-wire-liar. Who d'you think, the Sugar Puffs Honey Monster?

Dee I don't believe it. Barb never makes mistakes.

Ruth She does when she's had a row with her old man. In fact marrying him must have been one of them. He hits her you know.

Dee Oh yeah. She told you that did she?

Ruth Didn't have to. Haven't you seen her face?

Dee That was Monica.

Ruth Monica was already in seclusion, doped out of her head, even her dandruff falls in slow motion.

Dee So?

Ruth So no one else was put in seclusion. It was Pete.

Dee So what? It's not my problem.

Ruth Soon will be.

Dee Why, is he coming to work on our ward?

Ruth Not that I know of –

Dee Then I can't see –

Ruth Oh shut up trying to stretch the limited resources under your hair. What were you saying?

Dee Is he coming to work on our ward?

Ruth No before. Something about bums and museums.

Dee Oh yeah. Well, she trailed us round all these rooms and started to explain about all the stuff in the glass cases.

Ruth Little did you know you'd end up one.

Dee What?

Ruth A case.

Dee D'you want to hear this story or don't you?

Ruth Will it make a difference?

Dee (*sarcastic*) Yes, I expect it will change your life.

Ruth No, I mean if I didn't want to hear it.

Dee Any rate on the staircase was this –

Ruth I thought you said it was a glass case –

Dee No! On this wooden staircase was this –

Sharon Come on you two please, a little more work and a little less bunny.

Dee Statue.

Ruth Of course it is.

Dee What?

Ruth Me.

Dee What?

Ruth It's me.

Dee What??

Ruth You said 'Is that you?' and I said 'Of course'. As if I haven't got enough problems hearing voices. Don't wind me up about it. It's not funny.

Dee (*shouts*) Statues!! I said statues. As in exhibits of people made of stone, bird-brain.

Sharon Dee, I won't tell you again.

Dee Uh oh. She's remembered me name already. Don't bode well. (*Whispers.*) In this place were loads of nude statues and me and this little boy were making ourselves ill with laughing or rather trying not to laugh because we'd get told off for being rude. Then I climbed up the bannister when the woman's back was turned and stuck my bubble gum up her bum.

Ruth What the woman's?

Dee No the statue's. I tell yer, we were laughing so much –

Ruth Oh no.

Dee What's the matter?

Ruth I can't connect anything you're saying. I should have had my tablets. It's no good. My brain's completely –

Dee You're fucking hopeless.

Ruth I know.

Dee All it was, right, was when you had your hand up that bear's bum and we were laughing it reminded me of sticking the chewing gum in the statue's bum and that feeling of laughing when you're not supposed to laugh and how it really hurts but you can't help it until you're wheezing and puffing until you can't see straight.

Ruth Like when you stab someone.

Silence.

Dee No, Ruth. I'm talking about laughing. Jesus Christ, laughing! I don't think I've probably ever laughed like that since. Mind, could have something to do with the fact that I ain't had much to laugh at.

Ruth What about when you were on punishment and the nurse tripped over your foot and injected the mattress with largactil?

Dee No, this was totally different. Oh shut up and get on with your bear.

They continue to sew in silence.

Ruth Tell you what you could do with yours, give it to one of the blokes at the disco.

Dee Piss off will yer. (*Then.*) Why? I mean if you do, does that earn you brownie points?

Ruth They'd be <u>convinced you were getting better if you took that sort of interest in a bloke.</u>

Dee Maybe I should then –

Ruth Not in the state it's in though.

Dee Eh?

Ruth They'd think you was trying to make a statement about capital punishment.

Dee Yer what?

Ruth You said it yourself. You ain't got a head.

Dee No I never have. I certainly never got no favours handed to me on no plate. No one would deny that. Not that I made things easy for myself either. I'm not saying I wasn't difficult to handle. I was. I was never a frilly pink frock kid. I reckon I was born with a pair of Doc Martens in my heart.

Ruth Or your mouth.

Dee I was always hard.

Ruth Don't make me laugh.

Dee Cold. I wasn't cut out to be wet and feminine. I always liked toys that worked. But then I used to break loads of things. On purpose. I know it sounds like crap. Well, what's new, the majority of my life has been crap. I tell you my background makes that fairy story 'The little Match Girl' look like 'Dallas'. People don't have lives like mine. They get a break. They get a head. They –

Ruth (*rips the head off her own bear*) For Christsakes, here have mine.

Dee I'm not that fucking hard up.

Sharon *comes over.*

Sharon Ruth?

Ruth Oh shit. She's remembered my name and all.

Dee Don't forget she's new though. She'll be nice to us this week.

Sharon Ruth, there's a visitor to see you.

Ruth Me?

Sharon Yes. The Occupational Officer says I'm to escort you over, that is if you want to go.

Dee Course she does.

Ruth Oh shit.

Sharon What's the matter?

Ruth I've not finished my bear.

Sharon There's always tomorrow.

Ruth But I won't have anything to give them.

Dee Take the needle and that and sew the head back on while you walk over there.

Sharon I don't think you can take needles out of the room.

Dee No, but you can. Go on –

Sharon Come on then seeing as it's my first day –

Dee (*offers* **Ruth** *her teddy*) Here, take this one it's better looking.

Ruth (*takes it*) Oh. You're so hard.

Scene Four

Ruth *and* **Sharon** *walk towards the visiting room.* **Sharon** *is sewing the Teddy's head on as she walks.*

Sharon Do you have any idea who it is?

Ruth It could be one of three people.

Sharon Who?

Ruth D'you really want to know?

Sharon Course.

Ruth Well, it could be someone from a church I used to belong to. She comes at Christmas, Easter and once at Harvest Festival. She used to bring me things to eat but then they stopped that and she brought me tapes. (*Pulls a face.*) Mostly Harry Belafonte. She'd like the bear for the Christmas Fête or that. Or it could be my aunt. She usually comes at Christmas. She always brings me some bubble bath in a plastic container shaped like a person or a train or a mutant turtle or something.

Sharon Oh. What'll she do with the bear?

Ruth Give it to one of her grandchildren, I expect.

Sharon That's nice.

Ruth But I'm sort of hoping that it's my brother. He works on an oil rig so he can't come often. I don't know what he'll do with the bear. He's not married or anything but he'll be pleased.

Sharon (*about the bear*) Does this feel secure?

Ruth Yes. Thanks. Thanks.

Sharon Will you be disappointed, if it's only the woman from the church?

Ruth No. I'll be pleased to see her, you're pleased to see anyone in here, even strangers but if it's one of the others it'll be like an extra bonus.

Sharon I'll keep my fingers crossed that it's your brother.

Ruth Will you? That's nice of you. What do you make of it, here?

Sharon I'm not sure. It's only my first day. It's different.

Ruth You'll get used to it.

Sharon I hope not. (*As she opens the door.*) I must never do that. (*Gives* **Ruth** *the bear.*) Here don't forget the bear.

Ruth (*sees her visitor. Freezes*) No.

Sharon What is it?

Ruth Take me back to the ward.

Sharon Is that her, there —

Ruth (*screaming*) Take me back. (**Sharon** *tries to restrain her, they struggle.*) Let me go. Take me back to the ward.

Sharon Okay. I will. Come on stop struggling. (*Calls.*) Nurse? Could you give me a hand?

Scene Five

Jackie *unlocks a cupboard and takes out several pairs of high-heeled shoes and several cans of hair spray.*

Jackie I've not been here long and I've still got quite a bit to learn, Barbara reckons. But I know where everything is and what to do in most situations now. I am part of a recruitment drive. I was working in the B&Q Superstore in town previously. Before I left school I said I'd like a job working with people, meeting people and that. Jesus, aren't careers officers dead losses? You'd have to be out of your tree to think you meet people on the check-out. Re-bloody-diculous. Everybody knows what's entailed on a check out. Nothing. The only excitement you get is short changing people and refusing to open the till. That can be a bit of a giggle. Not that I ever did it, certainly not on purpose.

Now of course me mates all ask about me work.

Sometimes I exaggerate bits for their benefit but mostly I
don't have to. Especially if I'm on nights or weekends.
Christmas should be a riot. It's like the atmosphere in
here's got a life of it's own. Giving up your own socialising
time can be a bit of a downer. Take today, I've got to go to
the disco here this evening but there's always stuff that goes
on that you can have a laugh in the pub with your mates
about after. Some, a few people, really feel sorry for some of
them in here. They'd feel differently if it had been them on
the other end of the knife and got done in. You wouldn't be
laughing neither if it was your Mum or Dad that had been
killed. Them type of people think that if someone's talking
and not smiling that they must be sincere and they
practically worship programmes on Channel Four where the
burglars get more sympathy than the burgled and believe
the more horrible you are the more sorry we got to feel for
you. Well, I'm sorry but bollocks. Be fair, you can't go
around murdering people and burning buildings to the
ground without something happening to you. And you know
people talk of prison being a holiday camp? Well then, this
is a Euro Disney trip this is. It's not like prison at all. Hell
no. For one thing, you can't make yourself a cup of tea
when you want in prison you know.

Basically you get two sorts in here. One that's mentally
ill, usually manic depressive – most probably more
depressive than manic – or schizophrenic. Though if they've
been here a while they can swop 'em about a bit. So you
might have been giving medication for one then they decide
that they're another and you have to give a new lot of
medication. Anyway come to think, just cos you might be
schizophrenic doesn't automatically exclude you from being
depressed as well I suppose.

And then there's the other sort who are mentally
disordered. Psychopaths they call them. But I'm not sure
that they all are, because sometimes they can get upset and
cry and that, but anyhow their behaviour isn't right in the
head most of the time, whatever they choose to call it. I can
only describe it like their personalties are too strong in one
direction or the other. Let me give you a for instance. Like if
something goes wrong or you don't agree with it. You and I

might go along with it but not them. For example, my
Dad's a bit of a racialist, not as bad as some of them I've
met in here even, but he can sound off and that and I just
go 'Yeah, yeah' even though I don't happen to agree with
him. I mean that's what life is, compromise. If you were to
pick up on every little thing you would drive yourself mad if
you weren't already. You just can't go round all the time
saying what you think. Talk about one step forward, twenty
back. They reach the Parole Ward and then they blow it,
they just blow it and then they have to start back again. I'll
give them one thing though, there are no flies on them, not
where it counts. It's really unnerving but they know exactly
what button to push to wind you up. I don't know how. I'm
not squeamish. I can't afford to be, now I'm a nurse. But I
have got this thing about eyes, always have had, and
sometimes, you won't credit this, they'll just pop one out.
The stuff they get up to, slashing themselves, swallowing
stuff it's nobody's business. Of course it's all a rouse for
attention. Me heart's in me mouth every time I unlock this
cupboard I can tell you. Gawd, the Ozone layer is the last
thing in danger from these cans and the damage one of
these (*Holding stiletto heel.*) can do. Jesus. Makes his
crucifixion look like an act of kindness. But then like
everything in life, there's the other side. You see some of
them all dressed up, really making an effort and trying to
enjoy themselves and you feel a warm glow and think that's
what I like about this job. At the end of the day it's not just
a means to an end, like taking money for conservatories or
screws, it's about helping people.

Scene Six

The washroom. **Claudia** *and* **Ruth** *are getting ready to go to the
disco. Both wearing dresses and tights.* **Ruth** *has had a lot of
medication. Her speech is slow and slightly slurred. She is shaky in
her movement and her cardigan is buttoned up wrongly.*

Claudia (*putting on her make-up*) Where is that silly cow with
our shoes?

Ruth *tries to put her lipstick on. It misses her mouth badly.*

Claudia Ruth?

Ruth I'm all right.

Claudia How much PRN you had today?

Ruth It's all right. I'm all right.

Claudia How come you came back to the ward early? Eh? Did something happen at work?

Ruth Nothing happened. Nothing. Everything is all right.

Claudia Would you like a hand?

Ruth (*looks at her hands*) Yes, one that doesn't shake.

Claudia Look at the state of you. (*She takes her own hankie and wipes the lipstick off* **Ruth***'s face with it.*)

Ruth It's a ritual isn't it?

Claudia Wiping faces with hankies. Yes, it reminds me. (*Then.*) Of what I don't want to be reminded of.

Ruth It's always worst this time of year.

Claudia Don't I know it. If you can survive Christmas in here, there's hope. I'm all right until they play that 'When a Child is Born'. It's so blessedly poxy, it cracks me up.

Ruth I'm a carol bulimic, me. I've only got to hear the word 'Manger' and . . . (*She puts two fingers in her mouth and pretends to gag.*)

Claudia So lines from carols and hymns don't come into your conversation?

Ruth Not if I can help it. But then I can't help it. Ha. (*She starts to reapply her lipstick.*) I can't help nothing.

Claudia Come here, babe. Let me do it.

Ruth Did you kill them then? Sorry, sorry, sorry –

Claudia Take it easy. Who?

Ruth No one, no one. I know it don't do to talk about it.

Claudia My children? No –

Ruth It's just that I always thought well, seeing as a lot of the others don't talk to you and –

Claudia I like to keep to myself. It seems safer that way. But no, I didn't. I gave them away.

Ruth Is that why you're here?

Claudia That's the result of me being in here. They were, are adopted. And I agreed to sign the paper, five years ago now. I still feel torn. Some days I think, 'Yes, they've got a better life' but then at Christmas –

Ruth Christmas is a right frightening bastard.

Claudia You know the only thing I was ever really afraid of was losing them. When it happened I suppose I should have felt relieved. I sort of did but for the rest of the time I felt totally tormented. D'you know what I mean?

Ruth First you lost them then you gave them away?

Claudia I agreed that they went into care the first time I was in hospital.

Ruth What did you do the first time, then?

Claudia Went to my GP. The biggest mistake of my life. I see that now.

Ruth Why, did you stab him?

Claudia (*laughs*) No. I went because I was depressed. I was finding it really difficult to cope – I couldn't find a job which paid enough for the children to be minded. Me Mum had gone back home. She'd always helped out before. I was really unhappy. I needed something to change so I agreed to them being fostered while I was in hospital. There was no one else to look after them you see.

Ruth But you never got out?

Claudia Yes, I discharged myself after six weeks. The social worker promised that I could have my kids back if I got myself together. The doctor promised I wouldn't go back into hospital as long as I kept taking the tablets. It was like running in a dream and getting nowhere and then looking down and finding that someone has cut your feet off.

Ruth I hope you haven't told that to the RMO. Dreams about cutting bodies cause big setbacks.

Claudia I wouldn't tell him anything.

Ruth You still haven't told me how you did get in here or have I missed it?

Claudia No. I was so angry at the 'If-you-behave-well-enough-you-can-have-your-children-back' game that I chased the social worker across the balcony with a potato peeler. It was on the kitchen table. My neighbour had given it to me. He'd got a job lot. I don't even use them. And I didn't get a chance to use it on the social worker either. Didn't stop them sectioning me. See, because of my previous admission, I had a history of mental illness as far as they were concerned. And then they tried to charge me with GBH which was then dropped to actual bodily harm which then of course had to be reduced further as I only ripped her coat but by then the damage had been done. They transferred me here cos I was potentially violent.

Ruth Don't start to cry. (*She takes the hankie and starts to wipe* **Claudia**'s *face*.) Tell me what it was like being mad –

Claudia You what?

Ruth Wild, wild rage. Running along the landing.

Claudia Oh. I was screaming an' cussing her the way my Mother used to when she got mad. That alone would probably be enough to have me carted off but I totally let go. The anger took over. I felt completely exhilarated. I couldn't see straight. I could have killed her. It's just really lucky that I didn't.

Ruth Did you feel free?

Claudia I felt I was flying, I was so high.

Ruth We going to fly tonight ain't we?

Claudia Oh, yeah? What they changed your medication to then?

Ruth No I mean enjoy ourselves, dancing and that.

Claudia We're not going to be standing, never mind flying if that basket case Boggle-eyes doesn't put in an appearance with our shoes.

Ruth I'll go and find her –

Claudia Hey, and Sweetheart, why don't you ask if you can wear your other dress?

Ruth Why, is it better?

Claudia Yeah. You look great in it.

Ruth It's a ritual isn't it? (*She goes.*)

Claudia And don't go blabbing to – (*Then realises* **Ruth***'s gone. Starts to put her own make-up on.*) Not that anyone takes any notice. I wonder if my daughter has started to use make-up. Shut up. Shut up. It's Christmas.

Scene Seven

Chris, Claudia*'s social worker.*

Chris I still think about her. I know she's still in there, that Special Hospital, so called. I wish I didn't know. God, I wish she wasn't there. It was the worst day of my working life so I'm hardly likely to forget it. And I still can't think about it without feeling humiliated and embarrassed. I fairly flew across that open walk way. I know it's a myth that psychiatric patients are more violent than anyone else but Claudia was raging. It's also a myth that women who are angry are mentally ill, but it's the rest that's difficult to sort out. Like what is mental illness? I often catch myself standing on the escalators in the tube, during the rush hour wondering how come more of us aren't trying to stab each other. It sometimes seems to me a miracle that any social order exists at all. She had every right to be angry. She had every right to want her children back. We'd found them a very good foster home, with a Black family, with every intention that they should be reunited with her as soon as possible. It would have been very disruptive if they were taken away from the placement and returned to Claudia, if then she couldn't cope and they had to go back. It was only a matter of time. And my job was to make sure that the children's needs were being put first. I know that if they'd been returned to her there and then I wouldn't have being carrying out my statutory responsibility.

She wasn't well and she wasn't coping very well either. She was still on medication. But then I was at a mental health training day last week where this young woman was saying that when we talk about a drug's side effects we are minimising their power. We should all start calling them effects. And I thought yes, that's probably true and probably Claudia never should have gone into hospital in the first place and probably the drugs did make her worse and yes, I'd have been as angry and frustrated as her. I didn't want the police to be called. I didn't have any choice.

They arrived with the alacrity usually only achieved in soap operas. It turned out that they'd been raiding one of the flats two floors down. She ripped the sleeve of my coat and scratched my arm with a potato peeler. If they hadn't arrived I think I could have probably got away.

I can say and stick by this. She wasn't well enough to have her children back but she wasn't ill enough to go there. I knew that was on the cards. I minimised what had happened. I argued with the evidence. I almost went berserk when I saw GBH on the form. I went straight down to the police station. I got my own solicitor and eventually managed to get all the charges dropped. But I am now a link in a terrible chain of events which has taken years and two children from a young woman's life. And the worst thing is I don't see how I could have done anything differently. I never did anything wrong. I know I acted totally professionally and yet I feel bad. I still feel really bad.

Scene Eight

Claudia puts the finishing touches to her make-up. **Ruth** *comes in wearing her other dress and carrying two pairs of shoes and a can of hairspray.*

Claudia That's better. Did you remember my gel, girl?

Ruth (*taking it out of her pocket*) Here. I thought I might see Dee but—

She is interrupted by **Dee** *who puts her head around the door.*

Dee Somebody want me?

Claudia Get a move on.

Dee (*placing a tape recorder inside the door*) Now ladies I must have your full attention and admiration. So when I come through this door properly I want all eyes on me.

She switches the tape recorder on and goes out, shutting the door behind her. The song 'I'm Too Sexy For My Shirt' booms out. **Dee** *flings open the door and makes a grand entrance. She is wearing a dress. The dress is nice enough but* **Dee** *looks very odd in it. She is carrying a pair of high-heeled shoes. She starts to prance and pirouette around the room.*

All three of them laugh.

Ruth More like Mr Kipling than a tart.

Dee Barb and the tranx caught up with you, I see. (*Switching off the tape.*) And I hear it weren't your aunt but your step-mother what visited you.

Claudia I didn't know you had a step-mother.

Ruth I nearly didn't once.

Dee What, you mean —

Ruth Don't, don't, don't not now. We've got to enjoy ourselves.

Claudia True. Leave her be, Danny La Rue.

Dee (*to* **Ruth**) What did she want though?

Ruth She always said I'd come to a bad end, so I suppose she came to satisfy herself that she was right.

Dee After all this time?

Ruth I didn't see her. She's nobody. She's not here, not in the chair, silly mare, I –

Claudia Come on Ruth, let's concentrate on getting ready.

Dee But –

Claudia Leave it. (*Then to* **Ruth**.) Let's do your dress up.

Dee Don't waste yer time on her. She knows how to dress up. You both got to concentrate on me.

Claudia Are they paying you to be the drag act?

Dee You can cut that out. I'm relying on you two to transform me. I don't want no botch jobs. I want to be a bone-fide lady.

Ruth It's Friday evening; the plastic surgeon's gone home.

Claudia (*to* **Ruth**) That's better. (*To* **Dee**.) When was the last time you put a pair of heels on?

Dee What's that got to do with anything?

Claudia I thought so. We'll be lucky if we get you walking, but don't try thinking of dancing –

Dee All I'm asking is that when I emerge from here I look the part, cos you can bet your life that they're all outside there now, lining up ready for a big gawk –

Claudia You try those shoes on first.

Ruth They're Fiona's. Who let you have those?

Dee DIY Boggle-eyes sales girl of the year. Thrilled to bits that I was trying to make the best of meself.

Claudia Shame Fiona couldn't be here, she'd wee herself.

Dee (*puts the shoes on*) Now, let's see what all the fuss is about.

Ruth It's like a ritual isn't it?

Dee There. See, no big deal.

Claudia Now walk across there.

Dee (*lurches forward*) Oh fuck.

Claudia *and* **Ruth** *laugh. They each take one of* **Dee**'s *arms and help her across the room.*

Dee Me ankles feel like they could snap in half any second. Jesus, this is dangerous.

Claudia Now you walk back on your own.

Dee I don't see how I'm ever going to make it.

Ruth Don't be such a baby, even I can do it on medication.

Dee You could probably get a job in the circus.

Ruth Look who's talking.

Claudia Excuse me but do you two want to go to the disco or spend an evening talking about your career opportunities?

Dee Yeah, yeah Claud. Come on slap some of that gunge on me face. Come on, come on. If we do well over Crimbold we can't fail.

Claudia Hold out your hands. (*She squirts some foundation on to them.*)

Dee What do I do with it?

Claudia Rub it in all over your face. Gently. Okay, now close your eyes.

Dee *does so.* **Ruth** *bends down and pulls a hair out of* **Dee**'s *leg.* **Dee** *jumps, causing* **Claudia** *to accidentally poke her in the eye with the mascara brush.*

Dee (*screams*) Oh you bastards what are you trying to do?

Claudia Keep still.

Dee How can I? She's trying to flay me alive and you're trying to poke me bleeding' eye out.

Claudia Only cos you moved.

Dee (*to* **Ruth**) What's your bleedin' game?

Ruth I'm plucking your legs for you –

Claudia You haven't got time to do that Ruth. She's got enough there to stuff a mattress.

Ruth She can't go like that, they'll think she's just come from vandalising the raffia workshop.

Dee What am I going to do? What –

Claudia Hold still. I've brought a pair of my thick tights for you to wear –

Dee I just hope they go with the dress.

Claudia Match your personality perfectly though.

Ruth *laughs*.

Dee (*to* **Ruth**) That's better. It's wearing off a bit isn't it?

Claudia If I'm to put on lip gloss you have to hold your mouth still. Do you think you could manage that?

Ruth You need a belt on that dress. Here have mine. You know they don't like me wearing them.

Dee (*puts it on*) Ta.

Claudia (*standing back to admire her work*) There, what do you think?

Dee Oh blimey.

Ruth Fantastic.

Claudia (*to* **Dee**) Come here let me touch you up.

Dee Don't get an offer like that every day –

Claudia You are so predictable.

Dee Please, please tell that to me RMO. (*Then.*) We are on our way, Claud. Honest this is it.

Claudia Is it really that simple?

Dee Yeah, it really is especially for you, you're such a goody-goody.

Claudia You reckon? (*She takes a three-amp fuse out of her pocket.*)

Dee What's that?

Ruth It looks like a fuse from a plug.

Claudia You know how slow they are to escort us back if there's anything good on the telly –

Dee You're wicked.

Ruth We all are.

Dee *turns the music on: 'Holiday' by Madonna. They all dance and then exit, heads held high.*

Interval

Part Two

Scene Nine

The disco, complete with music (Lady in Red) *and lighting of sorts.*
(N.B. no strobe.) **Dee** *is kicking and fighting with* **Sharon** *and*
Barbara *who are trying to restrain her.*

Dee Will you just listen?? Fuck you. Will you?

Barbara *and* **Sharon** *have managed to restrain her.*

Dee Let me go, let me go, you fucking bastards. You arse
holes you fucking arse holes. I'll fucking kill you. Let-go-of-
me-

Barbara *and* **Sharon** *frog march her out.*

Dee Cunts, you fucking cunts.

Scene Ten

Sharon *sits on a chair. Takes her shoes off and starts*
rubbing her feet.

Sharon I've never liked discos anyway. I don't like dancing.
I can't see the point of it. I suppose I've never got over
being self-conscious about it. Watching people do it makes
me feel I'm watching a David Attenborough nature film or
something. It doesn't matter if it's New Age or Ballroom. It
makes me think of footage of scorpions' mating rituals or
ant-eaters' flea removing antics. I only ever go now if it's a
friend's birthday and that's where they've chosen to go. I've
certainly never had to go to one as part of my work before.
At least there was no question of being expected to dance. I
don't know why I wasn't paying attention to what was
going on. Uncharitable as it sounds I couldn't stand it.
None of it. It all suddenly seemed like a zoo and I wanted to
look away. I wanted to run away. Then the next thing I
know, Dee has her fist in another patient's face and we're
trying to restrain this mad tiger. I can't understand how she

could be so short-sighted. What did she think would happen? Well, that's just it, I suppose. She didn't think.

Scene Eleven

Thursday 26th December 1991. The day room. **Jackie** *has three breakfast trays on her lap and is sitting reading the TV page of the 'Mirror'. The television screen is blank.* **Barbara** *comes up to* **Jackie** *and looks over her shoulder.*

Barbara What are we missing?

Jackie Everything.

Barbara I've been on at him again. And I've written to the administrator.

Jackie You should ring the bleeding Home Office direct.

Barbara As if the week in between wasn't bad enough anyway. (*She starts to pick at a Christmas decoration.*)

Jackie Don't start taking the decorations down. It's only Boxing Day and it's unlucky.

Barbara Well, I don't feel very lucky.

Jackie I tell you one thing. I'd never have offered to work over Christmas if I'd known the telly wouldn't be working. How we supposed to do our job when the patients are so pissed off, with nothing to do.

Barbara Huh, half the ward is in seclusion anyway.

Jackie Half? Four.

Barbara Yes, okay. But over Christmas. What does that say for quality of nursing on this ward?

Jackie Come on Barb, you can't blame the nursing. For starters Monica's never been able to cope on this ward. She prefers seclusion anyway.

Barbara Umm . . .

Jackie And they should have kept Fiona on the Admission

Ward longer. As for that Ruth she's just a slag and she didn't learn that off any of us.

Barbara (*seeing* **Doctor Reed**) Jackie, she's mentally ill.

Jackie You what? She's a right slag I've heard you say that – Oh hello, Doctor Reed. (*To* **Barbara**.) What's he doing wandering round the fricking ward on Boxing Day?

Barbara Apparently, he's lost some opera tickets.

Jackie Well, he hasn't been anywhere near the ward in the last –

Barbara She was doing so well until –

Jackie Bye Doctor. (*Then to* **Barbara**.) Yeah, well she over-excited herself at the disco. In more ways than one. That's what done it. Until that butch cow, Dee put a stop to it.

Barbara No it was before that, that visit –

Jackie What, her Aunt upset her? Come off it, that is scraping the bottom of the barrel.

Barbara It wasn't her Aunt though, it was her step-mother.

Jackie Oh. Has she been before? Hang on, here wasn't it her step-mother that she attacked?

Barbara It would appear that it wasn't fatal.

Jackie S'pose that would have given anyone a turn after all these years. You don't s'pose the little slut thinks she did kill her and therefore that she saw a ghost?

Barbara No, she knows she's still alive, no thanks to her she nearly did kill her.

Jackie I wonder what she wanted after all these years, then?

Barbara Sharon said –

Jackie She's really trying to ingratiate herself isn't she?

Barbara I suppose she has to in her position.

Jackie With her colour you mean.

Barbara Well. Anyway. At least she's stopped wandering around doing the patients' sewing for them.

Jackie She's lucky you never grassed on her.

Barbara As if. Anyhow she reckons Ruth's step-mother started calling out after them, 'I just want you to know that I'm sorry.'

Jackie She must have meant sorry it happened. Nobody can be so weedy as to apologise for being stabbed.

Barbara Maybe she just meant that it was all right, that she was sorry for holding it against her.

Jackie Must be a bleeding saint.

Barbara It is the season of good will. Talking of which, Boxing Day breakfasts. C'on. Chop, chop.

Jackie I tell you I'm not going anywhere near that aggressive queer. I'm sorry I don't care how short of staff we are.

Barbara All right, give me Dee's. She's long since calmed down though. Will you go and find Claudia? She can go and clean them out.

Jackie *goes.* **Barbara** *goes over to the TV, tries several times to turn it on without success. She hits it. The phone rings, off.*

Barbara Oh go away, go away, it's bloody Boxing Day. (*She goes to answer it.*) I hope you haven't rung to talk about what's on the telly. () Oh. I do beg your pardon. I'm so sorry I thought it was an internal call. () Yes, in fact we were just talking about her. () Yes, we're all very concerned. () I'm afraid it did upset her. () Well, a little set back. () No, no, I'm pleased you called. But I'm sure you'd appreciate me being straight with you. () Sometimes we find with mentally ill patients certain people trigger off rather, well violent reactions in them. () No, I'm sorry you can't, not at present. She's really not up to it. () Frankly in the long run that would probably be for the best. I'm sorry to be so forthright but my job is to put my patients first.

Scene Twelve

Dee *wearing her own clothes in seclusion. She is hunched over, holding her foot and arm, rocking gently.*

Dee I never admit it but I can't really hack it in here in the way the others seem to. Of course I know it has something to do with that I was locked in a room for a few weeks when I was about three. I can't remember much about it, just a feeling, like trying to breathe through porridge. I try to make myself sleep. But it's hard.

And then just as you're about to drop off they poke their ugly mugs through the inspection flap or keep switching the fan off and on in the middle of the night. Breaks the monotony for them I s'pose, having someone screaming and shouting and carrying on. And that's when you have to try and keep your mind going because the grey blankness in here is like, when you imagine the universe, it's like being in the vast empty part. So I often distract myself by imagining my life as a film. I can see a picture of myself on the poster, a sort of cross between Martina and k.d. only younger. With the caption underneath. 'When the rescue services arrived, the nightmare began.' But I said I wanted help. I don't admit that to no one now. Oh, shit I could kill myself. Fancy admitting, in Holloway, that I wanted help. I'd have been out months ago if I hadn't opened my pathetic squealing gob. Shut up, shut up, shut up thinking try and get some kip.

An Angel appears behind her.

Angel Dee?

Dee (*turns*) Jesus.

Angel Try again.

Dee (*turns back*) Just piss off back where you came from. I'm a psychopath not a schizoid. I can't see things what aren't there. It's not in my diagnosis —

Angel But I'm your Angel —

Dee Don't tell me, I don't want to know what you are. You're nothing. You don't exist. My WHAT? You're my WHAT? I tell you one thing mate I've never seen a black angel.

Angel I've never seen a white one, duck.

Dee That's because they don't exist! There are no such things!! (*Then*.) Hang on, what d'you mean MY ANGEL? Call yourself an angel and I end up in hell. Holy fucking ghost you must be fuck awful at your job.

Angel My mobility was severely impaired by a wodge of Bazooka up my bum.

Dee Shit!

Angel Don't even think about it.

Dee After all this time, you still remember me?

Angel I've always been here. I'm part of you.

Dee I'm not talking to you. You're not there.

Angel I'm not going to go away until I've told you a story. –

Dee You can stop right there. You're an angel. This is Christmas. Let me tell you straight off I'm not having a baby for no one.

Angel Listen duck, Brown Owls have been struck dead for comparing themselves to the Virgin Mary never mind smack-head, bar-dykes who've made a career out of punching police men.

Dee Once! I did that once. He was really harassing me. Even then I had to jump off the ground to reach him and then I only got him in the throat and if you don't piss off I'll do the same to you.

Angel That's what you are doing to me.

Dee What are you on about?

Angel I told you. I'm part of you.

Dee Oh yeah?

Angel Your spirit.

Dee You don't much look like a treble vodka –

Angel That's not even funny. I'm the part of you that not only wants to survive but fly.

Dee Fly? ha! You won't even laugh at my jokes. Only I could end up with a spirit that's really a lump of stone.

Angel Petrified at an early age.

Dee I've always had the bum deal me.

Angel I know. Now, here comes the riddle.

Dee Oh, so corny.

Angel Listen cos I'm fading fast.

Dee Bleeding hell. Tinkerbell. Bleeding hell.

Angel Yes, a lot of the time it is.

Dee Yes it is. It is. I wish I was made of stone. Sometimes I feel so torn apart I imagine my flesh exploding and huge chunks of it careering round the ward. Oh, get on with it and leave me alone.

Angel Thank you. There is a child somewhere, who's very frightened. Someone is cutting into her, slicing at her body, slashing her flesh to the bone, stabbing to the tendon. They are freeing her of her life's blood. What have we got to do?

Dee Stop them.

Angel Go on then. (*She goes.*)

Dee But you don't understand. It's keeping me alive. Every other fucker's done things to me. I'm going to do things to myself for a change. Don't you understand? I'm creating order.

Angel *off. Laughs softly.*

Dee *holds up her hands to reveal a deep cut in her arm and a very bloody foot.*

Dee Where are you? Why don't you want to see?

Barbara (*voice off*) That's quite enough racket out of you. Quieten down. Breakfast's here.

Scene Thirteen

Ruth *in seclusion. She is wearing a strong canvas gown and sits with her hands over her ears to try and block out the voices.*

Voice Go on then. What's stopping you?

Voice Kill yourself. Kill yourself. Kill yourself.

Voice You'll have to do it sooner or later.

Voice Go on do what he says. I'll help you –

Voice Listen to them Ruth. Kill yourself –

Ruth It can be fatal to try and answer back. Sometimes I have to hum all the songs I know in order of how I learnt them to keep them out. Even then they can still seep in. I get so riled up. Nobody can wind me up like they can. It's my own fault. I let them in, in the beginning. They weren't like they are now, then. When they first started I was in here and they kept me alive. They were kind. They'd say things like 'Try and eat something' or 'Come on stand up and try and keep warm.' They called me a good girl then. They said if I listened to them I'd be all right and I did and was for a time, until they felt they were safely inside and then they turned nasty and it was too late. Now they call me all the time –

Voice Tart –

Voice Whore –

Voice Slut –

Voice Slag, slag, slag –

Ruth I can't understand why they call me a slag. They all do, voices and people. Maybe the voices spoke to the nurses

and told them to call me one. I can't understand. Why?
Why? Isn't that what they call natural, men exploring your
body, doing sexual things to you? Isn't that what we're all
supposed to aim for? Why then do you get called all these
names when it happens? It's happened all my life in much
worse ways in the past, much worse than any of the
category A blokes have done to me in here. There are
people out there who are having a great time who really
fucked me over.

Voice You're talking nonsense again.

Voice Rubbish.

Voice Trash.

Voice But you're a big girl now.

Voice *laughter.*

Ruth (*shouting over the laughter*) I'm not going to fight it, none
of it any more. Except the voices. I'm going to fight them.
(*Quieter.*) But otherwise if a man wants to do something to
me, anything, I let him. I hold my breath until it's over. In
here, I wake up most mornings and see a man in my room.
They never do anything. But every morning I get a fright.
It's their job but they never knock. I've been forcibly
stripped by six men in here and left naked without even a
tampon. I've been watched in the bath by men. They get
paid to do it. And some of them are really kind. This one
nurse, a man, kept me alive when I was in seclusion last
year. I was too far gone to be allowed even a strong gown or
a potty. My distress was too dangerous. I was left naked in
my own blood, shit and piss. But this nurse got me up each
day, took me to the toilet and bath. He couldn't have been
gentler and he never put a foot or any other part of his body
wrong but even if he had I wouldn't have done anything. I
can't connect myself to my body any more.

Voice No, you can't.

Ruth I don't want to anyway. What do I want to go
worrying about other people's carcasses for when I can see
their aura's. I know exactly what they feel. That Barbara

hates me. She's frightened of me. Not what I'll do to her but the bit of me that is her.

Voice She's bad. A very bad person.

Ruth Yes I know.

Voice Not her. You.

Ruth I'm not. I'm not fucking bad.

Voice You fucking bitch, slut, whore –

Ruth Leave me alone you fucking arse hole, fucker, bastard –

Voice She's disgusting. Fancy behaving like that. She's disgusting.

Ruth You're disgusting, evil whores yourselves. You disgust me vile, vile, vile, vile trial –

Claudia *comes in with a mop and bucket.*

Claudia Ruth?

Ruth And you can just get out of here you traitor.

Claudia Ruth, it's me Claud –

Ruth You think you can see me now do you? Sometimes you can and sometimes you can't. Well, I can't see you at all –

Claudia Ruth it's me Claudia, your friend.

Ruth You are not my Mother. Never call yourself that.

Claudia No. It's me Claud, come on.

Ruth (*returns to holding her hands over her ears, rocking her head from side to side. Mutters.*) My mother told me if I was good she would buy me a rubber dolly, sweet trolley, battered brolly, wrong, wrong. Start again. My mother told me. I can't. I can't.

Claudia I'm going to get someone. (*She calls.*) Barbara?

Claudia *goes.* **Ruth** *continues rocking and starts screaming.*

Scene Fourteen

Dee *sits in a wheelchair. Her foot is bandaged. She has several stitches in her arm. She is shaking involuntarily.*

Dee I could kill my body for giving me away. This is such an Alice Through The Looking Glass, arse-about-face existence. No one must reveal what they're feeling. Top show only. Smooth, total control.

  If emotion seeps through that's a sure sign of relapse in this topsy-turvy world. They can act out all the time, all they want but if we laugh and cry in the same day we end up with medication for manic depression.

Sharon *and* **Barbara** *come up behind her and* **Sharon** *starts pushing the wheelchair.*

Barbara (*to* **Sharon**) Sorry. I got delayed. Claudia had a spot of bother with Ruth. (*Nods towards* **Dee**.) Everything all right here?

Sharon Do they ever give lignocaine?

Barbara No.

Sharon The RMO's never give any pain-killer when stitching women up?

Barbara Never. Not for self-inflicted wounds. It only encourages them to go on doing it. Besides they can't feel it.

Sharon But they can. You should have seen the way her body shook afterwards.

Barbara They can't feel it when they do it. Pulling your own toe-nail out and slicing into your breast and arm with it would be a physical impossibility if she could feel it.

Sharon Imagine the pain she must have been in to do it.

Barbara Talk to yourself Barbara, what have I just been saying, she wasn't in any pain. She wouldn't have felt it.

Sharon Oh, yes she was. No doubt you're *au fait* with how a poultice works, a smaller pain to relieve a larger one. That's my point.

Barbara At least we agree that they can't feel it.

Sharon By the time it comes to being sewn up, they can feel it.

Barbara We'll obviously have to agree to differ.

Sharon Excuse me but if they can't feel it how would giving them a pain-killer encourage them to do it again, then?

Barbara I haven't got time to go all round the houses with you now, Nurse.

Sharon No, I don't suppose you do but for what it's worth I think that sewing up women who have cut themselves without the use of anaesthetic merely serves to reinforce the notion that they are shit.

Barbara Rubbish.

Dee People who never feel pain, seldom believe it can be felt.

Barbara What would you know? Just what would you know?

Dee Nothing. I read it in a book.

Barbara That's probably what gave you head-rot reading a book once.

Sharon Barbara, that guy over there, waving. Isn't that Pete?

Barbara Oh yes. I'll just go and have a word with him. You'll be all right, taking Calamity Jane back to the ward?

Sharon Yeah.

Barbara *goes.* **Sharon** *starts pushing the wheelchair.*

Dee Wait, I want to tell you something.

Sharon Tell me when we get back on the ward.

Dee It's important.

Sharon What is it?

Dee The truth.

Sharon Two minutes.

Dee I went to the disco –

Sharon Yes, yes –

Dee I got all dolled up. You saw me. I did it so I would be thought of as more normal and therefore more better I mean betterer. You know what I mean less mad. Am I making any sense?

Sharon Put it this way: I don't feel I should be part of Mensa before I let you go any further.

Dee So I'd made up my mind that I would socialise with the blokes and talk politely, not swear. So this bloke started talking to me –

Sharon Actually he was talking to Ruth –

Dee No, this was before that. The bloke I was talking to started telling me what he was in for. A whole host of right gory details and I thought yeah, who are you to judge, don't judge him because no one's in here for picking –

Sharon Daisies.

Dee Their nose. But then I saw he was getting off on it. I felt furious. Furious. Fur –

Sharon You felt furious.

Dee Yes, but I didn't do nothing. I just started to walk away. Then the next thing I see is that other bloke mauling Ruth and I couldn't stand it. She didn't want it. Why didn't you lot stop it?

Sharon Now you've got that out of your system perhaps you'd go back to the day room?

Dee Two things.

Sharon What?

Dee Did either of those blokes get banged up? No. They most probably got parole for showing such normal behaviour. Secondly, if I was on the outside and I made a relationship with a serial killer or rapist or both you'd consider me mad but that's what you have to do in here to prove you're sane. Now what's more loony, me or that?

Sharon You can't get away with hitting people no matter what the circumstances.

Dee You reckon? (*She stands up.*) In here you can get away with anything as long as you're not a patient.

Sharon Get back in the chair, Dee. Your foot must be very painful.

Dee Fuck off. I'll walk.

Dee *walks off.*

Sharon (*calls after her*) You'll only have to wait for me with the key. (*Then.*) Every day so far I've wondered why I took this job. What a week to start. Yesterday I peeled two BNP stickers off the Charge Nurses office window in the admissions block. So much for good will to all men. Barbara was shocked when I told her, I'll give her that. Most jobs I've had I've felt 'I wish my Mum could see me working'. I've not felt that in here yet.

Scene Fifteen

Ruth *in seclusion. One hand now covers a cut on the side of her head.* **Jackie** *comes in.*

Jackie Barbara said to come and get you. Come on stand up. Don't give me no nonsense. Don't start nothing. It's time for your bath. (*She sees the side of* **Ruth**'*s head.*) Hey, how did that happen? (*Looks at* **Ruth**.) No, you didn't do that, did you? It's like you've been hit with something sharp. Claudia didn't smash your head on the bucket did she? Hey, come on. This shouldn't have happened. If you'd done it to yourself well fair enough but you obviously never.

Ruth I like you.

Jackie You what? Me? Really?

Ruth I know where I am with you. You're what I expect you to be. I like that. I know where I am.

Jackie Oh. I'm not sure what to make of that.

Ruth Do you know about human rights?

Jackie How exactly do you mean like? (*Pause.*) I know about right and wrong and fairness an' that.

Ruth Course you do. Do you like me?

Jackie Like's got nothing to do with it.

Ruth Yeah, but do you?

Jackie What is this, twenty fricking questions? (*Then.*) It's difficult 'cos sometimes you talk daft, and that.

Ruth It's not something I like doing. I could curse myself for doing it.

Jackie I tell you one person who's probably cursing you right now and that's Dee –

Ruth Why, did I shout at her?

Jackie Na, but she's in seclusion for punching that bloke.

Ruth What bloke?

Jackie The bloke you was letting touch you up.

Ruth Oh. Is that why you don't like me?

Jackie I can't understand why you let him do it. It gives them all the wrong ideas.

Ruth Has anything bad ever happened to you?

Jackie Plenty. There was a time when – Oh no you're not worming any more out of me. It wouldn't be professional –

Ruth Bad things don't die you know. All the badness in the world never dies. It goes on and on –

Jackie Like someone else I could mention.

Ruth Someone's bad to you. You don't get the chance to be bad back but then you're bad to someone else because it has to come out. And they have to be bad and it goes on and on without hope, especially if you know the secret of being bad because that means you are mad and then there's only one way to stop it.

Jackie Come on we've had a nice conversation, don't spoil it. Let's get you in the bath and I'll bathe that cut for you.

Ruth Will you?

Jackie Yes, of course.

Ruth Why?

Jackie That's what I'm paid for.

Ruth You're not afraid of the badness then?

Jackie Of course not. Here we go. Have you made a New year's Resolution?

Ruth Yes.

Jackie That's good. See, things can't be all bad can they?

Scene Sixteen

Sharon *is in the office reading the patients' files.* **Jackie** *comes in*

Jackie Hi ya. Fag?

Sharon (*takes one*) Ta. I'm just reading Dee's notes.

Jackie Colourful, eh? If you'll pardon the expression.

Sharon (*decides to ignore it*) Except she's not done anything much.

Jackie Read on. She's been in prison three times.

Sharon For really petty offences –

Jackie Arson!

Sharon All of twenty pounds' worth.

Jackie Assault and she's only twenty-two.

Sharon That makes it worse. This place is the end of the road. No one gets referred on from here. She's twenty-two and she's ended up here.

Jackie You soon learn in this job not to get worked up.

Sharon I've been in this sort of job for ten years.

Jackie Oh yeah, I was forgetting. Tell you what though it's not all doom and gloom, Ruth's better.

Sharon Better?

Jackie Better than she was. Much better. I just gave her a bath. She got into her own night things without any help.

Sharon Where is she now?

Jackie In the day room. It's okay she won't do nothing.

Sharon How can you be certain?

Jackie She's talking sense. Well, for her. And she told me she spent her time in seclusion positively, thinking up New Year's resolutions.

Sharon That is a move in the right direction.

Jackie She's fine in the head, I tell you. On the head's a different matter. She's got a bloody great gash on it.

Barbara *comes in.*

Sharon How did she manage to do that?

Jackie She didn't did she. She never had the wherewithal. It's obvious. It must have been Claudia.

Barbara Did she tell you that?

Jackie Didn't have to. Claudia's the only one been in to see her.

Sharon But Claudia? Are you sure?

Jackie For my money, yes I am. Okay.

Sharon Don't look at me like that, either of you. I'm not going to stick up for her because of the colour of her skin. We're not like white people in that respect. Fairness comes into it. (*Gets up.*)

Barbara Where are you going?

Sharon To clean out Dee's seclusion room. If you're going to put Claudia in it, she's hardly the appropriate person to get it ready. (*She goes.*)

Barbara I didn't say –

Jackie Come on Barb. Dee was in there for punching a male patient in the gob and he wasn't exactly defenceless.

Barbara Do you ever try and put yourself in the patients' shoes?

Jackie Not likely.

Barbara Has it ever occurred to you that seclusion shouldn't be used as punishment?

Jackie But then most of them would get away with murder not that they haven't once anyway.

Barbara Would you take the drugs you have to give out every day?

Jackie Of course I bleeding wouldn't. I don't have to. My behaviour isn't a problem.

Barbara Suppose it was? What would you feel if you ended up here?

Jackie I never would. If I did then I'd deserve to be here and if I'd killed someone then really I shouldn't be alive. I think that's only right.

Barbara So you believe in punishment as a fair way of life?

Jackie Course I do. If you've done something wrong. Gawd, you're as bad as Ruth. All these boring questions.

Barbara Why, what did she ask you?

Jackie Nothing much. But it's not right is it if someone did something to her and they're not punished. What does that say to her? And it's all the worse because she doesn't really have the capacity to retaliate.

Barbara So what do you want me to do?

Jackie Bung Claudia in seclusion.

Barbara We don't have any proof.

Jackie Okay, let's go and ask Ruth.

Barbara In a minute. Finish your fag first.

Scene Seventeen

The washroom. **Claudia** *has found* **Ruth** *hanging from the high rail in the washroom.* **Claudia** *has her arms held up as far as they will go. She is trying to hold* **Ruth**'s *feet up.*

Claudia (*shouts*) Help! Help me. Would somebody please help her? Quickly!

(*Own thoughts.*) Please God don't make her dead. Please, Ruth don't die. I want to keep you alive more than you want to die. And I don't care how selfish that is. You are alive aren't you? Please still be alive. You can't have hanged yourself, not properly. I'd know. I heard somewhere that people shit themselves when their neck breaks. Why won't they come? Why won't they come? I don't want my lasting sodding memory of this place to be one of holding a corpse what shat on me. I don't care how much pain you're in. Don't die you selfish bastard.

(*Shouts.*) Where the fuck are you? You lazy godforsaken bastards. Help me.

Jackie (*off*) The language on her. Don't worry Barb, I'll deal with it. (*She strolls in. Then sees* **Claudia** *and* **Ruth**.) Oh fricking shit. Oh shit me. Shit. (*Shouts.*) Barb? Barb? Quickly. (*She presses the bell.*)

Scene Eighteen

Ruth's *step-mother*, Helen.

Helen I'd never intended going to visit Ruth, not in all
these years. I didn't see why I should, not after what she'd
done and it wasn't as if I was even a blood relation. In fact
she might as well have been dead for all I'd thought about
her. So the decision to go and see her came as rather a bolt
out of the blue. I was listening to Radio Four. I don't
usually. I can't stand those daytime programmes, 'Face
The Facts' and the like. It was an item about clichés of all
things. And I thought, 'Here we go, the ideas people at
Broadcasting House must be on holiday again.' Apparently,
the cliché which summed up the Seventies was 'corridors of
power.' I've forgotten what the Eighties one was supposed
to be but the one for the Nineties, according to this
programme is 'denial'. Well, 'corridors of power', that's
easy. Conjures up Watergate and miserable oak lined
tunnels but 'denial'. My mind went blank. Then of course I
thought 'Judas', 'deny', 'denial'. (*Pause.*) And then me. I
thought, 'me' and I had to sit down. I suddenly felt sick.

I suppose I am one of those people who try and make life
more palatable for themselves by skirting round little
details, like the brutal truth. I'm not a liar, not an out-loud
liar but a sort of avoider, omission maker. It's mostly an
internal process. If I don't like something enough I try hard
not to think about it. The more I don't like it the harder I
try.

When I first met him she was fifteen and quite odd even
then. They were odd with each other, a sort of hold I
couldn't put my finger on. His wife had left, just up and
gone and I thought (God, help me, part of me still does
think), how good of him to take them on. There was a boy
as well. I didn't want any children. It wasn't that I didn't
like them. I just didn't want any. At least I think I felt that.
Now it's really hard to discern what I denied and what I
didn't, but having believed at that time that I'd made that
decision I certainly was less than enthusiastic about looking
after two gawky rather wayward adolescents.

The day it happened shock blocked it out. I might have had to help shut it out but shock can block things out and keep them that way.

I came home from work unexpectedly. I went into the kitchen. My first reaction was to laugh. Awful. He was over her, mostly dressed. She was lying on the table her blouse open, her skirt up. For the merest fraction of a second I think she saw me but then a passive non-expression came over her face and I'm sure she wasn't aware of anything. She looked right through me. It wasn't put on. I walked out. He told me she'd been acting up. She would do that, regularly. And that she'd been rampaging round the kitchen with a knife. And all he'd been doing was trying to restrain her. Of course I believed him. She'd done it before, got a knife out of the drawer. It wasn't far-fetched. Of course I believed him. Of course I did. What a relief. The bit I'd had to work hard at was, well, all it amounted to really was a feeling, a very uneasy one, that it wasn't really like that at all.

Weeks before she stabbed me, she did a lot of negative things to get my attention but I acted like I hadn't seen anything. When she stabbed me it was like, like she was trying to stab some life into me. I know that sounds bonkers. It was so frenzied.

And it was just like that day. She saw me but after less than a second I swear she didn't see me at all.

It doesn't hurt being stabbed, not there and then. Too shocked I suppose for the body to take it in. Afterwards that's a very different matter. She was written off as a bad girl, always bad, took after her mother and even she abandoned her. So of course when this all came back to me I started to wonder what had happened to her. Then I wanted to see her and say something like, 'I know now. I understand why. I don't think it makes it right, what you did to me but I want to help, to make up for the years that I denied what was happening to you.' I didn't just go to the hospital on the spur of the moment. I thought about it for several weeks. Of course it gave her a shock. I tried to call out to her but after the momentary recognition she'd ceased to see me. I telephoned the hospital after Christmas but they said she was too disturbed to have visitors and perhaps, considering the effect I'd had, that it would be best . . . they were very nice about it. I thought I could write but then that too could make it worse, couldn't it? I wonder who I'm doing this for, me or her? Me, I suppose, isn't it? So perhaps sometimes it can be all for the best to pretend things are all right. And if I can't convince myself like I used to then that's my problem not hers.

Scene Nineteen

31st December 1991. The corridor outside the seclusion rooms. **Dee** *looks through an inspection flap. Her speech is slurred and her movement is slow because of the medication.*

Dee Claud, you got to start talking cos it's New Year's Eve and you're not doing yourself any favours. You're supposed to go to the Parole Ward next year. Tomorrow. (*Pokes a cigarette though.*) There you go.

Sharon (*about to walk past*) Dee, you must stop pestering Claudia. She might want to sleep.

Dee She's given up.

Sharon What? Fags?

Dee She shouldn't be banged up you know.

Sharon She assaulted another patient, Dee. Just like you did last week. You'd be the first to get on your high horse if she'd gone unpunished after you had to spend Christmas in there, surely. (*She starts to walk off.*)

Dee You people are full of shit, shit double standards.

Sharon I am not full of shit. Not that I could ever convince you of that. As far as you lot are concerned we're 'them' and we'll never be 'us' and you wouldn't be seen dead communicating with us not on anything remotely resembling a human level. In fact you don't think of us as having feelings at all.

Dee Stop talking shit.

Sharon It's very hard to continue to feel compassionate when you are constantly being told you're full of shit.

Dee You lot behave exactly how you like.

Barbara *walks towards them.*

Barbara There you are, Sharon. What are you accusing my staff of now, Dee?

Dee Being too free with their fists Barbs.

Barbara Let's get the record straight, the day I hit a patient is the day I resign.

Dee You mean the day you admit to –

Barbara Like being on your own do you?

Dee It says in Her Majesty's guidelines does it not, that seclusion should not be used just cos you don't like the look on a patient's face.

Barbara Her Majesty doesn't run this place. We do.

Dee Yeah, and I hope you sleep well at nights.

Barbara We do. Oh, we do. We go home as well. Where will you be going nine o'clock this evening? Cos me and my husband will be at a dinner dance.

Dee I tell you one thing I'm sure as hell glad your husband doesn't work on this ward an' all.

Barbara That's enough.

Dee Cos I've got a double standard. I don't mind seeing some men get hit but I don't like to see women hit.

Barbara Maybe you're even less well than we thought.

Sharon Barb, don't let her wind you up –

Dee (*to Barbara*) Obviously. Look I can hardly control my mouth never mind stand up straight. At least when I was an illegal junkie I used to feel great.

Barbara For your information so did I when I was your age, I used to feel great.

Dee What happened?

Barbara People like you. A job like this. Now get to the day room –

Dee I'm going . . . (*She goes.*)

Sharon Are you okay, Barb?

Barbara This is the last time I offer to work over Christmas. I can well do without it.

Sharon Overtime's handy though.

Barbara Yes, but my New Year's resolution is to have a bit more of a home life. (*She goes.*)

Sharon (*To the inspection flap*) Listen, Claudia, please start talking. I know you feel you've been treated unfairly but unless you put your side nobody's going to be able to decide one way or the other.( ) Okay. (*She puts her face right up to the inspection flap.* **Claudia** *spits at her.*) That's your top priority in life, is it? To spit on me. You think that's going to help you, eh? I didn't see you as stupid but I obviously misjudged you. (*She walks off.*)

Scene Twenty

6th January 1992. **Ruth** *sits in a wheelchair.* **Jackie** *brings her a meal.*

Jackie There you go.

Ruth Do you know when I can get up?

Jackie I dunno why you have to stay here. Nothing wrong with your legs?

Ruth No.

Jackie You're probably only in that so we know where you are then and don't have to watch your every move, every minute of the day.

Ruth I'm sorry.

Jackie What for?

Ruth Well, you seem to be angry.

Jackie Listen, I stuck my neck out for you. And I ended up looking a right dick-head didn't I? What did you want to go and kill yourself for anyway?

Ruth I . . . well . . .

Jackie Was it to do with that er . . . visit?

Ruth I expect so.

Jackie Did you not realise that she was still alive?

Ruth No, I did know she was. But when I did it I thought I'd killed her so it doesn't make much moral difference.

Jackie I expect it does – to her.

Ruth What does she want with me now?

Jackie Sharon spoke to her. She said she wanted to tell you that it was all okay.

Ruth Really? Well, you can tell Sharon to tell her that it's me that hasn't forgiven her. There are worse things than being knifed you know.

Jackie Really? A list of them isn't exactly springing to mind.

Ruth Being betrayed.

Jackie That's worse than being stabbed within an inch of your life? Do me a favour.

Ruth Yes, I am bad. (*To one of the voices.*) Yes, I am bad. (*To another voice.*) I've said I am, haven't I? Bad, bad –

Jackie Don't start that up again. It was wrong what you done and you must never do it again but you served your time now ain't yer?

Ruth How can I have? I'm still here.

Jackie You've been in here longer than you would have been in prison if you'd murdered her.

Ruth Yeah, but I'm not right.

Jackie You can't be that bad if you're aware that you're not a hundred per cent. It's just that you will keep giving yourself setbacks.

Ruth When I did it, I could hear someone screaming, like it was coming from outer space. It wasn't her and it wasn't me. I went out of the house and the air felt cold and my hand felt wet. There was blood pouring out of it. The handle had come off the knife and cut into my hand. I went into the chemist. There was a young girl serving. She put a bandage on it. Didn't charge me anything. Said I should go to the casualty department.

Jackie Yeah?

Ruth I walked there. I don't remember how long it took me or anything but I knew where it was because I'd been there before. I was sitting in the waiting area when two policemen came up to me. They asked me my name and I told them. They asked me where I'd just come from and I gave them the address. They asked me if I'd assaulted my step-mother and I said yes. The two of them just looked at each other. You see they knew I was mental because I was telling the truth.

Jackie Do you think you are?

Ruth There's something not quite right about me. Cos I killed the wrong one didn't I? When I was doing it I stopped seeing her. All I could see was him.

Jackie See you're still talking about killing someone. That's not going to go in your favour is it?

Ruth Yeah, I don't suppose I'd ever be allowed to join Friends of the Earth.

Jackie You're not helping yourself are you?

Ruth I've not had much practice in here.

Jackie Why do you allow yourself to be knocked around?

Ruth What do you suggest I do?

Jackie If someone smacks you, you smack them back but harder. You shouldn't let that Claudia get away with it. She struts around here like she's Miss Penwell Hospital '92.

Ruth *laughs*.

Jackie Yeah, she does doesn't she?

Ruth It wasn't Claudia.

Jackie Oh. Who was it, then?

Ruth You don't want to know.

Jackie Course I do.

Ruth You'll hate me if I tell you.

Jackie Of course I won't, tell me.

Ruth Barbara.

Jackie (*laughs*) Who was it really?

Ruth I told you, you wouldn't like it.

Jackie It's not a question of not liking it. I simply don't believe it.

Ruth And for your information it's not just me and it wasn't just the once.

Jackie Don't talk rubbish. I thought you were so much better.

Ruth When people don't believe me it drives me mad.

Jackie When people lie to me I feel crazy. For your information. (*She goes.*)

Ruth Me too, that as well. Me too. Don't go –

Scene Twenty-One

The nurses' office. **Claudia** *sits behind the desk reading her notes which are covered by a copy of 'the Guardian' which covers her face.* **Jackie** *storms in.*

Jackie (*thinking she's talking to* **Sharon**) Gawd, where'd you get that paper from? One of the posh old roosters on the gerri ward? That's where that Ruth will end up. Yer know there's no bleeding hope for her. There again, I s'pose if you can see and hear things what aren't there it automatically gives you a hand up when it comes to lying. The fact that she can't even tell what's fact and what's not makes her untrustworthy, don't it? Guess what? Guess what she reckons now? That Barb hit her. Yeah, that's right, Barb. Well, that's it as far as I'm concerned I've washed me hands of her. You was right you know to warn me not to get too emotionally involved. You know last week I actually thought I could help her. Huh, maybe it's me what's not right in the head, eh? Excuse me anyone home? What's so interesting in that paper?

Claudia The New Year's Honours List.

Jackie Oh blimey, you hoping you'll be in it one day then?

Claudia *laughs.*

Jackie What you laughing for? Don't they have Black people in there or something?

Claudia Maybe I am on it. After all, John McCarthy and Terry Waite are and I've been in here longer than they were –

Jackie Eh, yer what?

Barbara *comes in.*

Barbara Claudia, will you please get off my chair?

Jackie Who? (*Sees it's* **Claudia**.) Oh frick me, what the – I thought –

Claudia There's only two Black people on this ward, it's totally understandable that you'd get them mixed up.

Jackie I thought you were still in seclusion.

Claudia I still would be if someone hadn't decided to own up to the truth.

Barbara It was a misunderstanding, Claudia. I thought we agreed –

Jackie What were you doing in here on your own – ?

Claudia Barbara said I could. We've just made a little bargain –

Barbara I thought we'd come to an understanding. That the whole thing was an accident, a mistake.

Claudia Like me getting turned down at my tribunal was a mistake? It couldn't possibly have anything to do with this subjective, rubbishy nonsense I've just read in my notes –

Jackie Give those back. They're not yours to – Barb, what's the matter with you? Just tell her.

Claudia (*reading*) Walks arrogantly, talks in a loud voice, claims racism, paces up and down in her room at night, calls us white trash.

Barbara Claudia, we can talk about this later –

Claudia Later? Later? In another ten years perhaps? How long has this, this, fucking shit been following me around?

Jackie What you so wild about? None of it is lies.

Claudia Claims racism? What a laugh, what a laugh. You know what I'm called on the punishment block?

Jackie It's called intensive care actually.

Barbara Jackie.

Claudia Oh we know we can always rely on you Jackie to call a spade a spade.

Jackie Are you just going to stand there and let her get away with wagging her finger at you in your own office?

Claudia Yes, why are you, Barbara?

Barbara Claudia, I thought we'd settled –

Claudia That was before I saw this. My claim of racism was just the once. This is the 1990s and that white trash on your so-called intensive care ward call me Niggs, not just the once but repeatedly, like it was my name. I wouldn't care but as a insult, Nigger went out with the ark.

Jackie Yeah, but they don't mean nothing by it, it's only teasing, they say it nicely –

Claudia And the last time I complained about it was five years ago. I'd never have got on this ward if I'd even thought about racism. And this 'Talks in a loud voice' –

Jackie Huh, well, if you'd just listen to yourself –

Claudia You have heard nothing yet –

Barbara Oh I have, thank you.

Claudia I'm not going to keep my side of the bargain. You can't stop me. I'm going to expose this.

Jackie Plenty of people have read those notes over the years.

Claudia Not those. You –

Jackie Make sure you spell my name properly.

Claudia Not you, her. (*To* **Barbara**.) You making me carry the can for something you did.

Barbara This is old ground. I've already apologised –

Jackie You've apologised? To her? For what?

Claudia She's bashed patients around for years and got away with it but now she's decided to start blaming it on the other patients.

Barbara You have a choice Claudia. You are due on the Parole Ward at the end of the week. And you will get there if you leave the office now. If you don't you'll go back in seclusion, your disruptive behaviour will be well documented in that file and you know there's no one around who'll dispute it and what's more you know you won't get another chance to go on the Parole Ward this side of Easter.

Claudia I'm going but I'll make sure I spell every one of your names correctly. (*She goes.*)

Barbara I wouldn't bother wasting the life of the biro if I was you.

Silence.

Jackie It wasn't her?

Barbara What wasn't?

Jackie Ruth's cut?

Barbara No.

Jackie Who was it?

Barbara I think it must have been me.

Jackie You?

Barbara Yes.

Jackie You think?

Barbara Yes.

Jackie It was you?

Barbara My keys must have accidentally banged against Ruth's head.

Jackie You?

Barbara It wasn't intentional.

Jackie You bashed Ruth's head?

Barbara Afternoon, Doctor Reed.

Jackie (*smiles as he goes past, then*) Gawd, someone should put blakies on his shoes. Sorry but –

Barbara I didn't do it on purpose.

Jackie But you –

Barbara Look, for God's sake, Jackie. Why the big fuss? She tried to kill herself soon afterwards. She'd be dead now if it wasn't for you and me. I hardly think a graze on the head would have made any difference to a corpse.

Jackie But then you put Claudia –

Barbara It was you who told me Claudia had done it –

Jackie But you must have known –

Barbara I didn't realise I'd done it.

Jackie I'd have to be eight cans of lager short of a picnic to swallow that.

Barbara I didn't realise I'd cut her. And, of course the bruising didn't show straight away –

Jackie But you let Claudia take the blame, Claudia who'd just saved Ruth's life, who –

Barbara Who you saw in here just now trying to hold me over a barrel, when I'd gone out of my way to try and make it up to her.

Jackie Yeah well if it was me I'd want to smack you in the mouth.

Barbara So full of righteous indignation aren't you?

Jackie I believe in fair play, yes.

Barbara Don't make me laugh. You don't know the meaning of the word. You somehow think the rules and regulations in this place are fair, and in the meantime you decide to blow your ration of integrity over a little mistake.

Jackie All I'm saying is, Claudia was innocent.

Barbara Oh, yes? Look what was found when she was stripped. (*Holds up three-amp fuse.*)

Jackie What is it?

Barbara The fuse for the TV.

Jackie Her?

Barbara Just goes to show, no one in here is innocent.

Jackie Yeah, but that still don't . . .

Barbara You'd have had her put in seclusion for that though.

Jackie Well, yes.

Barbara So as she's already been in there she won't have to go again. That's fair –

Jackie But you? I mean, I never, not in a million years –

Barbara I didn't mean to hurt her, really I didn't. I was trying to get her to stand up. I did grab her roughly and her head bashed against the keys.

Jackie But to let Claudia –

Barbara She's hardly a defenceless victim is she? You saw how she was.

Jackie Yeah. Huh, I notice she didn't dispute the stuff about her being arrogant. She couldn't. Do you think she will complain?

Barbara So what if she does?

Jackie I suppose she's lucky we didn't threaten to get the police in over that fuse. It is stealing after all.

Barbara That's the spirit.

Jackie You taking the piss or what?

Barbara No, no. Just applauding your attitude, fair play, give and take, take and take, compromise, it's all right really –

The phone rings.

Barbara (*picks up phone*) Hello. () Yes it's me. (*To* **Jackie**.) It's Pete. (**Jackie** *goes.*) No, just Jackie. () She's gone. () Oh supper? I thought pork pies. () Just a joke. I didn't mean it. () What do you mean, what does that mean? You should know what 'Didn't mean it' means. It's one of your favourite phrases. () Nothing. Nothing's got into me. ()

What? You'll do what? Just what are you going to do?
Come over here and nut me perhaps? Why not, after all this
is a nut house. () Good question. Just who do I think I am?
And how did I become that person? Answers on a postcard.
(*She bangs the phone down.*)

Scene Twenty-Two

30th January 1992. **Dee** *sits in a chair.* **Sharon** *is standing at
the medication trolley. She is counting out tablets. She gives* **Dee** *a
cup of water and a fistful of tablets.*

Sharon Dee? PRN. Quite a spectrum of tablets today.
Look, all colours of the rainbow. (*No response.*) Come on you
don't want an injection. Come on be an angel.

Dee I can't. She's gone.

Sharon Who has?

Dee The angel.

Sharon Come on don't mess me about. You know we're
short-staffed this afternoon.

Dee Barb said she'd get me a glass of water.

Sharon She can't, she's had to go and see the administrator
but I'll get it for you.

Dee Please, would yer, I'm – I can't seem to stop being
thirsty.

Sharon Yes, I've said so haven't I? Come on, perk up, your
solicitor's coming to see you this afternoon.

Dee What for?

Sharon Your tribunal.

Dee I can't be arsed. Sorry, I mean bothered. Sorry, I
didn't mean to swear.

Sharon Let's hope these (*Meaning the tablets.*) pep you up
then. One, two, three down the hatch.

Scene Twenty-Three

Barbara *sits in the Administrators' office talking to an 'independent person' who seems very sympathetic to her.*

Barbara Well, I was expecting to see Mr Arnold. What are you, sort of like a floating administrator? () More independent? () Oh I see. () Well isn't this making rather a big deal out of it? () Well, with the stuff that goes on here all the time to take a little knock so seriously. () Yes, I appreciate that. () How did you find out about it? () Can't you? () No, I suppose not. () No I'm not denying that she got a light tap. I've already said as much but it wasn't what you think. () My keys knocked against her head. () She was just sitting there. () On her mattress. () In seclusion. Passive, well inert, except for her head which was rocking rhythmically from side to side like some great pendulum, on a Grandfather clock. Tick, tock, tick, tock and I hit her. () How? I took my bunch of keys and swung them round in the air several times – I swear to God if she'd said 'please don't' if she said anything even, then I wouldn't but she just kept doing it so I timed it for when her head came back to my side of her and bang, caught her full on the side of her head. () Oh, her head's all right now. Well externally. () It was only superficial, I assure you. () What did I feel?

   Regret, remorse, naturally. I feel disgusted with myself. () Then? I felt just the same as I've just told you. () Perhaps at the time I felt angry, I felt furious, in a rage. () Actually, when I hit her I felt like laughing. I did laugh. I felt full of glee, smug, pleased with myself and then I felt bad, very bad. I still feel bad. () No, I've not done it again. () No, she's never hit me. () (*Touches her face.*) Oh, that. My husband and I have rows every now and again. () Yes, sometimes but I hit him back. Besides this is where I slipped, anyway I didn't come here to talk about him. () I still feel angry. () More to do with the fact that she just took it. I'd feel relieved, validated if she retaliated. Do you know what I mean? (*Pause.*) Not long after that she tried to kill herself. () Of course I feel implicated. When someone, anyone you know tries to kill themselves you feel responsible

no matter who they are, never mind if it's your job to make
sure they don't, that you are paid to make sure they don't.
() Of course I find it difficult to cope with. Of course I do.
Wouldn't you? You'd have to be mental to think 'Oh God,
there's all these women in despair everyday all around me,
trying to kill themselves but that's nothing'. () Well, no it's
not exactly her behaviour I'm angry with but this blaming
everything on something else, on the past. It's no excuse is
it? () Oh well we're all entitled to our own opinion. But for
my money too much is made of it. What good does it do
carping on about these things? You've just got to get on
with life. She's no better now, Ruth. Lets blokes get away
with murder. () (*Long pause.*) I'm angry because she allowed
it to happen in the first place. () No, not me hitting her.
Him. () Him, who ever he was who abused her. I hate her
for it. () I hate it. () What is all this about? Why are you
picking on me? All these years and years of complaints.
People have done far worse things than catch a patient on
the side of her head with a bunch of keys I can tell you. ()
Well no, of course I'm not going to do it again. () Look I've
told you the truth, I thought that would be the last of it. ()
You can't discipline me not just for that. Come off it. What
is this?

Scene Twenty-four

*15th April 1992. The nurses' office which is decorated with
one or two 'home' made Easter bunnies.* **Sharon** *is now the
acting Ward Sister. There are three breakfast trays on her desk.*

Jackie *comes in.*

Jackie (*giving* **Sharon** *a packet of cigarettes*) There yer go,
Sister. Sorry, I was so long there was a right queue at the
shop.

Sharon Thanks. D'you want one? (*Opens the packet. Gives her
one.*)

Jackie Ta. I'll just have this and then I'll go and get her
majesty from the Parole Ward –

Sharon She can wait. The main gate have just rung to say the new nurse is on her way over. Would you meet her first?

Jackie Sure. I just saw Pete over the shop. He said she looks a right cracker.

Sharon Got a crêpe paper dress on has she?

Jackie Listen, I'm just glad he's still talking to me.

Sharon Look he knows that Doctor Reed overheard you. You didn't grass.

Jackie I hope so. Anyway I think he's okay about it cos he asked me if we'd heard from Barb.

Sharon Hardly likely if he hasn't.

Jackie That's what I said. Fancy, someone like her, leaving her husband and job without a word to no one.

Sharon She's a good nurse.

Jackie She'll be well fricked when it comes to references.

Sharon We all will, if they decide to take up every patient's little complaint.

Jackie They won't. Now they've been seen to do one they can sit back. Even then they wouldn't have done nothing if it was just Claudia. But then Ruth's Aunt wrote on that headed notepaper and Doctor broken Reed thought he'd chime in with his eavesdropping evidence. Bastard. Landing me right in the shit.

Sharon I bet Claudia regrets it more than you.

Jackie We warned her. It's not our fault she didn't believe it. Whatever else some of the staff in this place are they're loyal to each other.

Ruth *comes in.*

Ruth Can you, please come –

Jackie We've got a nice surprise for you –

Ruth Please it's –

Jackie Claudia's coming back. Remember you and her were always thick if you'll pardon the expression.

Ruth Please. Please will you come –?

Sharon We thought you'd be pleased. Ruth, what is it?

Ruth Dee.

Jackie What about her?

Ruth I don't know.

Sharon (*to* **Jackie**) I'll deal with it. Perhaps you'd go and meet the new nurse.

Sharon *and* **Ruth** *go.* **Jackie** *walks towards the audience.*

Jackie (*as if to the new nurse*) Oh, there you are. You found your way all right? I was just coming over to get you. Hello with the emphasis on hell. Welcome to Head-rot Hotel.

THE MADNESS OF
ESME AND SHAZ

The Madness of Esme and Shaz was first presented by the
English Stage Company at the Royal Court Theatre,
London in association with the Royal National Theatre
Studio on 10 February 1994, with the following cast:

Esme	Marlene Sidaway
Dena	Susan Porrett
Natalie/Lucy	Helen Anderson
Pat	Wendy Nottingham
Shaz	Tanya Ronder
Joan/Julie	Philippa Williams

Director Jessica Dromgoole
Designer Kate Owen
Lighting Designer Jenny Kagan
Sound Designer Paul Arditti

Characters

Esme	Aged 65
Shaz	Aged 33
Pat	Twenties
Dena	Esme's neighbour
Nathalie	Shaz's probation officer
Lucy	Admin. assistant for the DSS
Julie	Shaz's Psychiatrist
Joan	Police Officer

Part One

Scene One

Esme's *living room*. **Esme** *sits at her piano and has reached the last verse of a none-too-wonderful rendition of the hymn*, Dear Lord and Father of Mankind. *Always mindful of the neighbours above and below, it is neither full throttle nor full throated, however on '. . . Let sense be dumb, let flesh retire;' there is a persistent banging from the flat below and by the time she gets to '. . . Oh still small voice of calm' it is accompanied by a loud knocking on the front door.*

Dena (*shouts off*) Esme. Esme –

Esme *gets up and opens the door to* **Dena**.

Dena Esme, Esme, my love. . .

Esme I wasn't going full pelt, Dena. And it's only three o'clock in the afternoon.

Dena You know me, cripes, I don't mind. I really don't but Kenny's on nights and he can't have you pounding away, it's not fair.

Esme The thing is –

Dena It's just that these conversions, as you know, as you well know, aren't built for noise. You carry on like this and we'll have a repeat of the walls of Jericho on our hands.

Esme But Dena, it's not as if –

Dena Esme, please, you've got to make an effort to see it from our side. (*Touching the collar on* **Esme**'*s dress*) Now, that's a very nice bit of crocheting, yours?

Esme (*stepping back*) Yes.

Dena Certainly managing to fill your time.

Esme Mmmm.

Dena You've not been in long. Been to town?

Esme Just to meet Joyce –

Dena Is that your friend? Doesn't time just whirl –

Esme Does it?

Dena It only seems like three weeks since you saw her, not three months. And how's she taking to being pensioned off. I thought you met every three months –?

Esme Actually it has only been six weeks. She's off to Canada in a fortnight for a holiday so we brought our lunch forward. She's got family –

Dena Oh, that reminds me, my spare key. The decorators start the day after tomorrow. Let's hope so anyway because I've got the new hall carpet synchronised with its completion give or take a late start or a tea break or two. Isn't it exciting? Much better than a few days abroad. (*She goes over to the piano and picks up the sheet music while* **Esme** *goes and gets the key.*) Couldn't you just study the music and thereby cut down on so much trial and error on the actual piano?

Esme (*gives* **Dena** *the key*) I always promised myself that when I retired I'd learn to play –

Dena Esme, look –

Esme Don't worry I won't play it again today.

Dena Thank you so much. You know I don't like to ask. Now I don't suppose I could interest you in some raffle tickets –

Esme Dena, Dena, you know I don't –

Dena Agree. I know, I know, but they were always having lotteries and short straws in the Bible, weren't they? So I can't see what –

Esme As far as I can recall, none of the disciples won a time share or a microwave oven with a ten pence ticket in aid of 'Save The Children'.

Dena Maybe not, but then there's no mention of any of them needing a kidney machine.

Esme It's the principle, Dena.

Dena What, spending money? No, I'm pulling your leg.

Esme Getting something for nothing.

Dena And I thought you were one of the few left who did believe in the National Health?

Esme It's raffle tickets I don't believe in.

Dena I was only teasing.

Esme Oh.

Dena Don't worry I won't press you. I have to go, Kenny's tea will be burnt to a crisp –

Esme But I thought –

Dena He's going straight to bed after. Cheeri-bye-o and thanks a lot my love.

Dena *goes.* **Esme** *goes over to the piano and closes the lid. She picks up the block calender from the top of the piano and tears off the slip for the day.*

Esme (*reading the text*) 'Believe in the Lord Jesus and you will be saved, you and your entire household.' At least it doesn't say 'Love thy neighbour as thyself.' (*Knock at the door.*) Oh, no she's heard me. Either that or I made too much noise ripping it off. Please Lord forgive me if I find myself telling a lie of necessity. (*Calls.*) I'll be right there Dena. (*Opens the door to* **Natalie**.) Oh I beg your pardon. Sorry, I thought you were my neighbour –

Natalie Ms Huntley?

Esme Miss.

Natalie Oh, good. My name's Natalie Goddard. I'm from the probation service. (*She shows* **Esme** *her ID.*)

Esme You better come in. Don't tell me I've picked up something and not paid for it while shopping. No, I can't have. I . . . oh no, what have I done?

Natalie Please, please, Ms Huntley –

Esme Miss. Esme, Esme.

Natalie No, no it's nothing like that, you've done nothing. You've not done anything. It's nothing you've done. If you see what I mean.

Esme It's something I haven't done?

Natalie I did write to you making an appointment to come and see you but the letter got stuck in 'typing' and as I had to come out this way today I thought I'd just call in on the off-chance. I hope it's not inconvenient.

Esme Err . . . no. Not now I'm retired. Three months ago it would have been a different story –

Natalie Oh, how's that?

Esme I'd have been at work. I'm sorry, do sit down.

Natalie Thanks. Actually, I'm here about your niece, Sharon.

Esme Who?

Natalie Sharon?

Esme I don't have a niece.

Natalie Oh no. I'm so sorry. I expect someone at the Salvation Army's made yet another monumental clock up. You didn't have a brother called Edward or Ted Huntley?

Esme No.

Natalie I'm really sorry to have disturbed you. (*She gets up to go.*)

Esme Suppose I did?

Natalie But you just said –

Esme I did.

Natalie Yes, I thought you said you didn't –

Esme I did. Have a brother called Ted. Is he dead then?

Natalie I don't think so.

Esme Only you used the past tense.

Natalie Did I? I'm so sorry, we seem to have got a bit mixed up. I thought you said –

Esme I believe I have a brother. Did have. But we lost touch. So for years it's been as though I didn't have one. In so much as I've never mentioned him to anyone so if anyone asks it's easier to say 'no' than to come out with the whole rigmarole. I certainly didn't know he had any children.

Natalie Must have been quite a while ago. Your niece will be thirty-three this year.

Esme Oh.

Natalie I do apologise, this must have come as a terrible shock to you.

Esme Not really. I'm hardly likely to start missing her, am I. So, nephews? Do I have any of those?

Natalie Again, I'm sorry but I don't know.

Esme We hear heaps about adopted children trying to find their real parents –

Natalie Birth.

Esme Pardon?

Natalie Birth parents, that's what they, we, call them, now.

Esme Really?

Natalie Sorry, I interrupted you.

Esme I was only going to say, I didn't realise that it extended to real . . . err birth Uncles and Aunts. But she must have known about me.

Natalie Ah, well, it's not exactly like that. It's a titchy-witchy bit more complicated. Your niece is in err, a hospital. But she's well. She's not been well but she is now. Well. And well, she's due to be re –. Discharged, discharged but we can't find a hostel place for her for money nor money, ha. So we're checking to see if there's any relatives who are suitable for her to stay with.

Esme But –

Natalie Please, don't be alarmed. It obviously isn't suitable for her to stay with you. You don't even know her.

Esme What about my, err birth brother?

Natalie Well, always assuming he is alive, it's not appropriate either. She doesn't want to live with him.

Esme She's expressed a wish to live with me?

Natalie Not as far as I'm aware. She doesn't know we're contacting you, no point in raising her hopes if –

Esme She's well you say?

Natalie Oh yes. All the doctors agree.

Esme How long has she been in hospital?

Natalie Umm . . . thirteen years.

Esme Thirteen?

Natalie You see, that's why she can't come out and live on her own. She's been institutionalised. The adjustment would be too difficult for her to manage alone –

Esme She's been in a mental hospital?

Natalie Psychiatric. Psychiatric. As I said I don't think it appropriate.

Esme (*smooths out the text which is still crumpled in her hand and looks at it*) I could go and visit her, meet her, that couldn't do much harm –

Natalie No, but –

Esme I've not got much on. That's the trouble with retirement. No matter how much one looks forward to it beforehand, the luxury of the lie-in, like everything else becomes tedious after the first week –

Natalie Sounds like the sort of tedium I could just about endure.

Esme Yes, sorry. Fancy probation officers now finding

people's relatives, I expect you're having to do the job of several people these days.

Natalie Umm, not quite. It's –

Esme Sharon you say. What's her surname?

Natalie Last name. It's Huntley.

Esme She didn't marry either?

Natalie She didn't exactly get much of an opportunity. Not of course that marriage should necessarily be seen as an opportunity, as such, for everyone, anyone, I suppose, but then again –

Esme No, err yes, no, of course. Now which hospital did you say she was in?

Natalie Actually it's an RSU.

Esme Arrest you?

Natalie R-S-U. Regional Secure Unit.

Esme And what's that when it's at home?

Natalie A sort of half-way place between where she's been and the community.

Esme And where has she been?

Natalie An establishment for those with, umm, challenging mental health who have, err, have come off worse in a confrontation with the penal system.

Esme Like where?

Natalie Like . . . err . . . Broadmoor, for instance.

Esme (*the text falls from her hand and flutters to the floor*) For . . . for, what?

Natalie That's confidential information. She'll have to tell you that herself I'm afraid.

Scene Two

A week later.

Shaz (Sharon) *is in her room watching television. She is wearing a tee-shirt and tracksuit bottoms. Her arms are badly scarred.* **Doctor Morton (Julie)** *knocks on the door and comes in.* **Shaz** *grabs a sweatshirt which is lying on the floor and hurriedly puts it on.*

Julie What are you doing?

Shaz (*still watching the television*) Learning Australian.

Julie Do you mind if I sit down? (*She sits.*)

Shaz What's happened? Something fucking terrible's happened.

Julie No, why should it?

Shaz You coming to find me in the middle of the day and making yourself at home in my room for two things –

Julie I wanted to make sure you were okay –

Shaz Oh right. And now the bleeding hospital Social Worker's left I suppose you had no alternative but to ask here, at the horse's sodding mouth. How d'you expect me to be? By rights I should have left this dump precisely eleven months and twelve days ago but instead of being treated like the special case I'm s'posed to have been all these years everybody appears to have jumped off of my bleeding case all of a fucking sudden –

Julie Sharon –

Shaz No, don't try and bribe me with medication –

Julie Excuse me. Thank you. I wanted to find out how you are and to let you know that you've got a visitor.

Shaz Well, why didn't one of the poxy nurses tell me? Why have you had to drag yourself away from the main building? Oh Jesus God. It's not –

Julie It's your Aunt.

Shaz I did have an Aunt, then?

Julie So it seems.

Shaz What's she like?

Julie You'll find out soon enough.

Shaz D'you think she'll want me?

Julie Sharon. Shaz.

Shaz She don't. She don't.

Julie She didn't even know of your existence until last week. It's very early days.

Shaz Yeah. Right. Right.

Julie But I wanted you to be prepared, in case she doesn't come back to visit you again or in case you don't get on.

Shaz What's she like then?

Julie Well, she's a pensioner –

Shaz I guessed she must be. Christ, what d'you take me for?

Julie Oh yes, and her faith seems very important to her.

Shaz Oh, Jesus.

Julie Yes, her Christian faith.

Shaz He said –

Julie Who?

Shaz He, him, it. Her brother. Told me she left home when she was eighteen and they never heard of her again. So she must be quite game.

Julie That isn't the impression I formed, Shaz. She's a very quiet, nicely spoken, retired civil servant who's spent most of her life in the suburbs.

Shaz She ain't going to take to me then is she?

Julie Well . . .

Shaz Tell her I can't have visitors, eh? Or something. Don't sound like it's worth the fiasco.

Julie Shaz, I'll be straight with you –

Shaz Are yer?

Julie What?

Shaz Straight?

Julie Yes, as it turns out –

Shaz Shame.

Julie I meant I'll be honest with you.

Shaz I know, I know. Fucking hell, I was only mucking about.

Julie I think it highly unlikely that a woman in her sixties, who's lived alone for most of her adult life is going to start to share her flat with anyone. So I wouldn't build any hopes on that. But, I can't see any reason why she shouldn't like you. However if she doesn't, that could well be her problem, not yours.

Shaz I might not like her.

Julie Exactly. Are you going to give it a go?

Shaz But you just said it's highly unlikely –

Julie I meant, meet her –

Shaz Ain't got nothing to fucking lose.

Julie Maybe you could lose a few expletives?

Shaz Yeah I suppose that's not a bad idea. Come on then doctor throw me to the Christians.

Julie That's more like it. She's in the day room.

Shaz Aren't yer going ter come with me?

Julie I'm sure I'll find out how you got on soon enough.

Shaz Yeah, right.

Julie *goes.* **Shaz** *makes sure she's gone and then runs a hand through her hair and brushes the real or imagined dandruff off her sweatshirt.*

Scene Three

The day room. It has one small window with a bar across it on the outside wall. **Esme** *sits one side of a table which has several overflowing ashtrays on it. She takes a compact mirror out of her handbag and pats her hair in place.*

Esme (*shuts her eyes*) Dear Lord I know if this is your will, you will signal it in your own way. And please then give me the perception to hear you. Amen. (*She snaps the mirror shut and puts it in her handbag.*) Oh and if it's not too much to ask, and if it's also your will, please make her like me and help me take to her. (*She stops as Shaz comes in.*)

Esme (*extending her hand and trying to conceal her shock at* **Shaz**'s *appearance*) Hello, you must be Sharon.

Shaz Yeah. (*She sits down.*) They tell me you're me Aunt –

Esme They tell me you're my niece –

Shaz D'you think they made a mistake, then?

Esme Well, err I . . .

Shaz More like you're hoping they did. S'all right. S'okay. No sweat. (*She stands up.*)

Esme No 1 – . Please sit down again –

Shaz Wizz-e-wig, with me. What you see is what you get. It's a computer term. W.Y.S.I.W.Y.G. See.

Esme Do you do computer courses in here, then?

Shaz You must be bleeding, oh shit, sorry, joking. Na, no it was something I picked up off of the telly.

Pause.

Esme Do you have any hobbies?

Shaz Apart from watching TV you mean?

Esme Well, yes.

Shaz I enjoy listening to music and that.

Pause.

Esme I've got a piano.

Shaz Oh, really?

Esme It's second-hand.

Shaz Yeah?

Esme I bought it when I retired.

Pause.

Shaz Listen, it was nice of you to come and see me and that. I do appreciate it. We know what we look like now. Maybe I'll give you a bell when I get out, eh?

Esme Oh, they've found you somewhere to stay have they?

Shaz Not yet, but it's only a matter of time. Huh, only a matter of time. Hark at me.

On the word 'hark' the sun comes out. It shines through the window, causing the shadow of the bars across the window to fall in the shape of a large cross on the table. **Sharon** *doesn't even notice this. However, for* **Esme** *it's the sign she's been looking for but secretly hoping wouldn't appear.*

Esme (*shuts her eyes*) Oh, Lord, well if you're sure.

Shaz Sure? Well, nothing's –. Here, you all right?

Esme (*to* **Shaz**) I'm an old age pensioner –

Shaz Yeah. I know. Doctor Morton told me. Aren't you well then?

Esme (*to God*) Into thy hands I commend my spirit.

Shaz Do what? For Christsakes don't snuff it in front of me. They'd never believe it was natural causes.

Esme I have never suffered any ill health. In fact the

Personnel Officer gave me a certificate when I retired. It was one she made herself you understand. It wasn't anything official, a sort of jokey diploma, because I'd never had a day's sickness in all my working life.

Shaz Oh yeah? Nice. It was just that it sounded like you was chanting part of the burial service.

Esme Did it? Do you go to church then?

Shaz Only when someone I know, kills themselves like.

Esme I'm sorry.

Shaz So am I. Usually.

Esme You must think I'm a bit off my chump.

Shaz Yer what?

Esme It's just my way. I'm always shooting little prayers like arrows heaven-wards. I'm afraid it's something you'll have to get used to.

Shaz S'okay, I was warned you was religious.

Esme I live in a flat in Eden Park, which is approximately thirty minutes on the train, on a good day, from town. London. It has two bedrooms, a kitchen, bathroom and living room.

Shaz That's nice for you.

Esme Yes, I like to think it is. I do believe in God, and that we are all sinners but that God sent his only son, Jesus Christ to save the world.

Shaz I expect I'm a bigger sinner than you, though.

Esme And I have three house rules: that nobody wilfully damages me or my property, privacy in the bathroom, and that nobody blasphemes.

Shaz Very interesting. What you telling me for?

Esme Because those are the rules if you want to come and live with me.

Shaz Fucking hell. Blimey – Do what?

Esme I know you must be used to swearing and it will be hard for you to get out of the habit but I must insist that you don't blaspheme.

Shaz What did I say? What did I say? Fucking's only swearing, isn't it? It isn't in the Bible, is it?

Esme B-l-i-m-e-y-. It means God blind me.

Shaz Blimey, does it? Shit. Jesus. Sorry, sorry. Look I'll practice. Are you sure? I mean, you don't really know a thing about me.

Esme Well, you're my niece –

Shaz But, I mean, far be it from me to say but aren't you taking a bit of a gamble –

Esme No, I'm not. I don't believe in it. And I've been reassured that what I see is what I get.

Shaz But don't go imagining I look better with make up. I don't.

Esme What people look like externally is of no consequence to me. God, looks on the inside.

Shaz Oh Jesus. (*Then.*) Jesus, does as well I expect.

Esme Now, I suppose I'd better go and find Doctor Morton and give her the good news.

Shaz It will be all right? I mean it's true isn't it?

Esme Yes, of course.

Shaz But suppose you change your mind?

Esme I won't.

Shaz How will I know if things go wrong?

Esme Wrong? What on earth could go wrong? I'll come and visit every week from now until I can take you home.

Shaz But suppose – what I mean is, sometimes we don't get told that visitors are here or they say we haven't behaved enough to see them or that they didn't turn up.

Esme If you don't see me each week from now on until you're allowed to go, it means I've dropped dead. If that happens I'm sure Doctor Morton will inform you. If I am living and you don't see me, it means someone has told you a lie in which case I suggest you call your solicitor.

Shaz You've got a sense of humour, I like that.

Esme Oh good. Why, what did I say that was funny?

Shaz Take no notice. But suppose –

Esme I'm extremely unlikely to drop dead. I don't have that sort of life style. Don't worry I'll see you very soon –

Shaz I hope so Auntie Esme.

Esme Esme, will suffice just fine, Sharon.

Shaz Shaz. You can call me Shaz. Would yer?

Esme I'll try. Now which is the way back to Doctor Morton's office?

Shaz One of the staff will take you.

Esme Won't you?

Shaz Yeah. I would, I would. I ain't allowed. It's a locked facility, see?

Esme Oh. Yes, of course. Don't worry I'll find my way. (*Holds out her hand.*) Until we meet again.

Shaz (*shakes her hand*) Yeah.

Esme *goes.* **Shaz** *hugs herself.*

Scene Four

A month later. **Shaz** *and* **Esme** *sit opposite one another on an inter-city train. They are going home. They share sandwiches and a flask of coffee, which* **Esme** *has made for the journey.*

Shaz Don't they have buffets on trains no more, then?

Esme Yes, and they're still about as reasonably priced as the Fabergé Eggs.

Shaz Oh yeah? Tell you what, why don't I go and get us a miniature whisky to put in that? No, no, don't say anything, let me guess, you're teetotal, right?

Esme I suppose that there's still many things we don't know about each other.

Shaz Yeah, but I reckon it won't be too hard to guess a few of them, eh?

Esme (*Checks that they can't be overheard*) I told them at the hospital and your Probation Officer at Eden Park that you'd told me about what they term your index offence. They seemed most concerned that I knew –

Shaz You told a lie?

Esme It's what I call a lie of necessity. I always let the Lord know I'm about to do it.

Shaz It was a long . . . but . . . what? . . . . Now? You want me to tell you –

Esme No, no. Not now, no. I don't need to know, now. We have to get to know each other first before we can even begin to trust each other. In fact I don't need to know. At all.

Shaz I really value, like, what you've done. You might be teetotal but you must be all right. Either that or a bit garrety.

Esme The way you can really say thank you is to put your trust in Jesus. I know, I know. It's not obligatory but it's him you have to thank. I can't do anything without him.

The ticket collector, **Pat**, *comes along.*

Pat (*calling the length of the carriage*) Tickets please. Have your tickets ready please.

Esme *takes* **Shaz**'s *and her tickets and pass out of her bag. She gives* **Shaz** *her own ticket.*

Esme Here, that's yours –

Shaz Ta. (*She studies it.*) I hope I don't have to give it up –

Esme Why?

Shaz Souvenir of me new start, me new life.

Esme It's not a through-ticket. I thought we might get off in town. Do some shopping. Get you one or two bits and pieces. (*Lowers her voice.*) I thought perhaps a couple of bras.

Shaz I thought you said. You said, appearance doesn't matter because God looks on the inside.

Esme Bras are worn on the inside.

Pat Tickets, thank you.

Shaz Watchyer (*Peering at the badge pinned on* **Pat**'s *jacket, reading it.*), 'Pat. BR Ticket Conductor.' That's a bit unfortunate ain't it? Your name being Pat and that badge saying Pat right there on your tit. Like a Benny Hill joke.

Pat *looks at her, adds* **Shaz**'s *ticket to the pile and looks at* **Esme**'s *ticket and pass.*

Shaz Sorry, I didn't mean nothing by it. Don't talk ill of the dead an' all that. No offence. I was only trying to be friendly, make an effort and that, I don't suppose I could keep my ticket, for sentimental purposes?

Pat No, we have to collect all London tickets.

Esme Couldn't you make an exception? It's important to her.

Pat No.

Esme (*to* **Shaz**) Don't worry, we'll find you another keepsake.

Pat (*to* **Esme**) Two-fifty. You owe two-fifty on this ticket.

Esme Are you sure?

Pat Two pound fifty, please.

Esme But I've done this journey several times and that's what I've always been charged.

Pat Sure you haven't been getting the tickets out of the machine?

Esme No. Look you can tell it isn't out of the machine, they all have square edges.

Pat You've been under-charged. (*Holds out her hand.*) Two pounds fifty.

Esme (*gets out her purse and starts taking the coins out*) One . . . two . . . pound –

Shaz Listen, if she was charged that it's British Rail's fault not hers. Isn't it? If a shop puts the wrong price on something and you've paid for it, they can't come round your house demanding the difference.

Esme Sharon, it's all right. Two pounds, . . . ten . . . thirty –

Shaz No, put it away. For Christsakes. Oh shit. Bless me. Sorry. Don't let her treat you like a fucking criminal.

Pat Right, that's it. (*She walks off.*)

Shaz We was only stating our rights.

Pat *has already gone back up the carriage.*

Esme (*gets up*) You wait here, I'll go –

Shaz No sit down. Can't you see that's just what she wants.

Esme I could hardly fail to. If she said that'll be an extra two-fifty once she must have said it twenty times.

Shaz That's how they get to you. But if you give in to them, let them walk all over you, break your spirit, you're sunk.

Esme In my experience, giving in is part of life, especially over human error.

Shaz There was no need for her to speak to you like that though.

Esme We can rise above it.

Shaz Not if you're bloody sunk, you can't. The only reason I'm here now, is because despite everything they never broke my spirit.

Esme If they had, you might have actually got out sooner.

Shaz I might but I'd have gone back in there before you can say 'cheap fucking day return.'

Esme Don't look now. She's returning with the Senior Conductor. Oh that's odd.

Shaz What?

Esme They were both standing in the corridor whispering and pointing at us and now they've turned back.

Shaz See, they've decided to forget it. Just like you have about the bras I hope.

Esme I'm not going to force you to do anything you don't want to. Within reason. I just hope they're not ringing the police.

Shaz They'll have a job. The train won't get in for ages.

Esme There are phones on trains, you know.

Shaz Since when?

Esme I think about three years ago —

Shaz Go after them.

Esme Maybe you're right though and they thought better —

Shaz On the other hand she looked really hard at the destination on the ticket. She probably guessed I'm from the RSU. If there's one thing I've learnt it's that you never can second-guess a person's capacity for being bleeding spiteful.

Esme (*gets up*) And don't you make any remarks to anyone while I'm gone, especially not about their . . . top halves.

Shaz I was only trying to be friendly. I know I made a bit of a prat of meself but I didn't mean nothing by it.

Esme *goes.*

Shaz Please God, make it okay. Don't let anything happen now. I've not even been out half a day yet. Please. (*Then.*) Jesus? Jesus fucking Christ, she's got me at it already.

She looks up to see **Pat** *standing there*

Shaz My Aunt's gone to look for you. You must have passed her. Didn't you see her?

Pat I've been in the loo.

Shaz Is that where the phones are?

Pat Pardon?

Shaz She's just gone up there to pay you.

Pat I've come to apologise. She did pay the right money. It was my mistake.

Shaz You ain't rung the police then?

Pat (*laughs*) No.

Shaz (*sigh of relief, then*) Bloody cheek, it was like you were so sure –

Pat (*sits down in* **Esme**'s *seat*) I know, I've come to say sorry –

Shaz Only cos I suppose your boss said you had to –

Pat No he said, if you don't like the look of them, call the police.

Shaz You did like the look of us, then?

Pat Yeah.

Shaz Like that remark. What I said to you, I know it was out of order but I didn't mean it like that. I was just trying to break the ice –

Pat I know. I'm not really cut out for this job. I'm a bit short on social skills. Here. (*Offering* **Shaz** *her ticket.*) Here, you can have this.

Shaz Ta. Ta very much.

Silence

Pat You been a dyke long?

Shaz Pardon?

Pat I said, have you got a bike at home?

Shaz Yes and no.

Pat Sorry?

Shaz Did you? You just did ask me if? Didn't you? Yeah, I am and no I haven't – got a bike.

Pat You got a girlfriend then?

Shaz No.

Pat Oh.

Shaz You?

Pat No.

Shaz What is that about a bike? Some street code or something?

Pat No, that was like a cover bluff in case I'd got it wrong –

Shaz Oh. Right . . .

Pat Your Aunt's coming back.

Shaz (*turns her head, sees* **Esme**) Oh. Yeah. . . .

Pat (*stands up*) My phone number's on the back of the ticket.

Esme (*to* **Pat**) Now, it's quite all right. I've just seen your boss and I've paid him the extra two pound fifty and he says he'll forget the matter so I'd be very grateful if you'd stop harassing my niece.

Pat I do apologise, Madam. Good afternoon. (*She goes.*)

Esme I tell you I'm going to double-check all tickets from now on. Let's just hope the inspectors aren't out in force on the Mid Kent line.

Shaz Don't worry, Auntie err Esme. It's all going to be all right. I've got very positive vibes. A good omen.

Esme I think you'll find that 'Vibes' was a word that became defunct in the Seventies dear. And omens are a pagan concept. Come on let's get our things together so we don't have to start elbowing people at the last minute.

Scene Five

Two weeks later. The park.

Shaz *and* **Pat** *sit on the grounded aeroplane. Sound of children playing in the distance.*

Pat Have you ever wanted kids?

Shaz I thought you were going to say: 'Have you ever wanted keys?'

Pat Keys?

Shaz Yeah. One way or another they have played a key part in my life.

Pat Why, have you never had them?

Shaz Yeah. But I've never had a unique set. I've never lived on my own.

Pat Has your Aunt let you have your own set?

Shaz Oh yeah.

Pat Have you told her where you are?

Shaz Not exactly. That is no.

Pat Why?

Shaz Well . . . you know . . .

Pat Anyway, what's this got to do with keys?

Shaz Search me.

Pat But I thought you said –

Shaz No, it's what I thought you said. It doesn't matter. What are we going to do today?

Pat I don't mind. Anything.

Shaz Anything?

Pat I really like just being with you –

Shaz Do you?

Pat Yes.

Shaz Me too. With you, like. You know.

Pat No, what?

Shaz I like being with you.

Pat Let's drink to that. (*She takes a bottle of sparkling white wine and two glasses out of her bag and proceeds to open the bottle.*) Us liking one another.

Shaz Champagne?

Pat Only sparkling, you know fizzy plonk –

Shaz S'okay I understand what sparkling means.

Pat (*handing her a glass*) Do you like it?

Shaz Dunno. I've never had it. Cheers. (*She clinks glasses with* **Pat** *and swallows a mouthful.*) Yeah. It's nice. Sort of. It sort of just slips down don't it?

Pat Yeah.

Pause

Shaz (*takes another mouthful, then*) Why? Do you want kids, then?

Pat What I'd really like is a kiss?

Shaz Oh.

Shaz *looks at her but feels too awkward to move towards her.* **Pat** *moves towards* **Shaz** *and kisses her on the mouth and then pulls away slightly.* **Shaz** *leans forward and kisses her back.*

Scene Six

A month later. **Esme**'s *living room.* **Shaz** *stands, smoking a cigarette, flicking the light switch on and off.* **Esme**, *who has been collecting dirty washing comes in on her way to the kitchen.*

Esme How many more times? If you do that you'll fuse the bulb.

Shaz I haven't though, have I? I just can't get over being able to be in control of it. Anyway, don't fret, I'll be going out in a bit –

Esme You've had six weeks to adjust to being able to switch the light on and off (*Goes.*)

Shaz Someone's going to call for me.

Esme *hasn't heard this. She comes back into the room.*

Esme And you've left a full bath to go cold again.

Shaz It's having as much water as you want. It's strange, ain't it? I can't get used to it. And then I went and forgot and had a shower. Do I look okay?

Esme Don't get too used to it. Hot water doesn't grow on trees, you know. (*Doorbell. She goes to answer it.*) What now? We've not so much as dusted the piano –

Shaz (*following her*) Actually, I don't think it is Dena –

Esme *opens the door to* **Dena**.

Shaz Oh Dena. It is you.

Dena The very same.

Shaz What is it? Did you hear me drop the soap in the shower tray?

Dena I've not come to complain –

Shaz Good. In that case, here have a fag.

Dena Thanks. (*She takes one.*) I'm just returning my spare key. (*She gives* **Esme** *the key.*)

Esme Dena, I didn't know you smoked –

Dena No, but you know my Kenneth does. I can see you're going to end up with the same trouble as I've got if you're not careful. Nets a whiter shade of custard. But, as far as the new hall's concerned, it's now a no-go smokeless zone thank you very much. You must come and have a gander. Not now. Wait till I've got the carpet down. You'd think they'd have carpet fitters who could cut the bottoms off doors but no. I've got to arrange that separately. Bang goes my synchronisation out of the window.

Esme Won't you need the key for the carpet people, then?

Dena I'm not leaving them alone in there. Cripes, can you imagine? Giving them free range to scrape the underlay down my new eggshell? Not likely. It's not as if I'm not flexible. I told them, Friday's the only day I can't faff about with, not now Sandra's on a course and I'm the only one on reception. You would not believe the hoards of people who want a sick note for the following week and make sure they get it on Friday so they can enjoy the weekend.

Esme (*about the key*) You want me to hang on to it?

Dena Please. Suppose I lock myself out between now and then? Who would I turn to? Much obliged, Esme my love. What would we do without her eh, Sharon? Cheery chow for now. (*She goes.*)

Shaz D'you think her parents named her after that thing in the Flintstones?

Esme What thing?

Shaz That dinosaur dog thing –

Esme Wasn't that called Dino?

Shaz Dino! That's right. I tell you if she insists on calling me Sharon that's what I'll call her –

Esme She's all right in her own way. And she's been much better since you've been here. For some reason.

Shaz Before don't bear thinking about then. Esme I err –

Esme Does she often take cigarettes off you for her Kenny?

Shaz Yeah. She's so tight she squeaks when she walks.

Esme Does she?

Shaz Never mind. Esme, there's something I –

Doorbell.

Esme (*as she goes to answer it*) What's she forgotten now? Maybe her W D Forty. Is that what it's called?

Shaz (*is too distracted to appreciate* **Esme**'*s attempt at a joke*) I think that'll be . . .

Esme (*opening the door to* **Pat**) You! what is this?

Pat Shaz?

Shaz Come in, I'm sorry I didn't . . .

Esme I paid the difference. I only just threw out the receipt last week. That'll teach me to be so rash.

Shaz Esme, Pat is now my friend.

Esme Your –?

Shaz Girlfriend.

Esme Friend?

Shaz Yes.

Esme Girlfriend?

Shaz Yes.

Esme Your –?

Shaz We're lovers.

Esme What?

Shaz It's all right. Look –

Esme No it is not. You stand there calmly telling me you've given yourself over to vile affections.

Shaz Oh come on –

Esme There is nothing all right about Sin.

Shaz Esme, can't you just be happy for –

Esme (*dismayed*) Happy? Don't make me laugh.

Shaz Please –

Esme And I thought it was supposed to be a real trauma making revelations like that to one's relatives.

Pat It . . . err . . . rather depends how they're err taken. That is in my experience . . .

Esme Oh and have you had a lot of experience?

Shaz Auntie, Esme. Es. Look I'm sorry, right. Why don't –

Esme Why didn't you mention this before?

Shaz I didn't know if it would last did I? I mean I wanted to make sure and I didn't know how –

Pat I'm sorry Miss, err, Ms err, Esme –

Esme Miss Huntley. Oh, I see, the penny's beginning to drop, you thought that maybe you could use my flat as a trysting place.

Shaz As a fucking what place?

Pat Shaz! It means –

Shaz I know what it fucking means. I was making a fucking joke.

Esme Well, nobody's laughing.

Pause.

Shaz For Christsakes she don't need to use this poxy place. She has a four fucking bedroomed house of her own in bleeding Bexley Heath.

Esme Thanks to a great many pensioners being overcharged by two pounds fifty no doubt.

Pat No, I used to have a Saturday job in a betting shop while I was studying for my philosophy degree at Goldsmith's and I bet a whole term's grant on the outsider in the Grand National before last. It came in at one hundred and eight to one.

Esme So how has it come about that you're a ticket inspector?

Pat I'm trying to complete my Phd and it's central theme is journeys. Plus I find walking up and down gives me a lot of time to think.

Esme And you thought my niece would make a good chapter?

Pat Oh I love your niece.

Esme Not under this roof you don't.

Shaz Come on Pat, let's get the fuck out of here –

Scene Seven

An hour later. The park. **Shaz** *and* **Pat** *sit once again on the grounded aeroplane.*

Pat She'll be all right.

Shaz You reckon?

Pat She's just too highly strung.

Shaz She's too highly fucking principled.

Pat Prejudiced.

Shaz It was you saying you won that house in the Grand National what did it. She hates gambling. You couldn't have said anything worse.

Pat No, I left that to you. What was going through your belfry, coming out like that?

Shaz I thought you'd – I don't know, I thought you might disapprove if I just said 'friends' –

Pat Listen, from what you'd told me about her, I imagine the most exciting thing she's ever done is grow a geranium from seed. I didn't mean for you to just blurt it out –

Shaz What about all that cobblers you were giving me about the reclaiming of the word spinster bollocks?

Pat It's like Mary Daly says in that –

Shaz Oh shut up. Whatever it is I won't have read it. No, no it's okay, don't offer to lend it me. I won't get round to reading it.

Pat In that case I better change the subject. Why don't you come and live with me?

Shaz You what?

Pat In my four bedroomed, rented, shared house in Bexley Heath. You could have your own room though or you could share mine. I know there's several of us there but you'd have your own set of keys.

Shaz Is that a proposal?

Pat More like a proposition.

Shaz Sounds a bit sordid.

Pat (*on one knee. Rocks the aeroplane*) Shaz, lighter of my life. I was nothing before I met you. A half person wandering in the wilderness of loneliness. Let's fly together. Come. Share my life. And not necessarily in that order.

Shaz (*laughs*) Piss off you silly bat –

Pat Please, what do you say?

Shaz I'll have to ask my probation officer.

Pat *laughs*.

Shaz Actually, I'm not joking. I'm on licence.

Pat They've done away with those for dogs. Still, I suppose historically women have always been next in the line. Ask her then.

Shaz Shall we see how it goes?

Pat Don't you want to?

Shaz Yeah. Yeah but I . . . I want to be . . . be able to feel I've got something to offer –

Pat If I knew how to do it I'd be giving you a very old-fashioned look.

Shaz I mean a job or something. I owe –

Pat You don't owe me or anyone else anything –

Shaz You're joking. If I became head of ICI tomorrow, I would have to work until I was four thousand and forty to pay back all the money I've already had out of the state. Anyhow, I owe it to me, I think. At least, I'm beginning to think –

Pat Hey, you could do a degree. That's the only qualification you need for a philosophy degree. Thinking. I wish I'd done Women's Studies now. More interesting. You don't even have to hand in essays with philosophy. You just say you couldn't do them cos you were thinking, and you pass.

Shaz But I was thinking of trying to get a proper job. Though what chance I stand –

Pat Joe who I work with, does mini-cabbing as well, he's got five kids. They're not Catholics, he just doesn't like jonnies. I don't think his wife's a very well-read feminist somehow.

Shaz I don't want children.

Pat What? (*Then.*) Oh that was just pass-the-time-type conversation. I'm talking you and me, partnerships, not families.

Shaz Do you?

Pat No, not really. Any rate, the reason I was telling you about Joe in the first place was because of the mini-cabbing not his virility. He says he's the only bloke in his firm who's not just come out of prison.

Shaz Oh yeah. Except I can't drive. And I wish it was just prison that I'd come out of.

Pat I can teach you, if you want. Look, why give yourself a hard time? You've had a hard enough time.

Shaz You reckon?

Pat Don't you?

Shaz S'pose.

Pat What did you do? (*Pause.*) Did you kill the bloke who abused you?

Shaz How –?

Pat Did I know you were abused?

Shaz Yeah.

Pat Because you told me you were taken into care when you were a kid.

Shaz So?

Pat And I didn't hear you say that the authorities made a mistake, so that usually means abuse.

Shaz Oh.

Pat Don't look so worried. The fact that you killed him makes you nothing but a heroine in my book.

Shaz I didn't kill him.

Pat He survived?

Shaz I never even harmed no hair of his head.

Pat What happened to him?

Shaz I dunno. For all I know, he's still out there doing it.

Pat Bastard. How much better for so many people if you'd done away with him.

Shaz Don't try and make me feel guilty for not killing him.

Pat What did you do then?

Shaz I'm not sure –

Pat I've done things I'm ashamed of.

Shaz Have you?

Pat Yeah. Like I'm not a very honest person. Oh, I am with you. I couldn't say that if I wasn't but I'm not about loads of things. I often say the easiest thing, even if it's a complete lie.

Shaz You trying to tell me you're not doing a Phd?

Pat No, that's not a lie. Unfortunately. But I do just make up things, like that about winning the house in the Grand National. It makes my life more interesting.

Shaz You are strange.

Pat I hope I'm not too boring for you.

Shaz I hope. I hope I won't be too much of . . . of a . . . disappointment –

Pat I bet you didn't do anything really. Most women get locked up for losing their temper. Then dragged down by the system into the system –

Shaz I know what you're saying but it wasn't like that.

Pat Anyway, you don't have to tell me.

Shaz I think I do.

Pat No honestly. If you don't –

Shaz I think Natalie will probably insist on it as a condition of living with you.

Pat You didn't do dastardly things to British Rail staff, did you?

Shaz You're not going to find it funny. And you're not going to be proud by association.

Pat Whatever you tell me will make no difference to us.

Long pause.

Shaz (*without emotion*) Three years after I was taken into care my Mother died. I didn't feel anything. I thought. 'That's it then. My Mother's dead.' She'd not visited me in three years. I was in care because she put him before me.

Pat Women's conditioning is so strong.

Shaz (*without looking at her*) You won't find any easy answers for this in the books you've read.

Pat I'm sorry. Go on.

Shaz But when she died a feeling of hope went. Anyway several years later my Father married again. They had two children a boy, and a baby girl. I left care when I was sixteen. You had to. I got a job in an old people's home. I was –. Oh. I don't know. My behaviour was rather strange. I used to cut myself. No one ever knew. They told me I was very good at my job. They had no idea. I was – it was like I was very cut off. I decided to look for and found my Father. He was pleased enough to be reunited. I baby-sat for them. They gave me a key to the house. Sometimes when I knew they were out I would let myself in and write stuff with her lipstick over the mirror. Tip her perfume over the bed. Smear body lotion into the carpet. One evening I was babysitting. (*She stops.*)

Pat You, you killed the little boy?

Shaz No. I murdered the baby. Girl. I picked her up from her crib thing and held her. Squeezed her. Until she stopped breathing. When I knew she was dead, I sat down, turned the telly up and waited for them to come home.

Pat Why? Why her? (*Silence.* **Pat** *makes a decision here not to see* **Shaz** *again.*) It's very easy though, I mean it must be they're so fragile –

Shaz I meant to kill her.

Pat How do you know if you didn't know what you were doing, tipping stuff on the bed and –

Shaz Because I can remember that. I can remember –

Pat But it wasn't as if –

Shaz Pat, stop it. There aren't any excuses for what I've done. There are all sorts of rumours in there that they sterilise women who kill children. But nobody knows because it is too awful to talk about out loud.

Pat No wonder you don't want kids.

Shaz I can't have them cos I'm too fucking damaged but that don't justify nothing because I never wanted them anyway.

Pat What a shame you killed the wrong person.

Shaz There is no right person, there is no fucking right person . . . Oh, Jesus . . . (*She turns around and looks as though she might be sick.*)

Pat You okay? (*Then puts her arm around her.*) That's it. Take a deep breath of broken ozone layer. Hey, look, why don't we go on holiday? My parents have a cottage in the Dordogne. You'll like it there. I can show you where I spent my summers as a kid.

Shaz You . . . you don't . . . don't mind . . . It won't make any difference?

Pat No. No, it's only a temporary setback, that you didn't kill that fucking bastard. Everybody has the right to start again. You've not had a break.

Scene Eight

A month later. **Esme***'s living room.* **Shaz** *sits watching the phone and smoking. (The ashtray is full.)* **Esme** *sits at the piano.*

Esme Why don't you come over here and give it a go?

Shaz Do I have to?

Esme Have you got anything better to do than give the smoke alarm a nervous tick?

Shaz All right. I don't know why you're bothering. I can't read music or nothing.

She goes over to the piano. **Esme** *vacates the stool and* **Shaz** *sits down.*

Esme That's middle C. I've put the names of the notes on the keys, then written what they are in pencil on the music. You have to put both hands over the keys. Like this. (*She shows* **Shaz** *how to put her hands on the keys.*) That's it. Raise your wrists slightly, that's better. Now just follow the notes.

Shaz (*the sheet music is the hymn* The Lord's My Shepherd. **Shaz** *manages to play the first few notes with enormous pauses between them.*) Shit, this is just stupid.

Esme No, that's really good –

Shaz It's hardly Patsy Cline.

Esme Who?

Shaz For-bleeding-get it. (*She bangs her hands down on the keys.*)

Knocking on the door. **Shaz** *goes to the door and opens it to* **Dena.**

Shaz I only played about five fucking notes.

Esme Dena, I was just teaching –

Dena So I heard, as did my poor Kenny. I'd just got him down.

Shaz I have to do this Dena, it's part of my rehabilitation.

Dena But Sharon –

Shaz If you don't like it Dino you'll have to take the matter up with my probation officer.

Dena It's not me dear, it's Kenny.

Shaz Was that all?

Dena Err yes. But. No, I'll be off then.

She goes.

Esme There was no need to be rude. You need all the friends you can get.

Shaz Do I? Do I? I tell you what I don't need though. I don't need to do this crap no more. (*Slams the piano lid shut and goes back to the chair and sits down.*)

Esme Well, you can't just sit in that chair and smoke for the rest of your life.

Shaz Who says? (*Lights another cigarette.*) Fuck, it's me last one. Shit. Have you got a couple of quid till me giro comes?

Esme No, I haven't.

Shaz Don't be so stingy. That's the trouble with you. Christians, ha. Shall I tell you the trouble with Christians. S'posed to be blessed with the spirit, how come then they're all so fucking mean-spirited?

Esme *closes the piano lid and is about to go out of the room.*

Shaz You never asked me about her.

Esme Who?

Shaz Who do you think? Apart from you, who's the other person I know?

Esme Oh her.

Shaz Yes, her.

Esme I take it the holiday in France fell through.

Shaz Who told you –?

Esme First you ask me where the Dordogne is. Then you badger Natalie to get you the all clear for a passport. I don't have to have extra-sensory perception to work it out. So what happened, she got caught in Ladbroke's putting the excess fares money on the three-thirty?

Shaz Very amusing.

Esme And you've not heard from her since?

Shaz You know I've not. I told her. I told her about me. I thought it would be all right. I could sense the minute I opened my mouth it wouldn't be but I told her all the same.

Esme What do you want me to do about it?

Shaz I miss her.

Esme Oh.

Shaz I miss what should have been my life.

Esme You'll miss the rest of it, if you continue to spend it feeling sorry for yourself.

Shaz You've never even asked me anything. We're from the same family and you've never even asked me —

Esme I don't want to know anything about them. I made up my mind about that when I left.

Shaz Do you hate them?

Esme No, of course not. I don't hate anybody. I forgave them a long time ago. All it says in the Bible is, forgive those who do you wrong. It doesn't say anything about having them round for tea.

Shaz But why don't you want to know anything about me?

Esme Because, I think I can guess. I know, I expect somewhere, deep down.

Shaz How? How do you? How can you?

Esme I don't know.

Shaz What do you mean, then?

Esme Let's forget it.

Shaz How can I?

Esme Just don't think about it.

Shaz Please, talk to me, please.

Esme My father, your grandfather was a —. As a Christian I don't have the words to describe him. He was one of those men. When . . . when we were children, your father and I, he wouldn't leave us alone. You know to what I'm referring?

Shaz Yeah.

Esme And I suspect, I expect that my brother repeated the same pattern of behaviour when you were a child.

Shaz *looks down.*

Esme That's the difference between men and women. They can't seem to help themselves. Or rather they do help themselves. We don't –

Shaz No, no. We only destroy ourselves instead.

Esme Who has?

Shaz Oh look at yourself, preening at being the big martyr. We've got nothing to crow about, you and I. We're pathetic, slashed to bits. Don't bloody glory in our destruction.

Esme Speak for yourself. I'm far from destroyed, thank you. I don't even smoke. And I'm surprised at you sticking up for them. Still, the Lord works in –

Shaz The Lord? Pah! I'm not sticking up for them. Christ, I'm not that fucked. I'm saying that just cos everyone thinks it's all right to turn our own distress in on ourselves, it's a bloody big mistake for us to make a fucking virtue out of it.

Esme I'm not distressed. That's where hearing the good news of Christ has helped. I'm sure if you opened your heart –

Shaz If I opened my poxy heart, I'd bleed to fucking death. Oh Jesus. Jesus. Will you shut up talking about bloody Jesus.

Esme And will you stop taking his name in vain?

Shaz Christ! Talk about missing the fucking Godforsaken point. How many people do you know who can't fucking conduct their pitiful, miserable lives without shooting invisible arrow prayers to God the fucking father. Talk about infuckingadequate. It's you that's got the personfuckingality disorder. Jesus wept.

Esme Right. That's enough.

Shaz Oh yeah? And what are you and Jesus going to do about it then?

Esme I've warned you. One more blasphemy –

Shaz Yeah, yeah and Mary fucking Jesus Christ, Holy blimey Ghost, what?

Esme And, and you can just go –

Shaz Be a pleasure.

Doorbell.

Esme Go on then, it would be nothing more than relief to me. Go on. (*She gets up to answer the door. Over her shoulder.*) Oh, we might be mean-spirited us Christians but we still tell the truth. (*Opens the door to* **Natalie**.) Oh hello.

Natalie I was in the area and I just thought I'd call round to see how you both were getting on.

Shaz I'm not supposed to see you till Thursday.

Natalie I know. I thought I'd save you the trip. Besides I've got some good news. How are you both? (*Pause.*) Great about the passport wasn't it?

Silence.

Shaz You got a fag?

Natalie Reformed.

Shaz Eh?

Natalie Gave up. Two years ago. You should think about –

Shaz Don't bloody start. I don't want to give up anything else.

Natalie Ah, that's just it. You don't want to think of it as giving up anything, but think of it as giving something to yourself. Anyhow, I've not come here to preach at you.

Shaz You do surprise me.

Natalie No believe it or not I've got some more good news. You've got permission, in theory to move in with Pat. I know it's taken a little while, sorry but anyway, all I have to do is see you and Pat together and make certain she knows what you did and that there are no young children living in the house and that if any women in the household become –

Shaz Hold it. It's off. She –. I changed my mind. So save your breath.

Natalie I'm sorry to hear that. What –

Shaz Not now, eh?

Natalie So you don't want to move?

Shaz I didn't say that.

Natalie Where to?

Shaz Anywhere.

Natalie Oh?

Esme Bit of difficulty making the adjustment.

Natalie Still?

Shaz Yeah, what did you expect when you dumped me with this homophobic Jesus freak?

Natalie Shaz?

Shaz Ain't you got nowhere else I could stay?

Natalie Well, I – I. It isn't that difficult, is it? (*She looks at* **Esme** *for a denial but is disappointed*.) The answer is no, not really.

Shaz Great.

Natalie Surely things aren't that bad –

Shaz Yeah they are and you just made them worse.

Natalie How?

Shaz Listen, I don't want to talk about it now, right? I'll come and see you in your office on Thursday as planned, okay?

Natalie Fine. Yes, you do that. I'm sorry about this, err Esme.

Esme (*shows her out*) You are.

Esme *comes back into the room. Silence.*

Shaz Listen, if you lend us some money I'll pay you back when I can. And I'll go.

Esme Whose baby did you kill, yours?

Shaz His. So you see I'm beyond saving.

Esme I don't know. It has a certain Old Testament ring to it.

Shaz How can you? How can you say something like that?

Esme Like what?

Shaz Like that. Casual. Like it was just another commandment I broke.

Esme Well, I hope you haven't killed as many times as you've taken the Lord's name in vain, or we would have wasted a lot of time worrying about the population explosion. (*Laughs.*)

Shaz You're cracked –

Esme I'm beginning to think I might well be but I'm certainly not so clueless as to think they put you in one of those places for defiling God's name.

Shaz Can't you see? I'm as bad as him. Worse. Much worse. Nobody killed me.

Esme And can't you see the difference between doing something out of distress and doing something for pleasure?

Shaz If you'll just lend me some money and I'll –

Esme You'd be foolish to go, just go like that. You'll have them all on your back.

Shaz Huh, the only thing you'll miss is the money.

Esme What money?

Shaz The money they give you for looking after me.

Esme They don't give me any money for looking after you. You're thirty-three years old not a child. It's not a fostering arrangement.

Shaz You don't get nothing for looking after me?

Esme No, of course not.

Shaz So why, why are you doing it?

Shaz Don't think I haven't asked myself that.

Shaz You must get something extra.

Esme No.

Shaz Well, I don't get no extra money for rent or nothing. Hang on you must have savings. That must be it. Have you got a lot of savings?

Esme No.

Shaz Didn't you get no lump sum or that with your pension? You must of.

Esme Yes. (*Then.*) I gave it away. To charity.

Shaz You what?

Esme I didn't know about you, not then. If I had –

Shaz Na, no. Listen I don't want it. I wouldn't have wanted it. I'm not a charity case.

Esme I didn't say –

Shaz We can't have this. We're going down the Social first thing to sort this out.

Esme All right but here, take some money and get some cigarettes.

Shaz No, you're okay. I just gave up. Now let's get a pen and paper and see what our outgoings are. You got to be armed in your dealings with the SS.

Scene Nine

The next day. A booth in the DSS office. **Esme** *and* **Shaz** *sit facing* **Lucy,** *who is the last in a long line of DSS officers they have spoken to that afternoon.* **Lucy** *has also had a long day during which several* *people have physically and verbally threatened her. It is the first time* **Esme** *has been in a DSS office. She cannot believe how terrible it all is. This is one of the few things* **Shaz** *knows about so she is trying to prove herself, only of course, she isn't getting anywhere.*

Lucy And you've come out of where originally – ?

Esme We've been through this umpteen times –

Shaz Broadmoor.

Lucy Look maybe you should be claiming sickness benefit.

Shaz Don't try and get comical with me.

Lucy The last thing I feel like doing, believe me.

Esme My niece has come to live with me, having been in the Regional Secure Unit attached to Sunnymead Psychiatric hospital. My only income is a small pension from the civil service.

Lucy Well, if she's capable and available for work she should be signing on.

Shaz I am but I'm not getting no extra. If I was in rented accommodation I'd be entitled to claim extra from you –

Lucy From the DSS, yes. (*Then. Looking at the forms in front of her for the first time.*) Oh, is that your address? Eden Park?

Esme Yes.

Lucy I'm sorry, you're in the wrong office. I can't help you. You need to go to our –

Shaz Wherever it is we've been there at least twice today. They sent us here. This is our second visit here. The first time we saw the wrong person. You are the right person. This is the office we should be at; we've had the personal assurance of the Manager in the Godforsaken head fucking office.

Lucy I can't fucking help that can I?

Esme Now, just a moment.

Shaz (*to* **Lucy**) Well, do something about it.

Lucy Why don't you write in?

Shaz Suppose we were destifuckingtute?

Lucy It's not my money you know. If it was, I'd be destitute, cos I'd give it all to you just for the sake of my sanity.

Esme Shaz. There's no –. Here, let's go and buy you some cigarettes and come back another day –

Shaz (*to* **Lucy**) Wouldn't make no difference we'd still get treated like shit.

Lucy Well, if you insist on behaving like it that's up to you.

Shaz (*to* **Esme**) I told you I've given up.

Esme Listen, let's all calm down. My niece is a bit fraught. She gave up smoking yesterday.

Lucy I should think that's the least of her problems.

Shaz (*stands up*) You're well out of order, you are.

Lucy Oh and I suppose you're in full working order? Do me a favour.

Esme Aren't there such things as training courses to help public sector employees work with the public any more?

Shaz (*to* **Lucy**, *still standing, arm raised*) Say that again.

Esme Shaz, sit down.

Lucy Are you threatening me?

Shaz You obviously ain't in no state to help us, perhaps you'd get someone who could.

Lucy Be my pleasure. I won't keep you a moment. (*She turns to go.*)

Shaz You mean we'll sit here till they want to shut the office. You make sure you come back. With someone who can help us.

Lucy It's all gimme, gimme, gimme isn't it? You don't see another human being here –

Shaz Oh leave it out. We've spent the whole day in all the DSS offices in the South East to be told by ignorant-couldn't fucking-give-a-toss-types like you that we're in the wrong place.

Lucy Perhaps if madam wouldn't mind waiting a moment longer I'll see she gets dealt with. (*She goes.*)

Esme (*to* **Shaz**) Shall we just go home? Come on let's just —

Shaz Na. Between us we're entitled to more money. I want to make sure you're not out of pocket. That's all.

Esme But perhaps we would be better off, going home and writing a letter.

Shaz And waiting for eternity before we get a reply?

Esme It's just that I don't think it's a good idea to be so demanding of people, especially to their faces.

Shaz If you say 'please' and 'thank you' and 'do you mind if' and 'excuse me but' all the time, you might prove you're a polite person but you don't get no results. I learnt that in the bin. You have to shout up noses before you get any action.

Lucy *comes back on their side of the partition with* **Joan**, *a police officer.*

Lucy That's her there.

Shaz Oh shit. (*She tries to get out of the room but* **Joan** *bars the way.*)

Esme Shaz, try and keep calm.

Joan Has she actually assaulted you?

Lucy She hasn't had the chance. But her behaviour's been extremely intimidating.

Shaz Mine? Mine? Oh, come off it. Don't pissing well —

Lucy (*to* **Joan** *about* **Shaz**) See, see —

Joan Perhaps you'd like to come with me for a chat.

Shaz What? I ain't going anywhere with you.

Joan (*to* **Esme**) Are you all right, madam?

Esme Course I am. I'm her Aunt. She's not done anything –. She's given up smoking. I think that's – that accounts for –

Joan Threatening behaviour, is not nothing. (*She approaches* **Shaz**.) It would be best if you came along with me.

Shaz Just fuck off out of it.

Joan Look we know all about – (*She takes hold of* **Shaz**.)

Shaz You know all about what? What? Leave off of me. Will you let me go? (**Joan** *tightens her hold*.) Get out of my fucking face. I ain't going nowhere with you. (*she lashes out at* **Joan**, *punching and kicking*.)

Esme Shaz, try and be reasonable, we'll sort this out.

Joan We will indeed, at the station. (*She speaks into her radio*.) Dave, ditch the dosser outside, the real trouble's in here –

Esme The station? Listen, please let her go. She's not done anything wrong. She's just not like other girls, she's not very, placid –

Lucy Not placid? Not placid? No, she's bloody psychopathic.

Shaz (*struggling*) Just shut the fuck up.

Joan (*to* **Shaz**) Come on you're already looking at a charge of assaulting a police officer. That alone is enough to have you recalled.

Shaz (*screams and struggles*) Let me go. Fuck you. Let me go.

Scene Ten

A month later. **Esme**'s *flat. Three o'clock in the morning. There are piles of letters and papers everywhere.* **Esme** *is writing a letter.*

Esme Dear Shaz, I'm doing everything I can. I've tried on several occasions to visit you but they say you don't want to see me. I remember what you said about sometimes they don't tell the truth so I'll keep trying. (*She looks at the piano.*) I've bought you some Patty Cline music is it? I can't say I'm totally enamoured with it myself but I thought you might – (*She stops writing.*) How do I even know you're getting my letters? (*She picks up the phone. Dials a number from the long list in front of her.*)

We hear the recorded message.

Message This is the Special Hospitals Service Authority. I'm sorry but no one is available to come to the phone at the moment. Please leave your name and telephone number after the tone and someone will get back to you as soon as possible. (*Beep.*)

Esme Yes, this is Esme Huntley calling you on Monday sorry Tuesday morning at 3 a.m. This is the only time I can get through to you. It's about my niece, Sharon Huntley who was recalled to Secure accommodation without a trial or without anyone even listening to her. I would like her released and in the short term I would like to be able to visit her, as I seem to have been denied access. Failing this I would like a reply to one of my letters or phone messages. I'm beginning to wonder if I exist. Goodbye. PS Is there ever anyone of any use at home in the Home Office? Because if there is I'd like their name.

She puts the phone down. Dials another number. Gets another recorded message.

Message You have reached the Probation Service. The office is now closed. Please ring back during office hours. Which are nine-thirty to five-thirty, Monday to Friday. (*Beep.*)

Esme Natalie, it's Esme. I've not yet received your letter retracting bits of your report. I hope you haven't changed your mind. It was so unfortunate that you came to see us on that day. But really I didn't want Sharon to go back. Please would you come and see me or I could come to the office again. Please could you let me know when you'll be there.

She puts the phone down, goes over to the piano, leafs through the new sheet music; finds some, k.d. lang, sits down. Reads.

'Down to my last cigarette'. Sounds like your song, Shaz. Let's have a go shall we?

She starts to play but is disturbed by a knocking on the door. She opens it to find **Dena** *wearing* **Kenny**'s *coat over her nightie.*

Dena Esme . . . Esme.

Esme Dena.

Dena Esme. It's the middle of the night.

Esme Dena, why don't you go and fuck yourself.

Interval

Part Two

Scene Eleven

A week later. Night. **Esme**'s *living room.*

Esme What a day. What a day. One of the most exciting.
The most. It didn't start off that way but then I don't
suppose they ever do.

I was due to see Joyce for lunch. I did see her for lunch.
We talked about Shaz. She made me see that a lot of it was
all for the best. I didn't mind because Joyce is not a Dena,
not by a long chalk. Then she told me her news. She'd liked
Canada so much that she's emigrating. Going to live with
her family for good. I was really pleased for her. I was. I
was.

Even so it was a relief to be back on the train at Charing
Cross. I didn't even cough when some coarse woman
without tights or anything to read got on and lit up a
cigarette. And then it happened. I didn't realise, not till I
looked down at my hands and saw they were wet. Water
was falling from my eyes and splashing in dollops onto the
back of my hands. It was awful. The woman even put out
her cigarette. How can one cry and not know about it? I
shot a little arrow into the air. 'Lord, please get me back to
Eden Park as soon as possible.' The train broke down at
Catford Bridge. At first we all thought it was a bomb scare,
like one does. But it wasn't. We were just told to hang on
another half an hour for the next train.

There was nothing else for it but to come up from the
platform and collect myself in Catford.

I bought some tissues from the news-stand next to the
phone boxes. And I looked at them all empty and thought
how easy for someone, anyone to go in one and ring up that
place and say 'bomb scare'. I suppose in the back of my
mind, I thought Shaz could escape in the chaos. (*Laughs.*)
Ridiculous.

But then the front of my mind, as it were, wouldn't let go
of violent thinking. I thought about a shop in the Strand

which I usually cross over to avoid because there's always bunches of tattooed yobs and Rambo types, pressed up against the window which displays crossbows, knives, guns and what have you. It tries to pretend it's a sort of Army surplus, camping shop but a couple of rucksacks hanging from the door don't fool anyone. As I cut through Catford Shopping Centre, which is actually called Catford Mews, can you believe it? Who are these people who name these names. It's not even funny. I thought next time I'm in the Strand I'll not cross over, I'll have a better look. But then I remembered Joyce and that I didn't have any reason to go up to town now. I reached for a tissue and looked up to shoot an arrow. Then there it was, on the other side of the road, staring me in the face. The Catford Gun Shop. There at the bottom of an office block, called Eros House. And I said. 'Well, Lord, you brought me here'. I had a moment's qualm, because Eros is pagan but then I've never seen anywhere called Jesus anything. Of course, I suppose there's Jesus College but that's a far cry from Catford.

I looked in the window, checked that there weren't any customers in there and went in. By this time I was already feeling rather carried away with myself and wondered if this was the sort of thing that caused the onset of angina. The man behind the counter is very big but has such a gentle voice. I blurted out that I would like the most convincing replica he'd got. Yes, hand gun, that's right, one that would fit in my hand – under my pillow. It was easy, very nerve-racking but easy. He said did I live on my own? I said yes. He said how frightening it was now. I thought if you find it frightening there's no hope for the rest of us, Sonny. Actually, I didn't think that then. I thought of it just now. I was too scared to think of anything then.

Suddenly there I was, walking out with a replica Luger. (*She takes the gun out of her carrier bag, looks at it and puts it on top of the piano.*) I saw a little baker's, café thingy, in the mews. A cup of tea. 'You need a strong cup of tea, Esme,' I was saying to myself. I'd even started talking to myself in the third person to try and get a grip. I went in. On the counter there was a sign saying 'Take away'. 'Take away? Take away?' I heard my own voice inside my head shriek. 'Take

away? I could blow you away' and I had to hold a hand
over my mouth to stop the laughter spurting out and
remind myself that it was only a replica. I managed to buy
a tin of 'Seven-Up' instead and came home.

She starts to play Patsy Cline's 'Crazy' loudly on the piano.

I must calm down. I must go to bed. I've got to try and think,
sort everything out. Car. Why haven't I ever owned a car.
Ha, well, that's one thing I've still got in common with
Jesus. I wonder what time Estate Agents open? (*She looks for
the Thompson directory.*) There's probably a twenty-four hour
one these days.

*She finds the directory. Turns to the page with estate agents on it.
There is a loud knocking on the door.*

Esme (*putting down the directory and picking up the gun*) Howdy
Dino. (*She stops herself. Calls.*) Who is it?

Joan (*loud whisper through the letter box*) Miss Huntley? It's
the police.

Esme, *shocked, goes to the door. Then remembers the gun. Panics.
Puts it on the piano keys. Shuts the lid. Opens the door to* **Joan**.

Esme What's happened to her? What have you done?

Joan Who?

Esme Shaz. Sharon. My niece who thanks to you is back in
that hell.

Joan Miss Huntley, I'm sorry but she did assault me.

Esme What are you doing here? Is she dead?

Joan Nothing's happened to her. Not that I'm aware of
anyway. I'm here because your neighbour has made a
complaint about the noise.

Esme Dena? Dena rang the police? I don't believe it –

Joan Apparently, she says you were rather intimidating last
time she asked you to keep it down.

Esme So? Have you come to arrest me then, for playing the piano in my own home or have you got some unsolved bombings you thought you could fix me up with?

Joan Miss Huntley –

Esme That is the expression isn't it?

Joan Frame. That's more usual. It's just a warning. About the noise.

Esme It's my own –

Joan It's four in the morning –

Esme I've got that one somewhere. It's by someone called Faron Young. What sort of name is that –?

Joan (*seeing the sheet music*) Oh, you like Country and Western. (*Picking up the Patsy Cline music.*) Patsy Cline. Can you play this?

Esme Do you like it as well? What is it with you girls? It's really old.

Joan Don't you think she's original. She is the original. Can you play 'Walking After Midnight'? (*She goes to open the piano lid.*)

Esme (*putting her weight against the lid*) No! (*Then.*) But isn't that why you're here? To make sure I stop playing?

Joan Oh yes. What a long day. I need your word that you'll go to bed. Make no more noise.

Esme You've got it.

Joan Good. She died in a plane crash, you know.

Esme What??

Joan Patsy Cline.

Esme Oh her. (*Then.*) Can you try and get in touch with her?

Joan Through a medium you mean?

Esme No, Shaz.

Joan Haven't you rung the Unit?

Esme Yes, but they say she doesn't want to see me.

Joan If I was you I'd go down there. Be different when you're actually on the premises.

Esme I have but . . . (*Then, trying to get her to leave.*) Yes, yes, you're right.

Joan I'm sure. Now, you will try and keep the noise down won't you?

Esme Not another plink.

Joan Next time I'm in the area I'll call by and see how you got on.

Esme Okay and I'll play you 'When You Need a Laugh'.

Joan Or 'Have you ever been lonely'?

Esme Funny you know, I wasn't before she came to live here. Still it's too late to go into all that now.

Joan What you need is a hobby. Something other than the old joanna, to take you out of yourself, put a bit of excitement into your life.

Esme Yes, yes.

Joan I can't quite think what though. Umm, now what –

Esme Don't worry, I'm going to learn to drive.

Joan Perfect. I'll say goodnight then.

Esme Good. Goodnight.

Joan *goes.*

Esme (*picks up the directory, dials a number*) Good. A machine.

Machine 'You are through to the Eden Park office of Stephen Barnabus, Estate Agents and Valuers. Please speak clearly after the tone and we will return your call as soon as possible.' (*Beep.*)

Esme Yes, I would like you to call round tomorrow and

value my flat with a view to selling it. It's Flat two, ten
Roman Avenue and my name is Esme Huntley. And I'll be
in all day.

Scene Twelve

Several weeks later. Friday afternoon. Doctor Julie Morton's office.

Esme, *her handbag on her lap sits the other side of the desk.*

Julie Miss Huntley, I don't see what more I can do. You've
just heard me phone the Unit and they say she doesn't want
any visitors –

Esme Do you believe that?

Julie Yes. In fact she's been offered weekend leave. We've
done everything to try –

Esme Because I don't. I'd made up my mind the last time I
came down here, that if she wouldn't see me, then there was
nothing more I could do. You remember, it was you
yourself who suggested that I try and let go.

Julie I remember.

Esme But I can't get out of my mind, her telling me that
often patients wouldn't even be told they had visitors –

Julie Hard as it sounds, I know Shaz doesn't want to see
you.

Esme But I would like to see her.

Julie Miss Huntley, she doesn't want to see you. And she's
in no fit state to do so.

Esme What does that mean? What have you done to her? Is
she on the operating table? Are you planning to take part of
her brain away?

Julie No. It means emotionally –

Esme What about me? Emotionally? I was about to say I
haven't come all the way down here for the good of my

health but in fact that's exactly what I have done and I am not leaving until I've seen my niece.

Julie You're not being reasonable, Ms Huntley.

Esme Actually, I'm being extremely reasonable. If she doesn't want to see me, why doesn't she? What's happened to her?

Julie To tell you the truth I don't really know.

Esme Is she still here and alive?

Julie Yes, yes –

Esme Then I want to see her.

Julie Miss Huntley –

Esme Perhaps I haven't made myself clear. Doctor Morton, I am going to see my niece.

Julie And I have just spent the last fifteen minutes explaining –

Esme I didn't want to do this. (*She takes out the gun and points it at* **Julie**. *Looks up quickly and shoots an arrow.*) So? How else am I expected to save my entire household? (*Looks down quickly.*)

Julie Miss Huntley, Esme . . . this is. Please put that . . . don't . . . it's very stupid.

Esme Isn't it? Isn't it?

Julie Just put that down and we will –

Esme Listen to me. Save all your psycho-analytical brain power to help yourself. I've gone too far now to retract. I'm not going to put this away until I've seen her. I shall have no hesitation in using it.

Julie Just stop waving it in my face.

Esme Don't even look sceptical. I will shoot your brains over the walls. I will spatter your entrails across the filing cabinet. I will do things that make me ill and sick and I won't care because someone took away that fragile belief

which only Jesus made strong in me and seemed to hold my
sensibilities together. And that is the notion that I had
something to lose. But I seem to have lost even that now –

Julie *lifts the telephone and dials a number.*

Esme What are you doing?

Julie (*to phone*) Hello. Security? Yes, this is Doctor Morton.
Room –

Esme Don't. Don't do that. (*Pause. Then she throws the gun on
the desk.*) Sorry, sorry. I'm really sorry. (*Watches* **Julie** *pick up
the gun.*) It's not even real.

Julie (*to phone*) Yes, I'm still here. It's a false alarm. Yes, I
thought someone was trying to break in here but it's all
right now. I'm sorry to have troubled you. (*Puts the phone
down. To* **Esme**.) You were saying?

Esme I don't know what came over me. I feel – I feel – I
don't know what to say. I'm so sorry.

Julie (*picking the gun up and looking at it*) It can't exactly have
been a spontaneous outburst.

Esme No, I'd been planning it for ages but in the fantasy
I'd always imagined that we'd get away with it.

Julie What do you think you were doing, bringing this into
here? Really I should be calling the police.

Esme I don't know what's the matter with me. It's not my
job to know what's the matter with me. That's more up
your street.

Julie It certainly is not up my street as you put it, nor in
my job description to have the barrel of a gun shoved up my
nostril. How dare you come in here brandishing this?

Esme I don't know. I don't know. I really don't. Please
forgive me. I'm so sorry, I can't tell you. I don't know what
I was doing.

Julie Most of us, as you well know, have to take the
consequences of our actions.

Esme You and me maybe but mankind? In the main I think not –

Julie And when you were thrusting this in my face, it didn't sound to me like you weren't enjoying the power –

Esme Are you going to call the police then?

Julie Are you going to do this again?

Esme No.

Julie No?

Esme I promise. (*She gets up to go.*) Of course not. I'm so sorry. I really am. I'm just . . . hopeless.

Julie Well, don't leave it with me.

Esme You want me to take it?

Julie I've heard a lot about you. When you give your word I believe you. Besides lax as security obviously is, I don't fancy risking it being discovered in my waste paper basket.

Esme (*puts the gun in her handbag and turns to go*) Thank you for being so kind. I'll try and repay you, make a donation to the hospital. I'll – I'm so sorry –

Julie You must have wanted to see her very badly –

Esme Yes.

Julie Wait. Sit down. (*Pause.*) I'll take you over to the Unit.

Esme (*she sits*) You mean – I can see her?

Julie But the minute she protests at your presence you'll have to go.

Esme I understand. (*She stands up.*)

Julie Hold your horses, we're going to have a cup of coffee first. Sod the homeopath.

Scene Thirteen

A seclusion room. **Shaz** *sits with her back to the door wearing only a canvas gown. When she hears the door being unlocked she runs to the corner of the room and faces the door shaking. Her hands have menstrual blood on them.* **Julie** *and* **Esme** *come in.*

Esme (*shocked*) Shaz?

Shaz (*turning away, whimpers*) Oh. No. Get out. Go away.

Esme What is it? What have you done?

Shaz (*to* **Julie**) Please, can I have a tampon?

Pause.

Esme (*to* **Julie**) Have you got one?

Julie I'll go and get her one.

Julie *goes.*

Shaz Na. Don't go. S'okay – (*But* **Julie***'s gone.*)

Esme Shaz . . .

Shaz What are you doing here?

Esme Visiting you –

Shaz But –

Esme I knew they were lying –

Shaz I don't want to see you. I don't want you to see me –

Esme Why?

Shaz I didn't want you to, not like – oh shit.

Esme (*gets out a handkerchief and hands it to* **Shaz**) Here.

Shaz (*takes it*) Thanks. (*Wipes her hands with it.*)

Esme When Doctor Morton gets back I want you to tell her that you want to come home with me for the weekend –

Shaz But – (*She holds out the handkerchief to* **Esme**.)

Esme (*about the handkerchief*) It's okay, you hang on to it. Don't worry we'll soon get you out of here.

Shaz I love you.

Esme *takes a step back.*

Shaz I don't mean like that. I don't mean nothing sexual or nothing. I mean —

Esme I don't think I've ever loved anybody.

Shaz Yes, yes you have.

Esme No.

Shaz Jesus. What about Jesus?

Esme Jesus?

Shaz Yes, Jesus.

Esme Oh Jesus.

Shaz Me?

Esme You? I don't know.

Shaz You took me to live with you, you must have seen something good in me?

Esme No, that was because of a sign from God. (*Laughs.*)

Shaz Then you cared for me.

Esme Duty, duty, duty.

Shaz And now you've come all the way down here and you must have kicked up a hell of a row for her to let you see me in seclusion.

Esme Actually, one could argue that I did it for me. Now when she comes back, I want you to say, spontaneously that you want to go —

Shaz Where?

Esme Out of here.

Shaz I don't want to go.

Esme Are you demented?

Shaz And I don't want to see you again unless it's only because you love me.

Pause.

Esme If love is the longing for the half of ourselves we have lost, then all right.

Shaz Oh. (*Then.*) No, no I don't want to be the part of you that's raging and railing. I don't want to be the fucking nutter part, the anger you're too ashamed to feel. I don't want to be like that. I hate it. I'm totally out of control. I want to mean more –

Esme (*takes the gun out of the handbag*) If you don't shut up being so ungrateful, I'll kill you. (*Arrow.*) It was a necessity of breaking a promise.

Shaz Christ a fucking live –

Esme Watch it.

Shaz No, not you. You're the only good person left in the world –

The sound of the key in the door. **Esme** *puts the gun back in her handbag.*

Esme I'm warning you, don't you give me the piss around or you'll be leaving here in a wooden mackintosh –

Julie *comes in.*

Julie Sorry, I was so long. Shaz, they tell me that you weren't allowed any for your own protection –

Esme Protection? Ha. Ha. I mean how ridiculous. (*She nods to* **Shaz** *to prompt her.*) Shaz has something to ask you, haven't you, Shaz?

Shaz Please could I have weekend leave.

Esme We've been talking about it and Shaz would like to take up the offer.

Julie Well Shaz, this is positive. I'm pleased.

Shaz I . . . I . . .

Esme She didn't realise how much she missed me.

Julie (*to* **Shaz**) You seem a bit equivocal –

Esme *gives* **Shaz** *a threatening look.*

Esme Nonsense.

Shaz No, I swear I'll be good.

Julie Well, it'll take a little time to arrange. How about the weekend after next?

Esme No, this weekend, please – It's important. I've got things lined up. It's my birthday. (*Silent arrow, mouths 'Sorry Lord'.*)

Julie. But it has to be squared with her consultant and he's away until Monday.

Esme Oh please –

Julie She's not really fit to travel. Are you Shaz?

Shaz Err . . .

Esme I've got my car. (*To* **Shaz**.) I've learnt to drive. (*To* **Julie**.) It's not really my car. It's hired. Just for the weekend. I thought we could go, go and get some fresh air.

Julie Shaz?

Shaz Sounds dangerous –

Julie (*believing* **Shaz** *is joking, i.e. more like her old self*) That's better. (*Then.*) Oh what the hell. All right. Now, I'm going to tell the charge nurse that it's been sorted and all the paper work is in order.

Esme Thank you. Thank you.

Julie I must be mad. Now, whatever happens you must be back on the ward by supper time on Sunday.

Shaz (*to* **Esme**) Promise?

Esme Would you just calm down the pair of you and trust me.

Scene Fourteen

Esme *and* **Shaz** *in the car. There is no evidence that* **Esme** *has any dexterity behind the wheel.*

Esme Shaz, get that thing out of my bag. (**Shaz** *looks at her.*) Oh, it's not real. I didn't want to frighten you but I'd forgotten how stubborn you could be. I'm sorry, but I was at the end of my tether. Actually I wonder what happened to the beginning of it. It's history, obviously. Get it out of my bag. Would you look at that. They're not supposed to overtake in the lane on your side are they?

Shaz You're not supposed to be going at thirty miles an hour.

Esme Yes, I am. For your information that's the speed limit. I don't want to break the law.

Shaz This is a motorway.

Esme You can't be too careful, with these maniacs on the road. Just get my bag –

Shaz What do you want it for?

Esme To get rid of it. Just get it out of the bag and throw it out of the window –

Shaz We're in the middle lane! Pull over at the next service station and you can throw it away there.

Esme I can't do that.

Shaz Why?

Esme There's something wrong with the mirrors. I don't think they work properly.

Shaz What?

Esme I don't trust them. They only seem to register one car in three. It's really disconcerting.

Shaz (*looking out of the window*) Okay. It's clear. Pull over now. (*The car veers violently across the lanes.*) When did you pass your test?

Esme It's next month. You know, when I went to hire it the man asked for my driving licence, of course. I said I'd forgotten. I meant I'd forgotten that I needed one. He must have thought I'd just forgotten to bring it. Mind you, I had to leave rather a hefty deposit but lucky wasn't it? Not that I really approve of luck but I don't think God would want his hand in that sort of dodgy deal especially as I still haven't got the hang of how to steer in reverse. I think you must have to have a sort of ambidextrous mind for that. But it's wondrous the places you can get to by going in a circle.

Shaz *looks at her open-mouthed.*

Esme Yes, nice surprise isn't it? Don't worry this is just the start. I can't tell you, these last few weeks I've even managed to amaze myself.

Shaz You're fucking verging on the hard shoulder.

Esme No, for the first time in my life, I'm verging on feeling alive.

Shaz Pull out or we'll be stopped by the police —

Esme But this lane is lovely and empty.

Shaz Because you're not supposed to drive in it!

Esme Don't you want to hear my plans for us —

Shaz Only if they include me getting a bus back to the hospital —

Esme You don't want to go back there at all —

Shaz But you promised —

Esme Well, it was a promise of necessity. I've got something much better in mind.

Shaz What, driving us straight to heaven?

Esme I thought you might like some sea air. (*She is interrupted by the sound of another car hooting loudly. To the driver.*) Huh, what's the matter with your eyesight? I'm old enough to be your Grandmother.

Shaz I think it's more to do with you pulling out in front of him and then dropping your speed.

Esme Oh, I see.

Shaz No, don't accelerate. He's trying to pass you –

Esme And they say it's women who keep changing their minds. Well, what do you say –

Shaz Keep your eyes on the road.

Esme About us going away –

Shaz As long as it's not further than Whitstable and we can go on public transport.

Esme Oh, I think we can do better than that.

Shaz Whatever, whatever but I must be back on the ward by tea time on Sunday. And I'd actually prefer it if it wasn't a medical ward. Brake!!

Esme (*breaking*) Now which peddle is that? Just kidding. That was a joke.

Shaz *reclines her seat and shuts her eyes.*

Esme What are you doing?

Shaz Praying.

Scene Fifteen

An hour later. **Dena**'s *flat.* **Esme** *and* **Shaz** *come in.* **Esme** *is clutching a large Marks and Spencer carrier bag.*

Esme For goodness' sake buck up. There's nothing to connect us with a discarded fake Luger and a sanitary towel bin in a Blue Boar blooming service station. Go on, go and freshen up.

She empties the carrier bag and hands **Shaz** *a new pair of shoes, a pair of light trousers for the trip and a silk shirt.*

Esme There I thought you'd like them. Notice the absence of a bra. Now, quickly go and have a shower and put these on.

She almost has to push **Shaz** *into the bathroom.* **Shaz** *goes. Sound of shower running. As soon as the door is closed,* **Esme** *goes over to the piano and opens the front panel under the keys and takes out stacks of neatly piled five and ten pound notes and stuffs them in the now empty carrier bag. (It's the money from the sale of her flat, minus the cost of travel, car hire etc. In total about sixty-eight thousand pounds.)*

Esme (*calls to* **Shaz** *over the sound of the shower and the rustling of money*) Do you know for one awful minute I thought you didn't want to get out of there. I don't know what we'd have done without the car. Left Luggage departments? They look at you like you were asking for two pounds of semtex and a box of matches. What a nightmare. Not that I'd risk putting everything in the boot. According to Dena, vandals break in for a packet of fags now. (*She has finished packing the money.*) Talking of which we're a bit behind schedule; we don't want her to arrive back and find us in her flat. (*Listens.*) What are you doing?

Esme *hears only the sound of the shower, becomes suspicious, starts rattling the door, puts her shoulder against it and opens it. She pulls* **Shaz** *out, still dressed in the clothes she was wearing when she first came in.* **Shaz** *has a large gash in her left forearm which she is trying to cover with her right hand.*

Esme What are you doing? We're cutting it very fine. (*Sees the blood seeping underneath the hand. Silence.*) I know. I know you're in a lot of pain. I don't know how to make it better. But true to form I'm trying to do my best.

Shaz *starts to cry.* **Esme** *goes to make a move towards her but cannot touch her.* **Shaz** *looks around her.*

Shaz I don't even know where I am. I don't remember –

Esme This isn't my flat. It's Dena's. I thought you needed a wash and brush up. She doesn't know we're here.

Shaz But that's your piano.

Esme I gave it to her. I sold my flat. All my – our worldly goods are in the car. Come on now before someone breaks into it –

Shaz I can't –

Esme How deep is that?

Dena *comes in.*

Dena What? What, what are you doing in my flat? Esme, Esme? How could you?

Esme I came to return your key. Then I realised it was Friday and you'd be at work.

Dena Doctor Knutsford's ulcer burst. There didn't seem much point hanging on after I'd put him in a minicab and cleared the surgery. (*Then.*) Why didn't you put it through the letter box like any respectable –

Esme I thought it was such a shame that Shaz hadn't seen your new hall.

Dena You? My? – (*Sees* **Shaz.**) Get your arm away from that dado rail. It hasn't been varnished yet. My carpet! What's she done?

Esme She cut herself.

Dena How?

Esme I just told you.

Dena (*to* **Esme**) Bathroom.

Esme *goes into the bathroom.*

Dena First Aid box in the vanity unit. (*To* **Shaz.**) Give that here.

Shaz *has no intention of letting* **Dena** *touch her but* **Dena** *grabs her arm anyway. Then to* **Esme** *who gives* **Dena** *the first aid box.*

Dena I won it in a raffle. (*She takes out what she needs.*) Mind you it cost me ten pounds' worth of tickets and you can buy them in Boots for five seventy-five. (*She deftly dresses the wound. To* **Shaz.**) Whatever you've done girl, you're not going to be able to cut it out. You've either got to live with it or do away with yourself altogether.

Esme Dena. Leave her be.

Dena Leave her be? I wish I could. Shame you didn't think to tell her to leave my carpet be. How dare you come into

my flat without my permission? Fancy letting her out in this
state. They didn't let you out did they? You've escaped.
That's it, isn't it?

Pause.

Shaz Ring them. Ring the hospital. Tell them to come and
take me back, please. It's okay. I won't do anything.

Esme No. Shaz. Shaz.

Dena Oh, ring them? Just like that. On my phone bill?
Well, it's long distance isn't it? And no doubt they'll keep
me hanging on for ages while they verify the story. (*To*
Shaz, *about* **Esme**.) I'm not her you know. I haven't got
M.U.G. written over my forehead.

Esme She hasn't escaped. They have let her out.

Dena You know what's missing from this country. No
responsibility. No bloody collective responsibility that's
what, and why? Because no one's prepared to pay for it.
That's the NHS for you. No payment. No responsibility.
They just want it for nothing. Esme, you didn't even leave
me a forwarding address.

Esme That's why I came back, to return your keys and say
goodbye properly. Shaz, put your clothes on and leave the
door ajar.

Shaz What happened to the rule about privacy in the
bathroom?

Esme I seem to have had a bit of a rule-breaking afternoon.
And I've got a log-jam, backlog, of arrows relating to
duplicities of necessity.

Shaz *goes into the bathroom.*

Dena There's not enough hot water for a shower.

Esme Don't worry, we haven't got time for that. (*To* **Dena**.)
Here, take this towards the raffle tickets.

Dena (*taking the ten-pound note*) Oh the devil has got into you
today. I never thought I'd see the day when you contributed

to raffle tickets, albeit posthumously. It's true though, what
they say. You reap what you pay for.

She's interrupted by a knock at the front door.

If that's Kenny, forgotten his key and he finds (*Nods towards
the bathroom.*) her here, I'm for the high jump.

She opens the door to **Joan**

Dena Oh. Can I help you, Officer?

Esme Oh Lord, Lord. (*Silent arrow.*)

Joan Oh hello, Miss Huntley. So the two of you were able
to patch things up. I'm so glad.

Shaz *comes out of the bathroom, dressed.*

Joan And you've got your niece back.

Shaz Oh God. (*To* **Esme**.) Sorry, sorry.

Joan (*thinks she's apologising to her*) You shouldn't have
clocked me like that but if the truth be told, I was gutted
that it meant you ended up back there.

Dena You'd have preferred her to do a stretch in Holloway.
Just a quip. Fuzzy felts, huh. I ask you. No humour. Don't
get me wrong, I'm all in favour of community policing. God
knows we pay enough for it but if my Kenny sees you –

Joan I'm afraid this isn't a social call. Do any of you know
anything about the 'Micra' outside?

Esme What about it?

Joan Apart from the fact that the plonker seems to have
parked it perpendicular to the pavement, we have reason to
believe it's a stolen vehicle.

Esme Stolen –

Shaz Stolen –

Joan Yes, can you believe, someone who's half inching
them, then hiring them out. The audacity. It could only
happen in south east London.

Dena Do you mind, this is a suburb.

Joan Rest assured, our intelligence informs us that he's operating from Catford –

To **Esme**'s *and* **Shaz**'s *horror* **Joan** *gets out her radio.*

Dena Never mind about your intelligence, what are you going to do about my new neighbours?

Joan I have warned them about the noise.

Dena It's not made the slightest impact. Can't you arrest them? There must be a law against people using handcuffs and the like in domestic carnal pursuits.

Joan I'll get someone out from the station about the car and then I'll have another word with them.

Dena Do. Esme, with you, I didn't know when I was well off. Now it's bed springs and clanking all night long. It's like living in jail.

Joan Actually, this doesn't seem to be working. I'd like to use your phone.

Dena Do the police get free phone calls?

Joan The police get very uneven tempered if obstructed in the course of their duty.

Dena Oh, come through –

Esme (*arrow*) Please God – (*Appeals to* **Shaz**.) All our worldly goods.

Shaz (*suddenly bangs her hand on the top of the piano*) Whose is this?

Dena Now, I did offer her something for it –

Shaz (*positioning herself between* **Joan** *and the door to the room where the phone is*) Not that – this. (*Picks up sheet music.*)

Dena Oh Esme can have that back. Not my cup of char at –

Shaz (*brandishing the music in* **Joan**'s *face*) Would you buy this out of a sense of duty?

Joan Now, it's that sort of in-your-face attitude what's working against you out here –

Esme (*snatching the music from* **Shaz**) Time to get your own back, Dena. When St Paul was in jail he sung. (*To* **Joan**.) Now what would you like?

Joan Let me just make this call –

Esme (*to* **Joan**) Anything. Anything, you want.

Dena (*to* **Joan**, *nodding towards* **Shaz**) You'd probably be calming down a very volatile situation.

Joan What about a little burst of Dolly Parton then?

Shaz Don't you mean big bust?

Dena I'll say this for her, she is a wag, your niece.

Shaz What about 'I Will Always Love You'?

Esme I can't play that one.

Dena What about 'Country Roads'? I know you can play that, as does my Kenny and half of Eden Park, no doubt.

Esme *starts playing. They are interrupted in the middle of the second verse by a loud and persistent banging from the upstairs flat.*

Voice Off Shut the fuck up.

Dena (*shouts back*) You'd do well to take your own advice. (*Then to the others.*) Perverted fornicators.

Joan Leave this to me. Don't go on without me. I'll be right back. (*She goes.*)

Esme Come on Shaz.

Dena Where are you going?

Esme I'm taking Shaz away –

Dena Don't leave me here. If Kenny comes back and finds the Police Federation's answer to Tammy Wynette in his hall he'll go berserk.

Esme I'm sorry but we'll miss the –

Dena I've missed you, too. Even her.

Shaz Me? You missed me?

Dena At least you kept old Esme in order. She was terrible after you went. Tell you what, why don't you come down the British Legion for a drink one Friday?

Esme Thank you but – Shaz, are you coming?

Shaz Yeah.

Dena Look at you two, foot loose and fancy free, not like me, stuck here having to make Kenny's tea. Hey Esme, do you think we could put that to music?

Esme Another time, Dena.

Dena (*to* **Shaz**) I mean that about the Legion.

Shaz You're on.

Esme Goodbye, Dena.

Dena Now listen, take care. And if you can't be safe be frugal.

Scene Sixteen

The next day. **Shaz** *is on the deck of a cruise liner in the Mediterranean. She is wearing shorts but still has a long-sleeved shirt on.* **Esme**, *holding several deck quoits comes over to her.*

Shaz They didn't have no newspapers then?

Esme Of course not. Where would they get them from, on a boat, in the middle of the Mediterranean? Anyway you're not due back till tomorrow.

Shaz They'll catch up with me.

Esme I doubt if they'll report you missing once the Health Authority adds up how much money they'll be saving.

Shaz Course they will and it'll be in all the papers.

Esme So what? They won't have any idea where to find us.

Shaz What about that Police Woman?

Esme Oh yes. And we gave her a big clue, didn't we.

Shaz What? What?

Esme By the end of next week, I expect half the Kent Police Force will be combing the Blue Ridge Mountains of West Virginia. (*Laughs and starts humming 'Take Me Home Country Roads'.*)

Shaz It's not some light-hearted prank or nothing. It's terrible. This is terrible. What we've done is terrible.

Esme We? It was me. Don't think you'll get any of the credit. Look if they find you, I've told you I'll say I kidnapped you.

Shaz As if I'd go along with that. Not that anyone would believe us even if I did.

Esme Stop fretting. They wanted to let you out anyway. Now come on. (*Handing her the quoits.*) Let's have a game of quoits.

Shaz Yeah and if one goes a bit wide of the mark and lands on those two snogging over there, we'll be had up for coitus interruptus.

Esme Don't let them put you off.

Shaz At the risk of appearing overly ungrateful I have to say that despite its name a cruise is a very heterosexual experience.

Esme Are you going to play or what?

Shaz I might if you tell me where we're going.

Esme Limnos.

Shaz What's that when it's at home?

Esme It's a Greek island. Don't worry Mitilini is just across the bay.

Shaz Where? It sounds like a bleedin' place out of the bloody Bible.

Esme It does get a fleeting mention but it's better known for its poet. I thought you might have heard of it.

Shaz You know me. I ain't heard of nothing.

Esme Sappho?

Shaz Must be a class act. They all are, those ones who only have one name – like Madonna.

Esme We're going to stay on the island next to the one where she was born.

Shaz Oh. And when are we going home?

Esme We're not.

Shaz Not?

Esme No. We're going to learn a new language instead.

Shaz But I don't like foreign food.

Esme That's why I decided we'd try and start a pizza place or something.

Shaz Oh really. That's all right then. (*Pause.*) Come on, when are we going back?

Esme Shaz, we're not. We're going to stay there –

Shaz What? What? Have you completely –? We can't just –. What would we live on?

Esme The money from my flat.

Shaz As soon as you ask the bank for that they'll be on to us before you can say unbalanced deficit.

Esme It's in the Marks and Sparks carrier bag. You know I think what happened in Dena's flat was a true miracle.

Shaz Miracle? I tell you what was a miracle, getting through customs.

Esme They had their chance. I can't help it if they were more interested in searching those poor youngsters who looked liked they had some sort of gum infection.

Shaz Is this on the level?

Esme I think it might be against man's laws but God hasn't given us any sign of disapproval, so as far as I'm concerned it must be the right thing to do.

Shaz (*laughing*) I can't believe it. I don't believe it. (*Then she puts her hand to her chest.*)

Esme What's the matter?

Shaz I dunno. It sort of hurts in here. It's a feeling I can't remember. (*She stretches her arms in an expansive gesture.*) I feel good.

Esme Oh. Well, whatever it is I do wish you'd wear a bra.

Shaz You should take yours off, in this weather.

Esme If I do, will you wear a tee-shirt or something with short sleeves?

Shaz I can't. I can't.

Esme Yes, you can.

Shaz No.

Esme Why?

Shaz I don't want to.

Esme Lots of people think battle scars are something to be proud of.

Shaz But I ain't done nothing to be proud of.

Esme I'm proud of you.

Shaz Are yer?

Esme Yes.

Shaz But they're so ugly.

Esme (*starts to roll up one of* **Shaz**'s *shirt sleeves*) How will they ever heal otherwise?

Shaz (*starts to roll up the other one*) Come on then, let's go mad.